W9-AMM-619 $11.95

THE BAJA BOOK III

A Complete New Map-Guide to Today's Baja California

By TOM MILLER

and

CAROL HOFFMAN

With Foreword By   RAY CANNON

Elmar Baxter   Charles Larson

Editor   Illustrations

Cover Photo Courtesy
Dr. C. W. Larson

Photographs for Baja Spacemaps®
From NASA Earth Resources Technology Satellite

BAJA TRAIL PUBLICATIONS, INC
PO BOX 8088, HUNTINGTON BEACH, CALIFORNIA 92615

THE BAJA BOOK III...A Complete Map-Guide to Today's Baja California. Published by Baja Trail Publications, Inc. PO Box 6088, Huntington Beach, CA 92615. ISBN 0-914622-07-1 All rights reserved. No part of this book may be reproduced in any manner whatsoever without written permission from the publisher, except by reviewers who may quote brief passages to be printed in a magazine or newspaper.

DEDICATION

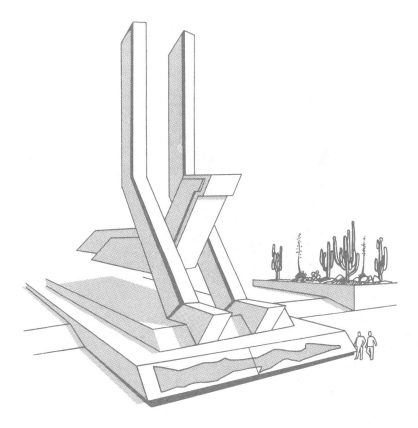

THE BAJA BOOK III, like its earlier editions, is dedicated to the true adventurers who have come to the Baja California peninsula over the past 300 years...and left such a rich heritage; to the travelers who followed to appreciate the beauty of this frontier land...and returned to spread the word; and to the people of Baja who today are our hosts below the border.

ABOUT THE AUTHORS

Tom Miller is a lifelong aficionado of Baja California, a saltwater angler who has held a number of world records, and active participant in numerous conservation programs.

For many years, Miller maintained a trailer home south of Ensenada before building a palmthatched ramada on a remote beach south of La Paz. During the more than three decades since he made his first trip to Baja, Miller has logged many tens of thousands of miles throughout the entire peninsula — exploring, charting, photographing and taking notes. The result has been well over a thousand articles on Baja California that have been published in prominent daily newspapers, the weekly Western Outdoor News (where his columns ran for nearly 18 years) and a variety of magazines, including Outdoor Life, Field and Stream and California Angler. Today, he is widely recognized as the leading authority on recreation/travel in Baja.

The original book, **The Baja Book**, written with Elmar Baxter in 1973, was the first of its kind, and a roaring success. It was superceded some years later by **The Baja Book II**. Today it is **The Baja Book III** which contains the distilled experiences and knowledge of "Sr. Baja" and his new co-author, Carol Hoffman.

Carol's attention was first drawn to Baja, interestingly enough, by the first edition of **The Baja Book** within weeks of the opening of the Baja Highway in early 1974. In the many trips since she has demonstrated a sensitivity to details which bring into closer focus the roadlog and services portions of the book. She has also shown an unerring eye for those very special spots that every Baja traveler looks for. A welcome addition indeed.

Elmar Baxter's busy schedule did not allow time for participation in the exhaustive research and writing chores entailed in **The Baja Book III** as he did when he co-authored the first two Baja books, but we are fortunate to keep him on the team as editor.

FOREWORD
By RAY CANNON, Author of *"The Sea Of Cortez"*

There is a wondrous feeling about driving down the full length of the new 1000-mile highway through the mountain range that forms the Peninsula of Baja California.

The casual observer can read much of the history of the earth in the vast stretches of volcanic pinnacles and craters — primordial formations created as lands cooled, catastrophic earthquakes escarpments, primitive fossilized life forms, and on down to the middens of aboriginal man, remnants from the advent of the Spaniard — and finally to a period shortly after the 1849 Gold Rush, when Baja California and its past was all but forgotten for almost a century.

But even emptiness has left its thumb prints on the unrecorded history. Once-thriving mining towns are now seen as ghost towns. Roaring, bellowing cattle ranches are today heard as the lowing of stragglers on distant hills. *Camino carretillas* (cart-roads) have been eroded into gullies and gulches. Former *haciendas* and mine structures are crumbling rapidly. Observers who examine closely can find excitement in all that's old and be enthralled by the ageless enchantment of nature's untouched beauty. While seeing is reward beyond appraising, there is even more joy in the deep inner feelings of breathing clean-scented air and the delights of a warm, tropical climate, all in a freedom unique to most *norteamericanos*. Most of the good, the wonderous, the enchanting that Baja California has to offer would be missed without a knowledgable guide. This book provides that guidance.

The Baja Book and its mapping was done by knowledgable men who studied the roads, especially the new Transpeninsula Highway, for the express purpose of creating this fine, informative volume. No one should venture into Baja California without a copy in hand.

(Though Ray is no longer with us we find ourselves unable to change the Foreword of this third version of **The Baja Book**, such has been — and still is — the effect of this dynamic man on the peninsula of Baja California. We choose to leave it stand for **The Baja Book III**, and most likely **The Baja Book IV, V** and **VI**, when they come.)

ACKNOWLEDGEMENTS

We are most grateful for the encouragement provided by the Governors and their staffs of the states of Baja California and Baja California Sur. Thanks, too goes to the many federal agencies who contribute to the well being of the Mexico visitor. Their cooperation over the years has been most helpful.

Much credit must go to my partner on the first two Baja books, Elmar Baxter. Not only did he contribute to the writing of our original Baja roadguide, but his guidance in the public relations and media portions of the promotion had made the difference between a so-so-selling book and one which has become an acclaimed success.

Juanita Roland of the EROS Data Center, U.S. Department of the Interior, was extremely helpful in selecting the original ERTS satellite space photographs of Baja California used in our maps. A similar use of satellite imagry in mapmaking has yet to be seen.

Among others who have made significant contributions are Luís Bulnes, Luís Coppola, Anita Espinoza, John Fitch, Ricardo Garcia-Soto, Jorge Gleesen, Luís Klein, Bud Lewis, Shirley Miller, Ed Pearlman, Alfredo and Gail Ramirez, Tony Reyes, Mac and Mary Shroyer, Bob and ChaCha Van Wormer, Al and Dorothy Vela, Chuck Walters, Walt Wheelock, Anita Williams and Clemente Wilson.

The authors would also like to express their thanks to Pat Brumm for her consummate editing skills and patience.

The outstanding illustrations continue to be the work of the very talented Charles Larson, who has accompanied us on several tours of the Baja peninsula. Cover design and layout is by Frank Steven Tiscareño, a young and talented new light on the graphic design horizon. Type Unlimited's Yvonne Davis massaged her many computers and typefaces to give us the current look.

Muchas Gracias, to you all.

CONTENTS

THE
BAJA
BOOK
III

7

MEXICO 1...WHAT'S IN A NAME?

HIGHWAY 1
NORTH OF
SANTA INES

Romanticists call it "The 1000 Mile Dream." Patriots named it for Benito Juarez. Geographically speaking, it is the Transpeninsula Highway. In Spanish it is the *Carretera*. The padres knew it as *"El Camino Real"*. To mapmakers it is officially Mexico 1. *Campesinos* speak of it as *Numero Uno*. Wags label it the Frijole Freeway. To those of us who had waited its completion for more than 20 years, it is simply the Baja Highway.

For 1058 miles it threads serpentinely like a narrow black band from the United States Border at Tijuana along the 800-mile length of the Baja California peninsula. Sometimes it skirts the cool blue Pacific, other stretches carry up *arroyos*, across *barrancas*, rising to an elevation of 3200 feet before it plunges again to alkaline deserts. Its mid-section touches the warm waters of the Sea of Cortez before recrossing to the Pacific drainage north of La Paz. Below La Paz it passes the Tropic of Cancer on its way to Cabo San Lucas, land's end, where sea finally meets ocean.

Baja California is like Alta California in the U.S.-cut on the bias. Geographically once part of the Mexican mainland, it angles sharply to the east as it juts southward. La Paz near the tip is actually east of Phoenix, Tucson and Salt Lake City.

A two-lane paved highway designed primarily to open *"La Frontera"* and to link both Bajas to the U.S. with truck transportation, the Baja Highway is, for nearly 400 miles, about 20 feet wide. Much of this stretch, between El Rosario and San Ignacio, has few shoulders. Turnoffs are rare. While all of Mexico 1 must be driven with extreme caution, this particular portion must be approached with extra care by operators of wide vehicles. Most of the peninsula is still open range and one must watch for livestock.

Driving after dark can be hazardous, as witness the crosses and monuments seen along the roadside. If an approaching vehicle flashes its lights at a bridge or narrow area, it means that they intend to proceed through. You had better slow down or even stop, pull as far over on the right as possible and allow the oncoming driver to pass. Rules of the road regarding who has priority on the up or down-grade mean little here. Caution is the best rule to follow.

The State of Baja California, occupying the northern half of the peninsula nearest the border, is on Pacific time, changing with the seasons as we do in California. The State of Baja California Sur is on Mountain Standard Time and does not change time.

BAJA—A FRAGILE PARADOX

The 800-mile long peninsula known as Baja California has long had the reputation of being rugged and hostile, and with good reason. It took the Spaniards 162 years, from the first attempt by Hernán Cortés in 1535 to Padre Salvaterra's 1697 landing in Loreto, to establish their first permanent settlement in Baja. After another 150 years, the Spanish influence was still limited to small communities around the few remaining active missions, plus scattered tiny ranchos. Chroniclers of those times commented on the inhospitality of the land, which today is still known as *"La Frontera"* by many residents of mainland Mexico.

Nothing is more awesomely rugged than raw desert land. Baja has repeatedly been characterized as being a barren wasteland...yet the peninsula, and especially the ocean around it, is full of life. Despite snowy two-mile-high peaks in its northern portion and small, scattered oases, it is classed as a desert — with rainfall figures ranging from near 10 inches in the southernmost regions to less than 2 inches in many areas further north.

As those who visit the great deserts of the Southwest have discovered, this environment is one of the world's most fragile. So tenuous is life here that the destruction of only a few plants can leave scars for generations.

If you are drawn to Baja for its uncluttered landscapes, try to keep them that way — uncluttered. Though the stark beauty of Baja is eroding a bit in some areas with the increased traffic, there is still much to protect and to preserve for generations yet unborn.

Baja California is, since the opening of the highway, moving from a primitive environment demanding great resourcefulness from its residents...towards a modern, effective society through improved transportation, communications, industry, housing, education — and tourism. But none of these changes has or probably will alter the basic friendly attitude of the Baja native. *"Mi casa es su casa"* is a way of life to the Mexican. "My house is your house" is an offering of friendship and respect that is well to remember.

If you enter Mexico without preconceived prejudices, if you can throw away the key to the clock and forget the calendar in this land of little hurry or worry, if you can embrace the Baja Californian for what he is, a pioneer in a *poncho* not very different from our own Western past...then you will love Baja, perhaps even as much as we do.

BAJA IS BORN

CIRIO

There was a time, 20 million years ago, when no peninsula extended 800 miles southeastward from the western edge of the North American continent. Baja fossils show that what later became a peninsula was once part of a land supporting verdant jungles filled with life forms typical of that era. Palms, ferns and other lush vegetation towered over the 50 foot duckbilled hydrosaur, a gigantic tyrannosaurus-like creature, and other reptiles in a steamy setting of erupting volcanoes and torrential rains.

In that era the earth was not at rest and her uneasy writhings tore loose a great chunk of the North American continent. Fueled by convulsive upliftings of rocky strata and an occasional collapse of the ocean floor, the landmass began to move northward. From time to time entire ranges collapsed into the sea, only to rise and again become covered with deep layers of volcanic outpourings.

The tip of Baja California is believed to have once been located on the west coast of Mexico between Acapulco and Puerto Vallarta. Today those orginal geographical neighbors are a good 300 miles apart and in the void between them has formed the Sea of Cortez. Even today the Baja peninsula moves northwestward along with California, toward the Bering Sea at almost one inch per year.

THE HISTORY AND PEOPLE OF BAJA

Baja has answered the many challenges to its existence by creating an environment completely unique in the western hemisphere. It affords a ruggedness, magnificence and variety of scenery to delight anyone with a love of the outdoors. From unexpected alpine meadows near the 10,126 foot Picacho del Diablo to the barren escarpments plunging downward toward the Sea of Cortez and on to *Finisterra* — Land's End, there are countless places of scenic and scientific interest throughout Baja.

The millions of years have left stories for all to read: the towering cinder cones, strange plants and jagged granitic and basaltic outcroppings are obvious to the untrained eye, while the skilled observer has studied the history of Baja through the widespread fossil beds and Indian middens near such towns as Ensenada, San Quintín, San Felipe and the mountains south of La Paz.

Conservative estimates place the arrival of man on the Baja California peninsula at about 10,000 years ago. The land forms were basically as they are now, but there was more water in this post ice-age period. Increased vegetation and animal life around lakes and their drainages provided the hunters and gatherers with a varied food supply.

By the time the Spaniards arrived over 400 years ago, the peninsula was considerably drier, and the lakes had for the most part disappeared. In 1535, Hernán Cortéz led a colonization attempt near La Paz, but his followers were driven out within two years by lack of water, inadequate supplies and natives made hostile from severe treatment.

Stories of great treasures of gold, pearls, and a race of Amazons ruled by a beautiful queen, Calafia, continued to excite explorers, and in 1540 Hernando de Alarcón visited the northern peninsula when he sailed into the mouth of the river now known as the Rio Colorado. He wrote of the native people there, was well treated and received food from them — as did Don Juan de Ornate, who visited the same area in the early 1600's and called the river people Cucapa. Ornate received gifts of corn, beans and squash from the Cucapa, which indicates that at this early period these northern Baja California people were practising agriculture.

Padre Eusebio Kino attempted to missionize the native people of the southern peninsula in 1683 and 1685, but it was not until 1697 that Jesuit padre Juan Maria Salvaterra established the first permanent non-indigenous colony on what was still thought by many to be the "island" of California.

Kino also visited the Colorado River delta in 1702 and observed small *rancherias* near the river growing corn, beans and pumpkins. The padre charted the region as a peninsula in 1705, but his map was rejected in Europe. It was not until Padre Fernando Consag sailed completely around the Gulf of California in 1746 and Jesuit Weneslaus Linck traveled from California across the Colorado River into Sonora that the dispute was finally settled.

It is generally believed that most of the earliest inhabitants of Baja California arrived via gradual or spasmodic immigrations from the north and
that their movements came about through cultural pressures or climatic
changes. Some scholars, however, pursue the possibility of ancient transpacific contacts with Baja California, especially in the southern portion.

The native people of the peninsula were accustomed to using stone
for their tools: in ancient times, crudely formed scrapers and choppers,
later, fine projectile points and equipment for grinding foods, portable
metates and bedrock mortars. They used wood to make dart throwers,
spears, and later bows and arrows — as well as hunting sticks similar to
the Australian boomerang.

Along the coasts on both sides of the Baja California peninsula are
numerous extensive clam shell middens. They are much in evidence
between Ensenada and San Quintín and in the region north of Bahía
Magdelena. The piles of shells graphically tell the story of a tribe's arrival
in the area and their subsequent harvesting of the larger clams. As the
supply diminished, smaller and smaller ones were taken until it became
unprofitable to remain. They then moved to another spot, to return again
after the clams had replenished themselves.

Available evidence indicates that the inhabitants had little clothing.
Women wore simple skirts of agave cactus fiber cordage or willow bark,

and people protected themselves from winter's cold with deerskins or rather intricately contrived capes made of the skins of small animals, mostly rabbits. Historians and anthropologists also mention unique capes of human hair which were used by shamans for ceremonial purposes.

Native housing consisted of simple brush or rock shelters, some of them open to the sky, and caves. Household equipment included carrying nets of agave fiber in the northern and central peninsula, and nets and mats of palm fiber in the southern portion.

In the north, over 2,000 years ago, the people learned to make thin-walled, hard-fired ceramic pots and bowls for cooking and storage. The northern and central people were also familiar with the art of basketry. Mexico has recently expanded its program of archaeological investigation in the peninsula, and it is important that visitors be aware that all archaeological pieces (such as stone tools and arrowpoints) are considered part of the national heritage and may not be removed. There is an ongoing campaign seeking the return of archaeological material already out of the country.

Ethnobotanists are learning from the surviving Indian people of northern Baja California that their forebearers possessed a vast knowledge of plant usages for food and medicinal purposes — from wild grass seeds, to pine nuts, acorn and cactus fruit, as well as various roots. Protein sources varied from insects to large animals such as deer and bighorn sheep.

These insects and animals — as well as fish, human figures and geometric forms — appear in paintings and carvings on rocks in many places along the peninsula. The most unusual and impressive paintings are those found in the central section, where larger-than-life figures of men and animals are painted in red and black. The figures dominate whole landscapes from the towering walls and ceilings of their rock shelters.

Radiocarbon dates on material from these caves have been reported by Dr. Clement Meighan to indicate the presence of people there 500 years before the coming of the Spaniards. Several excellent books have been written about the rock art of Baja California by Dr. Clement Meighan, Campbell Grant, and Harry Crosby.

As resident Indians in the missions of the southern two-thirds of the peninsula died off, their places were taken by people from the mainland, who have lived and worked in Baja ever since at fishing, cattle herding and mining.

Over the years, immigrants also came from Spain, England, France, Russia, Germany, China and the United States to add to the present-day population of Baja California. Many of these still maintain surprisingly strong identies with their homeland while others have been completely absorbed by Baja.

Today the thousand or so surviving descendants of the original 40,000 who populated Baja California are concentrated in the northern third of the peninsula — living for the most part in the mountains of the San Pedro Martír or the Sierra de Juarez and along the Río Hardy. They identify themselves as as Kiliwa, Pai Pai, Cochimi, Cucapa and Kumayai, many of them still speaking their ancient Yuman-Hokan dialects. Some even retain their several thousand year-old heritage, which helps them survive in an otherwise hostile environment.

BEFORE THE BORDER...YOUR TOURIST CARD

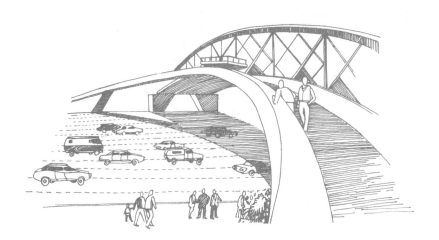

To drive the transpeninsula highway, Mexico 1, beyond Ensenada, you will need to obtain a Mexican Tourist Card. By law one is also required if you drive anywhere beyond the so-called Border Zone, or if your stay in Mexico is more than three days (72 hours).

Mexico issues two types of Tourist Cards. Both are free. One is valid for single visits of up to 180 days; it can be filled out beforehand and then validated upon proof of U.S. citizenship. A Multiple-Entry Tourist Card is valid for 180 days and is required when you apply for a Mexican hunting license, as you must log both **in** and **out** along with your hunting permits. For this one you must provide three 2 x 2 inch passport photos.

In either case, you may obtain the forms from the Mexican National Tourist Council or Mexican consulates in major cities. Single-entry permits may also be available through airlines ticket counters serving Mexico, Mexican auto insurance offices, some travel agencies or the Mexico West Travel Club.

Proof of citizenship can be a passport, birth certificate, voter registration, naturalization papers, baptismal certificate, affidavit of birth, discharge papers, or armed forces ID card. Such proof must be presented for every member of your family and should be carried throughout the trip. (It should be noted that U.S. Immigration officials can also ask for proof of citizenship before allowing you back across the border.) Children under 15 may be included on their parent's card, but separate cards are advisable, just in case they should return home with someone else.

Minors under 18 traveling alone or with persons other than their parents must not only obtain a Tourist Card but also present a notarized letter of consent from both parents or guardians. If the minor is with only one parent, a notarized letter of consent from the other parent is required.

Canadians and citizens of most other lands must present passports or birth certificates when applying for their tourist cards. At times citizens of some countries are not allowed in without a visa issued by a Mexican consulate, currently that list includes citizens of South Africa and Taiwan.

PERMITS APLENTY

Normally entry permits are required for each vehicle, including trailers and boats, entering Mainland Mexico. However, under current regulations, if you plan to stay within the confines of the Baja California peninsula you need only concern yourself with a boat permit.

If you decide to use one of the ferries linking Baja to the Mainland you will be required to obtain permits for all of your vehicles. There's no charge but you must present your U.S. driver's license and proofs of ownership on automobile, motor-home, trailer, boat, etc. If you don't own them, carry a Notarized Affidavit from the legal owner(s) showing that you have their permission to have the rig in Mexico.

HUNTING LICENSES

The quality of wing shooting for dove, quail, pheasant, duck, geese and brant in Baja California and nearby Sonora/Sinaloa is such that it attracts hunters from all parts of the U.S. and Canada.

The procedure for obtaining hunting licenses, gun permits, etc. is taxing, to say the least, and few people take it upon themselves to do all of the running necessary to get the papers. We strongly recommend that the leg-work be left to people in that business, such as: Mexican Hunting Association, 3302 Josie Ave., Long Beach, CA 90808, Phone (213) 421-1619; Mexico Services, PO Box 66278, Los Angeles, CA 90066, (213) 398-5797; or Romero's Mexico Service, 1600 W. Coast Highway, Newport Beach, CA 92663, Phone (714) 548-8931.

Should you want to do it yourself, here are the steps involved:

You will need up to 14 passport-size full-face photos, proof of citizenship, and a character reference (in duplicate) from your local police department. Also have the serial numbers, calibers and makes of the shotguns you wish registered. Next, go to a Mexican Consulate — where you will also be issued a multiple-entry tourist card — and request a Consular Gun Permit application.

Once filled out, the gun permit is taken to the Mexican Game Department (SEDUE) in either Tijuana or Mexicali. There you will purchase an application, which must be paid for in another office, then returned with the receipt for further signatures. Then it is taken to the Military Commandant's office, where it is signed, duplicated, and re-signed by the appropriate officials. (Here you may have to leave the papers and return another day.) Then you go back to the SEDUE where it is validated and the permits issued. All fees must be paid for in pesos and vary from year to year. A truly exhausting experience! Total cost is about $120, plus your time.

Latest information on seasons, bag limits and U.S. border regulations on the importation of game is available through the above-named organizations, or at the Mexican Consulates and U.S. Customs offices.

An increasingly popular way to avoid the hassle is to book one of the package tours where guns, guides, permits and accommodations are included. One such company is Wild Wing Adventures, 16000 Ventura Blvd. Suite 200, Encino, CA 91436.

FISHING LICENSES

Permits to fish from a commercial passenger-carrying sportboat in Mexican waters are usually included in the price of the trip. However, if you fish from a private boat, or from the shore, you will need to buy a standard Mexican fishing license. They are available through the Mexico West Travel Club, 2424 Newport Blvd, #91, Costa Mesa, CA 92627, (714) 662-7616; a number of tackle stores near the border (including some in the Los Angeles area); and at the Mexican Department of Fisheries in San Diego. They may also be purchased at some fisheries offices in Mexico, but supplies are spotty. Prices vary as the peso fluctuates, but they are less expensive than a California state fishing license. Boat permits too are very reasonable.

Each person 16 years or older on a private boat must have a license, whether fishing or not, when in Mexican waters.

Possession of cabrilla, lobster, oysters, pismo clams or shrimp is forbidden, though you probably will not be bothered if a small amount is used for immediate personal consumption. Possession of a totuava is now permitted under certain circumstances, but they are considered an endangered species by the United States, thus they cannot be brought into the country.

Anglers may catch a total of 10 fish per day — and no more than five of one species — but only two roosterfish or dolphinfish (dorado), one sailfish, marlin, swordfish or black sea bass. Releasing of fish is encouraged and is widely practiced. See Tom Miller's **Angler's Guide To Baja California** for more details.

Fishing and boating is restricted from December to April in Scammon's and Black Warrior lagoons as they are areas where California gray whales come to calve and mate. Check with local authorities for current regulations.

ABOUT INSURANCE

Automobile insurance in Mexico is confusing to many visitors, yet it is of vital importance. Simply stated, Mexican law does not recognize ANY insurance except that written by licensed Mexican insurance companies and their representatives, no matter what your American policy says.

To be fully protected while in Mexico, you must carry Mexican insurance on your car, trailer, boat (if trailered) or any other item you might be hauling. If the car, but not the trailer, is insured and you are in an accident, your car insurance is no longer valid — same as many policies written in the United States.

Should you become involved in an accident while in Mexico, you are considered liable under Mexican law and both parties are held equally guilty regardless of the circumstances until the matter is legally resolved. Lacking proper coverage, your vehicle can also be impounded and fines levied. Your Mexican policy guarantees, in Spanish, that you are able to pay damages up to the limit on the policy in case you are found to be at fault.

In the event of an accident and you are without Mexican insurance you may be brought to the police station for a hearing. If no one was injured or killed, you will be allowed to leave if you can pay for the damage and possible fines. If you are unable to pay, you probably will remain in custody and your car will be impounded.

If the accident involves injury or death to any party, you may be placed in protective custody until responsibilities are established by the authorities. Legally you can be held for up to three days before your case is heard. Bear in mind that an accident of any kind in Mexico is considered a felony, not a misdemeanor.

All of the above is based on the legal system known as the **Napoleanic Code**, wherein one is held to be guilty until proven innocent — as opposed to our **English Code** where the reverse is true. The Napoleanic Code is prevalent through much of Europe and most of Latin America.

Mexican insurance rates are based on the value of the vehicle and length of stay. For example, full coverage for a 10 day trip in a $8,000 car from the local automobile club runs about about $70. Members of the Mexico West Travel Club (see end of book) can qualify for substantial savings on both short term and annual policies through special group rates.

If you return sooner, refunds are available from most carriers. Some also offer credit if you stay in a recognized trailer park and have the manager sign a statement that your trailer/motorhome was not moved over a certain period. Ask your insurance carrier for details.

A variety of long term policies are also available for those who spend more days over a 12 month period, etc. Again, check with the carrier.

REGARDING ACCIDENTS IN MEXICO

1. Report any accident you may have to the nearest authorities.
2. City police have jurisdiction only in cities, not on highways.
3. Do not panic and do not pay anyone.
4. Show your Mexican insurance policy to competent authorities, but do not surrender your Mexican policy without a receipt for same.
5. If anyone is injured or killed, the parties involved must go to jail until guilt is established.

IT'S THE CUSTOM

Mexican Customs regulations are similar to those in other countries. The whole of Baja California, however, is a Free Zone and your vehicle or goods are less likely to be searched there. When you enter mainland Mexico by ferry, though expect a vehicle and luggage inspection.

Time was when the *"mordida,"* which translates as "death bite" and means a small bribe or tip, was common practice around larger towns, particularly along the border. The Mexican Government has been cracking down on this tradition in recent years while at the same time increasing the incomes of officials to compensate. Unfortunately, a runaway economy helps keep the practice alive. So if an outstretched palm should appear at times, be prepared to part with a small amount of money to speed you on your way. After all, it is part of the culture of many of countries of the world. But then, have you ever tried gotten a good seat at a Las Vegas show without slipping the host a $20 or $50 bill?

By law you may take only one quart of liquor into Mexico along with a "reasonable" amount of tobacco products. Though you probably won't be searched in Baja, it doesn't make sense to try and bring in cases of booze, or dozens of cartons of cigarettes. Don't bother to bring your own beer, it is very inexpensive and the tastes world famous. Wines of good quality are also available in Mexico. Inexpensive too are rum, brandy, gin, vodka and, of course, tequila, but Scotch, bourbon and Canadian whiskeys are very expensive.

You are allowed to bring in one still camera and one video camera per person, plus 12 rolls of film for each. Usually you may carry more, but professional photographers are supposed to have permits.

Americans may not take large quantities of new goods across the border without paying duty if it appears it might be for resale. However, a supply of simple gifts like paper and pencils, erasers, gum, candy, cookies or balloons will not be questioned and they make a big hit with the children you meet. Used but clean clothing in smaller sizes is always appreciated and may find you a friend for life.

Tips are also appreciated for services rendered, but don't be suprised if they are refused with a smile in this simpatico land.

When returning to the U.S.A. you may bring back up to one liter of alcoholic beverage per person. An American law, it applies to all persons over 21 crossing the border, whether in a car, bus, plane or walking. Currently, U. S. citizens may bring $400 worth of goods back into the United States duty-free. Special regulations apply to many handcrafted items and art objects.

FUEL FOR THOUGHT

All gasoline in Mexico is sold through the government's production and marketing monopoly, Pemex (Petroleos Mexicanos). When planing your trip into Baja California, you should consider the following:

First—Once out of the border towns, you should carry *pesos* to buy gasoline, as dollars are not always accepted and can be very confusing.

Second—Gasoline is usually plentiful along Mexico 1, except between San Quintín and Santa Rosalía. (We will provide special tips on this in our roadlogs).

Third—The unleaded premium, or *Extra* gas in the silver pump is intended for cars with catalytic converters. Costing a bit more, it also has a higher octane rating, and can be used to "boost" the performance of the leaded, lower octane-rated **NOVA** Plus.

Fourth—Fuel prices are the same throughout Mexico, and will roughly approximate the same costs found in the United States. You will find variations (in dollar values) because of the *peso* fluctuation in relation to the dollar, but generally, the above rule of thumb works well.

Both gasolines appear to work satifactorily in almost any car, if the spark is retarded and a good quality octane booster such as "Moroso" is used. We find that the combination reduces pre-ignition "pinging" rather effectively. Remember too, that gearing down under stress conditions will always make it easier on your car's motor.

Fifth—Diesel fuel in Mexico is widely available and its quality has improved greatly over the past few years. Today most knowledgable diesel engine owners use double filters on fuel lines anyway, but in Mexico this is a particularly good idea, for impurities can slip in more easily in a desert environment where dust and wide temperature fluctuations exist.

Sixth—Butane supplies are best found in the larger towns near the border or in La Paz. Only limited supplies may be available in between, and shortages sometimes occur everywhere during the winter months. We do not recommend attempting to drive LPG-powered vehicles very far into Mexico, as the supplies are not that reliable. White gas is difficult to obtain, so bring what you need. Kerosene (petroleo para lampara) is usually found in the smaller native grocery stores.

MORE POWER FOR BAJA

At *Cerro Prieto*, a few miles south of Mexicali, geothermal wells are being tapped to produce a significant portion of the electrical energy for the residents of the Mexicali Valley.

The intense heat that underlies the region is manifested on the surface by varicolored bubbling fumeroles, some of which emit high-pitched whistles and long plumes of steam. The field is currently the second largest geothermal generator in the world, and is still being expanded.

THE GREEN ANGELS OF BAJA

Motorists in need of a helping hand on Baja's paved roads will find that and more in the fleet of specially-equipped green pickup trucks which patrol Mexico's main roads at frequent intervals. Called *Angeles Verdes*, or Green Angels, it is their job to assist motorists in trouble.

Each vehicle carries a crew of two, at least one of whom speaks English. They also can provide a limited supply of spare parts, gas, oil and water. Minor repairs can often be made right on the spot, at no charge, except for parts, which are available at cost.

A push or tow is also provided as necessary, again without charge. This motorists' service is provided by the Mexican Government as part of its program to make visitors welcome and help make their stay as carefree and enjoyable as possible.

However, we must emphasize that this complimentary service should not lull the motorist into driving in Mexico with a vehicle in need of repair or service. If you plan off-road sidetrips, make sure your tires are in top shape, carry a five-gallon can of water, another of gas, and an adequate tool kit.

The Green Angels patrol the highways in Baja several times daily, so you may have to be patient. Fortunately, many of the truck drivers of Baja are also generous with their time and talent, and often beat the *Angeles* at their own game.

The Green Angeles, or *Angeles Verdes* of Mexico are another way of saying "welcome to Baja."

HEALTH HINTS

There are some things you can do before you leave home which will help you have a healthy Baja vacation.

Be sure you are up to date on your tetanus boosters. This is a good idea no matter where in the world you might be going, even across town to fish or hike.

Take take along a good First Aid Kit (see section on First Aid, page 173). Extra eye glasses and sufficient medical prescriptions to last your stay are also suggested. If necessary, most drug prescriptions, or their Mexican counterpart, are available in Baja's larger towns, along with medical and dental aid. You might also want to check with your health insurance carrier to see if their benefits go with you. (Incidently, medical, dental and optical services are much less expensive in Mexico, and some visitors come just for this.)

Everyone leaving for a foreign land should be sure they are in reasonable health. Don't risk spoiling your trip, schedule your medical and dental chec-kups before departure.

Contrary to widespread belief, the same type bacteria and viruses that can cause the tourist intestinal problems flourish on both sides of the border. The villain is called E. coli, and is found all over the world, but with varying severity of symptoms. In Mexico, it is simply called *"turista."*

That particular intestinal affliction endured so frequently by tourists has almost as many colorful names as victims. And it may well be avoided completely, if certain simple precautions are taken.

Mostly, it is a matter of not overdoing in strange surroundings. Don't go overboard on heavily-spiced dishes, don't overindulge in food and drink, don't overexert or undersleep. Avoid water unless bottled, unless you know that the water is potable. Go easy on fruit and vegetables. Enjoy the great fresh seafood of Baja, but if something tastes funny, don't eat it there any more than you would at home.

Should E. coli get to you, the illness may last up to three days. Symptomatic treatment can be made with Tincture of Paregoric or one of the diarrhea medications. Small amounts of fluid at frequent intervals, consomme, beef tea, soda pop are helpful to get you over the worst. Avoid spicy foods, milk, dairy products, orange juice and eggs for a few days.

Amoebic Dysentery is far more serious, and a physician should be consulted immediately. But this malady is far, far rarer even than the infrequent *tourista* in Baja California.

There are a number of preventatives and remedies readily available almost anywhere in Mexico. Lomotil is considered among the best. If caused by infectious bacteria, Oxabid is said to be preferable. Remember that nearly any medication can have side effects, so if possible stay away from any of them.

Some U.S. doctors freely prescribe antibiotics such as erythrocin as a preventative. This is fine, but some classes of these drugs can cause sun poisoning — a more severe malady than what it is intended to prevent.

Remember, you are changing your entire enviornment and that may be a cause, not just the water, etc. Most cases occur during the first few days; after that your system adapts.

Interestingly, Mexicans encounter E. coli when they travel north into the United States. Wonder what they call it?

A WEATHER REPORT

Much of northern Baja California has a climate similar to that of Southern California. Both are basically semi-tropical desert, with verdant valleys, high mountains and hot, dry deserts.

The cool Pacific currents make Baja's west coast much cooler than the same latitude on the Sea of Cortez, just as Los Angeles is cooler than Palm Springs.

Climate in the north coastal region of Baja, with Ensenada as the hub, offers warm days and cool nights in summer — in winter, cool days and chilly nights. There is considerable fog along the beaches, with a 10 inch average rainfall coming during the winter and early spring.

Along the Cortéz, Baja is pure desert from Mexicali south to Bahía de Los Ángeles. Summers range from 90 to 110 degrees, with warm and sometimes humid nights. Temperatures cool off to a more comfortable level in spring and fall. Winters days can be balmy, even quite warm, but strong chilly winds are also a fact of life during that time. From just south of the 28th parallel — the border between the two states of Baja California and Baja California Sur — the climate becomes more sub-tropical. Summers are hot and humid, winters cool enough for an evening sweater after a day in the 70's. Spring and fall are close to perfect. Rainfall is scant, most coming from late summer storms. They, however, though often brief, can be violent and release torrents into the arroyos. Most Baja resorts are now air-conditioned, while others are so situated that they make the most of prevailing breezes. Generally, the peninsula is less humid than its counterparts across the Cortez on the mainland. Despite higher temps and humidity, more and more visitors are finding summer travel in Baja's "hot zones" to be easily livable. In some areas, such as Cabo, it is even becoming crowded in August and September.

WHAT TO WEAR

Here in Baja there is little need for concern over what to wear. Here they keep it simple. First, get comfortable in clothes appropriate to the season, and this usually includes a wide-brimmed hat — see previous page. Next, keep in mind that Baja's culture still doesn't include bikini-clads wandering anywhere but on the beach or around the pool, so bring coverups. Loose, wraparound skirts for visiting in town is also a good choice, although pants and shorts on women is becoming more accepted.

Dressing for an evening out is simple, just get comfortable, with *Guayaberas* for the men and casual dresses for the women sure winners. Rarely is anything more required. If you see a tie, it will likely be on the maitre 'd. There are few places in the world where you can purchase better casual clothing at better prices then in Mexico, so take advantage of it. Plan to buy some of your holiday wardrobe as you go. You will be glad you did.

Aside from clothing, you should bring the needed toiletries as supplies are limited locally. Don't forget sunscreen products, insect repellant, vitamins and prescriptions, extra eyeglasses, plus a small, basic first aid kit.

If you will be camping don't forget to have a sturdy, wind resistant sun shade. Nothing makes a vacation seem so long as to have to huddle together inside your vehicle in order to get out of the sun.

BYOB—BRING YOUR OWN BOAT

In the years since the completion of the Baja Highway the numbers of boats entering Baja for fishing and other forms of recreation have increased expotentially. And as their numbers have grown the Mexican government is working to make it easier for the visitor. Currently you need only show legal ownership and purchase an inexpensive annual license for your trailerable boat from any of a number of outlets. Rates vary according to size.

Papers for any private ocean-going yacht must be obtained through the Mexican Consul or a yacht clearance broker. Listing all crewmen and passengers, along with particulars about the boat, they are presented to authorities at your Mexican port of entry. Two brokers are Romero's Mexico Yacht Service, 1600 W. Pacific Coast Highway, Newport beach, CA 92663, (714) 548-8931; and Mexico Services, Box 66278, Los Angeles, CA 90066, (213) 398-5797.

On-the-road insurance for trailerable boats must be purchased when you buy policies for the rest of your rig. An uninsured boat being towed by an insured vehicle violates the terms of your Mexican auto policy, rendering it null and void. Some policies here in the U.S. have similar restrictions. You may also obtain on-the-water liability and/or hull coverage through Seguros Olmeca. More information and rates are available from the Mexico West Travel Club, 2424 Newport Blvd, Suite 91, Costa Mesa, CA 92615, (714) 662-7616.

FOR YOU PILOTS

If you fly your own plane, you are under a new set of rules. When flying to mainland Mexico, flight plans must be sent in writing to the nearest International Airport, even if you plan to overfly it for a more distant destination. Your final ETA should be included. This is an FAA requirement, to aid the U.S. radar in sorting out your "blip" from others who may not be authorized to be in the area.

When flying to Baja you must file a flight plan with the FAA, then clear immigration, etc. at one of Baja's international airports with no intermediate stops permitted enroute. International Airports are located at Tijuana, Mexicali, Loreto, La Paz and Los Cabos, with announced plans for Mulegé (a good chance) and San Felipe (don't hold your breath).

If the plane's owner is not aboard, the pilot must carry a notarized authorization from the registered owner. Tourist cards and proof of citizenship are required, just as they are if you drive. Upon leaving Mexican territory, clearance must be obtained from FSS.

Check with a Mexican Consulate regarding other regulations. **"Airports of Mexico and Central America"** by Arnold Senterfitt is a valuable reference for pilots heading for the peninsula.

Most airfields indicated on our Baja Photomaps are dirt, usually maintained by the nearest inhabitants, so don't expect too much. Their condition also varies with weather, usage, etc. Always make a fly-over before heading for a landing. Veteran Baja pilot Arnold Senterfitt suggests you give these a High Look-Low Look-Close Look approach. You can't be too careful when using Baja's dirt landing strips.

As with your automobile, you should carry Mexican insurance on your aircraft. Again Seguros Olmeca and the Mexico West Travel Club can help you there.

DIVING IN BAJA

The reefs and coves of the Sea of Cortez number among the premier places in the world for the diver. Hundreds of species of sealife may be found in sometimes bewildering abundance. There are, however, a number of restrictions that must be heeded.

It is illegal to possess a speargun if you are using Scuba equipment. However, it is permissible to use one when free diving. You may **not** take lobster, abalone, pearl oysters or cabrilla. It is also necessary to have a valid Mexican fishing license if you take any form of sealife. The rules are strictly enforced and the penalties can be severe, so confine most of your activities to looking; it is still great.

Dive centers with compressors, etc. are found in Mulegé, Loreto, La Paz and Cabo San Lucas. The Mulegé Divers in, of course, Mulegé is especially recommended. Several hotels have compressors, including Hotel Punta Pescadero in the East Cape and the Hacienda at Cabo. There are also dive boats for charter in La Paz and Cabo San Lucas.

TALE OF A PEARLER

Most noted of the early Cortez pearlers was Francisco de Ortega, who in 1633 produced his chart of the Sea of Cortez in which he named the larger islands, bays, points, etc. His nameplaces are still in use to this day, despite later attempts by other navigators to rename the landmarks in the Cortez. — Ray Cannon

SURFING AND WINDSURFING

Judging from the number of boards seen in Baja it is obvious it is a surfing hotspot. Any time of the year all manner of vehicles can be seen on likely beaches. Baja is becoming the home of the true "endless summer," except much closer to home. Rapidly growing in Baja too is the subculture of windsurfing. Though their needs are a bit different — reliable breezes and small waves — they too are finding their version of year-around action.

Some of the formerly out-of-the-way breaks are secrets no longer. One, Punta Santa Rosalillita has a right break that can be ridden for up to 1-1/2 miles on a heavy west-southwest set.

Summer storm systems south of Baja create good shore breaks on at least a dozen beaches between Hotel Palmilla and Boca del Tule, 20 miles east of San José del Cabo.

IF YOU TAKE A CAMERA

Take plenty of film — you'll need it. Hot weather can play havoc with your color film and it is important to store it in as cool a place as possible, so don't put it in direct sunlight or the glove compartment. The bright sunlight of Baja makes it advisable to have a polarizing filter, and a medium yellow filter is a plus for black and white photography. Be extra careful to protect your camera from the fine dust found almost everywhere off Baja's main highways. Ditto for salt water.

A PET PROBLEM

To bring a pet into Mexico, you should have a veterinarian's certificate of good health and rabies shot within the last six months entered on a visa form by the Mexican Consulate.

THE PESO STORY

Since September of 1976 when Mexico's economic policy caught up with her and she was forced to devaluate the *peso* for the first time in many years, it has been of one economic crisis after another. As to when or where it will stop nobody knows. We've quit trying to guess.

Suffice it to say that while everything seems to remain about the same in dollar costs, the number of pesos marked on the product soars. It surely is much harder on our Baja hosts than it is on us. We can only hope that their government gets things under control soon.

On the inside back cover we've tried to fashion a *Peso Exchange Barometer* to equate the value of *pesos* to dollars at a variety of exchange rates. We hope that the *peso* will not outstrip this one, but won't bet on it.

Dollars are accepted through most of Baja, and a bit less so on the mainland. For the sake of simplicity we recommend you exchange dollars for *pesos*, a few days supply at a time, at the banks. Open weekdays from 9 a.m. to 1:30 p.m., they exchange at the going official rate, while hotels, etc., tend to offer a bit less.

Since 1980 Mexico has has a Value Added Tax *(IVA)* of 15 percent on the mainland, six percent in Baja. Added to most goods and services (but not gasoline), it is usually included in the price. It's not a ripoff, just a way of raising money, like our sales taxes and other use taxes throught the world. If you have any doubts, just ask and they will explain it.

SIDETRIPS AND SHORTCUTS

In 1973 when the Mexican Government completed Mexico 1 and officially opened Baja to tourism, they announced a master plan of road development intended to establish scenic, recreational and commercial routes throughout the peninsula.

Since that time, some roads have been paved beyond Mexcico 1, such as to Bahía de Los Angeles, between Cabo San Lucas and La Paz via Todos Santos, and from Ensenada to San Felipe, but most of the activity has been in building hundreds of miles of graded gravel roads where none existed before.

In the process, there has developed an interesting series of sidetrips, at least one of which should catch your imagination—

Sidetrip No. 1...is all paved, adjacent to the border, and about four driving hours in length. Begin in Tijuana and take the toll road along the Pacific south to Ensenada, then north through Guadalupe and past olive groves and vineyards to Tecate. From here you may return to Tijuana or cross the border at Tecate, some 38 miles east of San Diego.

Sidetrip No. 2...is best taken over several days, and this too is all paved. Beginning in Ensenada, take Mexico 3 east into the mountains past huge boulders, cattle ranches and farms. Then come miles of mountain vistas as you move southeastward toward the Mexicali-San Felipe highway (Mexico 5). As the road drops into the desert bordering the Sea of Cortez an almost-manicured desert comes into view with the magnificent two-mile high Picacho del Diablo as a backdrop. San Felipe, only 30 miles south of the intersection, has numerous accommodations.

Some 127 miles to the north is Mexicali and California's Imperial Valley. For a spectacular drive, follow Mexico Highway 2 west from Mexicali up the precipitous eastern escarpment of the Sierra Juarez and then pine-studded highlands, finally arriving in Tecate.

Sidetrip No. 3...between Laguna Chapala and San Felipe, should be reserved only for hardy travelers with rugged backroad-proven equipment. Portions of it trace the old La Paz road before Mexico 1. Though the approach roads are paved there are only a few miles of paving between the end of Mexico 5 and the Baja Highway at Laguna Chapala, plus lots of washboard, sand and rocks. Some improvements are being accomplished, but its gonna take awhile. (See pgs 52-53, 58-59 and 62-63 for maps and logs.)

Crossing searing desert sands and traversing treacherous hillsides, the road leads to miles of virgin beaches and bays, old mining areas and palm-lined arroyos. Along the way are forests of elephant trees, cirios and giant cardons at their best. Water and fuel are almost nonexistent and the climate harsh, but the rewards are there for those willing to make the effort.

Sidetrip No. 4...takes us through the Vizcaino Desert past the largest evaporative salt works in the world, bustling fishing villages and tiny encampments which appear to have been bypassed by the rest of the world. (See pg 89)

Sidetrip, No. 5...paved, it goes from La Paz south along the Pacific side through Todos Santos and Pescadero to Cabo San Lucas on Mexico 19. The return trip comes back up the Cortez past the East Cape before winding through the mountains and back to the La Paz plain, a total of about 240 miles.

Sidetrip No. 6...is the newly constructed sand and gravel roadbed that follows the Cortez-facing Baja beaches from La Ribera to San José del Cabo. Along the way are some of the most beautiful, and remote, beaches to be found anywhere. Be sure that you are self sufficient as you'll find no services over the 64-mile journey.

SIDE TRIPS — SHORT CUTS

(POINT TO POINT
DISTANCES SHOWN
IN MILES . . .)

TIJUANA
39
TECATE   MEXICALI
1
2   126
134
ENSENADA   127
134   SONOITA
1   124   NOGALES
3   140
84   SAN FELIPE   SANTA ANA
SAN QUINTIN   PUERTECITOS
56   15
109   106
SANTA INES   PUNTA FINAL
70 47
4
PUNTA PRIETA   BAHIA de LOS ANGELES
7   41   HERMOSILLO
GUERRERO NEGRO
88   81
SEA
SAN IGNACIO   GUAYMAS
44
SANTA ROSALIA   OF   148
38   NAVAJOA
MULEGE
CORTEZ
PACIFIC OCEAN   83
100
LORETO
N   LOS MOCHIS
89   TOPOLOBAMPO
CIUDAD CONSTITUCION
137   270
TO MAZATLAN
LA PAZ
66
TODOS SANTOS   51   5   BUENA
VISTA
51   SAN JOSE del CABO
SAN LUCAS

TO PUERTO VALLARTA →

CORTEZ CROSSINGS

An essential part of the way of life in the lower half of the Baja Peninsula are the oceangoing ferries which regularly criss-cross the Sea of Cortez. For the most part designed and built in Europe, these ships are by no means small. They hold up to 100 or more cars, trucks, trailers and boats, and have a variety of accommodations for passengers. The crews are courteous, but in general fail to keep the ships up to acceptable cleanliness standards in the passenger salons, bathrooms, etc.

Currently there are three routes being serviced on a regular basis — Santa Rosalia-Guaymas, La Paz-Topolobampo and La Paz-Mazatlan. There is also a twice-weekly run between Cabo San Lucas and Puerto Vallarta but lately it has not kept to its announced schedule. Depending on which ferry might be on the run accommodations range from reclining, airplane-type seats in an open salon, bunk beds in nonprivate cubicles on the lower deck, to regular shipboard cabins with beds, toilets and showers.

At presstime the announced schedule was as follows:

Santa Rosalia to Guaymas — 11 p.m. departures, Tu, Th, Sa; arriving at 7 a.m. the following day; Guaymas to Sta. Rosalia — 10 a.m. departures Tu, Th, Sa; arriving 6:30 p.m.

La Paz to Topolobampo (near Los Mochis) — 8 p.m. departures, Mo, We, Th, Sa; arriving at 4 a.m. next day; Topo. to La Paz — 10 a.m. departures Mo, Tu, Th, Fr; arriving at 6 p.m. the same day.

La Paz to Mazatlan — 5 p.m. departures daily; arriving 9 a.m. next morning.. Mazatlan to La Paz — 5 p.m. departures and arriving about 8:30 a.m. the following day.

As there is presently no U.S. office for ferry reservations, you should make them in person at the respective ferry offices at least one day in advance. The ferry office in La Paz, located downtown on Madero Avenue and Victoria can take reservations for all ferries. Unfortunately we have found them not very reliable. All of the other offices are located in the ferry terminals.

If you wish to call ahead, their numbers (dialed from the U.S.) are: La Paz 011-526-822-0109 and -5677; Santa Rosalia, 011-526-852-0013 and -0014; Cabo San Lucas, 011-526-843-0079. English is not spoken in any of the offices, so plan on doing it all in Spanish. As you may be delayed for several days if reservation loads are heavy, plan on enjoying the sights of the region. Most terminals are located within an easy drive of camping spots.

How much do they cost? In the Mexican economy today, it is impossible to be specific, but you might figure less than $50 for a 28-foot rig from Sta Rosalia to Guaymas; $75 between La Paz and Topolobampo or Mazatlan; and $80 between Puerto Vallarta and Cabo. Passenger rates, salon class are only a couple of dollars for any of the voyages. There is a rumor that there may be a more deluxe "Turismo" class ferry going on the Puerto Vallarta run soon. It will be premium priced, and better maintained. Time will tell.

When the Cortez ferries first began their runs the passengers aboard found the atmosphere around the stern-located lounge and restaurant much like a minicruise ship and spent the sunset hours watching the sea glide by. A welcome break while someone else does the driving. Let us hope that the "Turismo" ferry will revive that ambiance.

ONE LAST NOTE: Once you've parked your rig on the ferry, you cannot return to it, so be sure to remove whatever you will need during the trip.

BAJA PHOTOMAPS

In 1973 when we began the Baja Book series we found that while a broad selection of maps of the peninsula existed, the physical contours — shorelines, landmark locations, etc. — varied rather widely from one to another. It became obvious that all were incomplete by today's standards. Clearly, the time for guess-mapping has passed.

In late 1972 NASA launched the first U.S. satellite program devoted exclusively to the study of earth resources from space. Carrying special cameras and sensors to provide data relating to agriculture, forestry, land use, geology, hydrology, geography, environmental science, etc., the ERTS (Earth Resources Technology Satellite) Pathfinder was sent into a 568-mile-high orbit.

From this platform in the sky the ERTS cameras looked down on a Baja California as never seen before by man. Constantly recording the electronic EKG's of the earth with its bank of camera systems, Pathfinder radioed back thousands of images for study by scientists throughout the world.

For the first time this long narrow peninsula that encompasses the states of Baja California and Baja California Sur could be clearly seen at a single glance — a great ragged finger clawing the Pacific. Using special films, virtually every land detail was captured.

The authors discovered that they could visually detect surf breaking on the sandbars at the entrance to Laguna San Ignacio. Farmland became easily identifiable — even hundreds of miles of the Baja highway could be seen! Surely, the key to mapping Baja was to be found in these remarkable images.

From thousands of prints we selected a complete, nearly cloudless set of photos of the peninsula. Once secured, thirty-five of these images were pieced into a great nine foot high montage of Baja California.

Next came the painstaking process of transferring the many notes and sketches secured over thousands of miles of driving through virtually every corner of the vast peninsula into an easily-understood map. Using a second color, the data was overlaid onto the actual photographs, thus preserving every detail of the original pictures.

The end result was scaled into 45 full-page Baja Spacemaps®, each covering about 70 air miles of Baja at a scale of one inch to 7.8 miles.

BEFORE-YOU-CROSS-THE-BORDER CHECKLIST
Make sure you have the following, if applicable:

- Proof of citizenship...
- Tourist card...
- All vehicle registrations and/or proof of ownership or notarized permission...
- Notarized permission for children other than your own if they are under 18...
- Mexican insurance...
- First aid kit, sunscreen & insect repellant...

- Emergency water...
- Propane tanks filled — it's sometimes hard to find in Baja...
- Written confirmations on any hotel reservations...
- Fishing and hunting licenses, guns and tackle...
- If you have doubts, reread the BEFORE THE BORDER section, pages 14-23...

NOTE: Don't forget to turn off the gas and lights; put the cat out; lock the house — and take **The Baja Book III...**

HOW TO USE THE BAJA SPACEMAPS and ROADLOGS

All Baja Spacemaps have been coordinated with matching Baja Roadlogs in a mile-by-mile manner on facing pages so you can locate your position on the appropriate Baja Spacemap at any time. Note that roadlog entries start with the nearest kilometer marker. Now you can readily determine how many kilometers, thus miles, you are from nearby towns, etc. The use of the space photos also pinpoints arroyos, beaches, camping and fishing spots, etc. in a manner never before possible.

All maps are shown in the same relation to magnetic north — as indicated by the compass arrows — so that your view of the countryside will remain consistent.

The small maps of Baja in the margins of each roadlog page are marked to show your general position in the peninsula. Page numbers of connecting maps are given in the margins of every Baja Spacemap.

To accommodate the roadlogs we find it necessary to repeat three maps (pages 30 & 32, 62 & 64, 120 & 122). Note that several times the roadlogs direct you to turn back a page. This is because of the East to West path of the highway (Tecate to Ensenada, pages 34 to 32; Loreto to Ciudád Constitución, pages 108 to 106 and 104; and San José del Cabo to Cabo San Lucas, pages 124 to 122).

Baja Spacemap keys are as follows:

Paved highway	🐾 **Beachcombing**	⛪ **Missions**
Unpaved road	◤ **Diving**	🏝 **Resorts**
Minor road, not for standard cars.	🐟 **Fishing**	〜 **Surfing**
	★ **Gas Stations**	⎯ **Sailboarding**
⚓ **Anchorages**	🔫 **Hunting**	🚐 **Trailer Parks or Camping**
⊂ **Clamming**	▭ **Landing Fields**	

Page Guide for Baja Spacemaps

Spacemaps in West-East
Sequence, North To South

**Maps on Pages 30-32
62-64 & 120-122 are
repeated to
accommodate
roadlogs.**

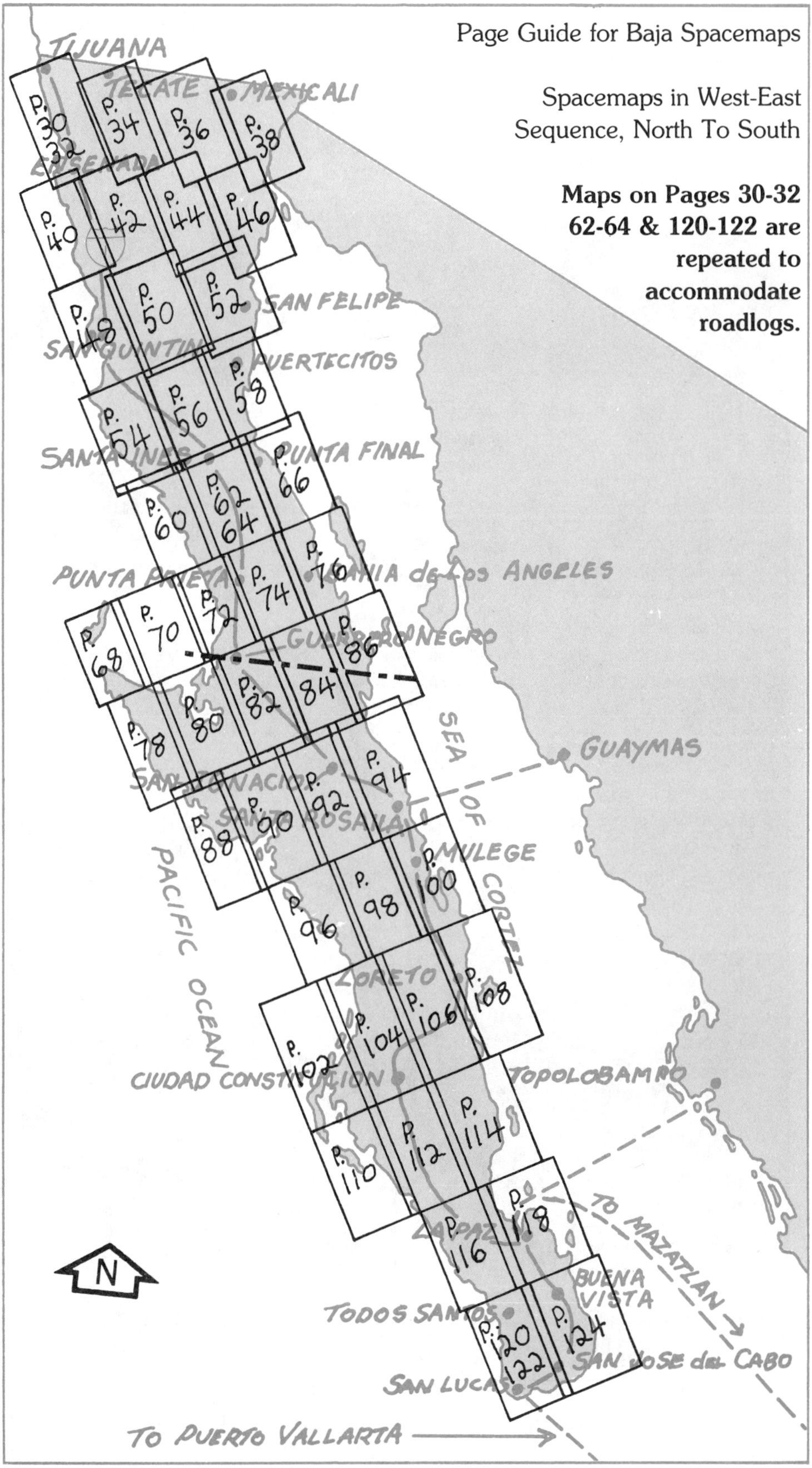

TIJUANA
TECATE · MEXICALI
P. 30/32
P. 34
P. 36
P. 38
ENSENADA
P. 40
P. 42
P. 44
P. 46
P. 48
P. 50
P. 52
SAN FELIPE
SAN QUINTIN · PUERTECITOS
P. 54
P. 56
P. 58
SANTA INES · PUNTA FINAL
P. 60
P. 62/64
P. 66
PUNTA PRIETA
P. 72
P. 74
P. 76 BAHIA de LOS ANGELES
P. 68
P. 70
GUERRERO NEGRO
P. 86
P. 78
P. 80
P. 82
P. 84
SEA
SAN IGNACIO
P. 88
P. 90
P. 92
P. 94
GUAYMAS
SANTA ROSALIA
OF
MULEGE
P. 96
P. 98
P. 100
CORTEZ
PACIFIC OCEAN
LORETO
P. 102
P. 104
P. 106
P. 108
CIUDAD CONSTITUCION
TOPOLOBAMPO
P. 110
P. 112
P. 114
LA PAZ
P. 116
P. 118
TO MAZATLAN
BUENA VISTA
TODOS SANTOS
P. 120/122
P. 124
SAN LUCAS
SAN JOSE del CABO

N

TO PUERTO VALLARTA →

SAN DIEGO

0   5   10   MILES

0   5   10   15   KM

PLAYAS DE TIJUANA

SAN YSIDRO

ISLAS
DE LOS CORONADOS

TOLL GATE

TIJUANA

CALIFORNIA

BAJA CALIFORNIA

SAN ANTONIO

LA MESA

MEX 1

MEX 2

ROSARITO

TOLL GATE

POPOTLA

PUERTO NUEVO

Bahia Descanso

CANTAMAR

HALF-WAY HOUSE

Mision El Descanso

PACIFIC OCEAN

LA MISION

LA SALINA

Mision San Miguel

BAJAMAR

EL MIRADOR

GUADALUPE

SAL SIPUEDES

MEX 3

TOLL GATE

ISLAS
TODOS SANTOS

EL SAUZAL

Bahia de
Todos Santos

ENSENADA

Punta Banda

ESTERO BEACH

EL CIPRES

LA BUFADORA

See Page 34

N

TIJUANA — ENSENADA

0   **K0**   As you cross the border into Tijuana (pg. 126) pass under the International Arch and, following the "Ensenada Cuota" sign, keep in right lane and bear left as road curves. After following a couple of the cloverleafs you end up going west on divided road next to the border fence. Shortly you will go up a steep hill and then west again.

5.7   **K9**   Mexico 1D curves south at intersection with Playas de Tijuana road.

6.2   **K10**   Toll gate. This is first of three located between Tijuana and Ensenada. Due to rampant inflation, no telling exactly what the toll might be in pesos, but it is reasonable. Restrooms.

14.2   **K22**   Resort development of San Antonio Shores is on right. On hill to left is KOA campground and trailer park.

16   **K26**   Road curves gently inland past truck gardens. Visible to right is power plant, desalting facility for Tijuana's municipal water system, and a large tank farm.

18.5   **K29+**   Rosarito Norte sign; road right passes through Roarito Beach (pg. 130). Road coming in from left (north) is old, non-toll road. Not recommended as it is usually crowded.

21.7   **K34+**   Road right to Rosarito Sur and non-toll *"libre"* road that parallels divided Mexico 1D for next 20 miles past numerous resorts, trailer parks, restaurants. Second toll gate just ahead. Restrooms.

33   **K53**   Cantamar turnoff from toll road.

41.2   **K65+**   La Misión turnoff. La Fonda hotel and restaurant is nearby. Marvelous view, good food. American colony of La Misión is adjacent. *Libre* road continues south under toll road, turning inland past ruins of Misión San Miguel, up into hills and 20 miles later rejoins Mexico 1. Continue south on 1D.

45   **K72+**   La Salina turnoff to several beaches with camping facilities and good fishing (perch and corbina). Just to north is new, exclusive, and expensive mobile home and trailer resort.

48   **K77+**   Jatay turnoff to Bajamar resort development. Highway continues winding through rocky terrain with scattered brush and agave cactus.

51.7   **K83+**   El Mirador turnoff. A small parking area from which there is a magnificent view of the Todos Santos islands, Punta Banda and Pacific Ocean. Road ahead should be taken with caution as too much speed could be a problem.

61.8   **K99**   Toll Gate. This is the last one. Just ahead is San Miguel village and *libre* road from La Mision (see above).

62.5   **K100**   Ensenada *libre* road rejoins highway. Proceed past various factories and warehouses. Several new residential and hotel developments are also beginning to show.

64   **K102**   Side road to right is Mexico 3 from Tecate. Proceed past more motels, campgrounds and the cannery community of El Sauzal.

69   **K109+**   Follow road right at fork to *"Muelle"* (breakwater 126) past shipyard and Ensenada.

70.5   **K112**   Enter downtown Ensenada (pg. 130) at first signal. Divided road right bypasses downtown traffic.

End of log...

T
H
E

B
A
J
A

B
O
O
K

III

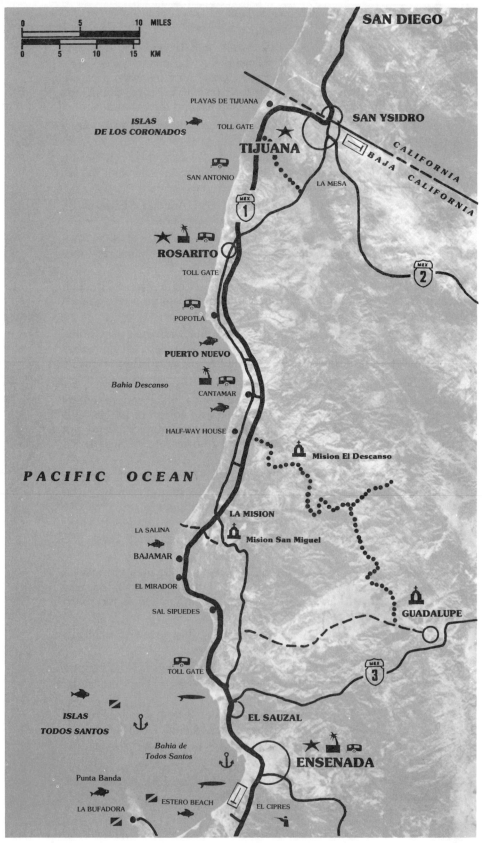

See Page 34

TECATE — ENSENADA (from page 35)

49   K79   Road right is to Guadalupe, 1 mi. (pg. 130). Road winds at times but easy driving. Continue past farms and *ranchos*.

61   K98+   Pass small settlement and cross narrow bridge. Road goes sharply to left, 30 mph then follow canyon down toward Mexico 1, 7 miles north of Ensenada. 65.6 K105 Junction with Mexico 1. *End of log...*

TIJUANA - MEXICALI

0   K184   As you cross the border into Tijuana (pg. 126) pass under the arch and follow signs indicating the road east to Mexicali and racetrack. This should be Paseo de Tijuana. At traffic circle go south on Blvd. Cuauhtemoc to Agua Caliente Blvd, then head east past racetrack.

4   K178+   Agua Caliente Racetrack just to the south. You won't find a kilometer marker near here, but if there were one it would be just east, and read 178. Continue east through large and crowded La Mesa suburb.

10.5   K167   Wind uphill and sharp to left, 25 mph, just before reaching dam.

11.2   K166   Rodriguez Dam - part of the water supply system for Tijuana. Continue upgrade.

16.5   K158   The small town of El Florido. Several dairies hereabouts.

24   K146   Road south leads to Presa Carrizo, a dam and lake in Tijuana water supply system. Area is known as "Cañada Verde."

29.4   K136+   Famous health spa, Rancho La Puerta is on right.

31   K134   Enter rapidly growing city of Tecate, continue straight. Right branch parallels other, and leads to Ensenada road at signal past brewery. (page 123).

33   K131   On left is Panadería El Mejór. This could well be the best bakery in Baja. Everything is great, and "Open 24 hours!" Leave Tecate and begin winding upgrade.

(continued on page 35)

See Pages 30 & 32

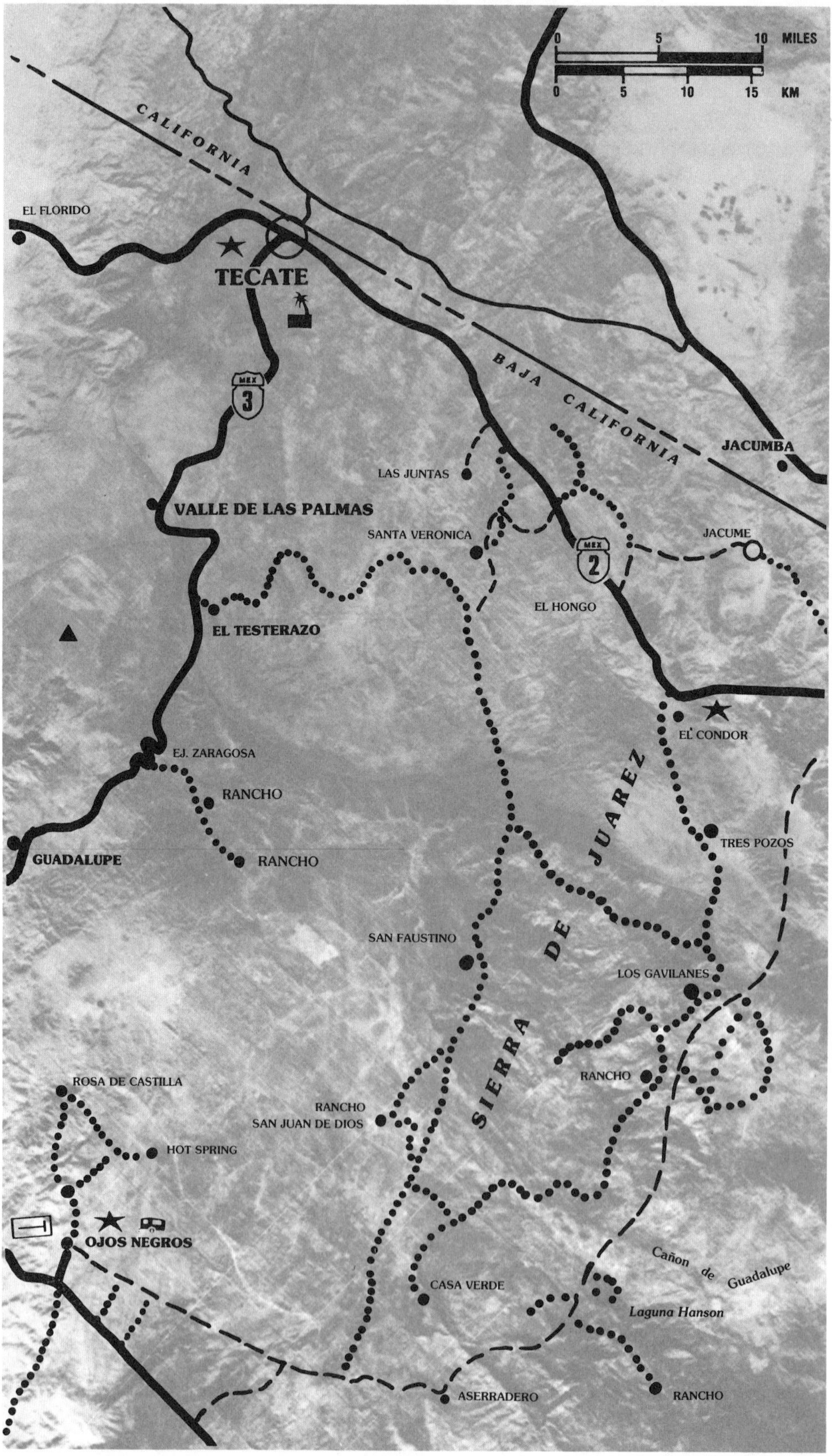

See Page 36

CALIFORNIA

EL FLORIDO

★ TECATE

MEX 3

BAJA CALIFORNIA

JACUMBA

LAS JUNTAS

VALLE DE LAS PALMAS

SANTA VERONICA

MEX 2

JACUME

EL TESTERAZO

EL HONGO

EL CONDOR ★

EJ. ZARAGOSA

RANCHO

RANCHO

GUADALUPE

TRES POZOS

S
I
E
R
R
A

D
E

J
U
A
R
E
Z

SAN FAUSTINO

LOS GAVILANES

RANCHO

ROSA DE CASTILLA

RANCHO
SAN JUAN DE DIOS

HOT SPRING

★ 🚐
OJOS NEGROS

Cañon de Guadalupe

CASA VERDE

Laguna Hanson

ASERRADERO

RANCHO

0   5   10 MILES

0   5   10   15 KM

See Page 44

N

TECATE — ENSENADA

0   *K0*   Leave Tecate on Mexico 3 highway south past park and several large buildings on left. Cross railroad tracks and begin climbing out of valley. Watch speed on curves and approaching vehicles.

5.7   *K9*   Rancho San Lorenzo on right.

8.5   *K13+*   Road winds up hill, 30 mph. Continue uphill.

10   *K16*   Top of grade.

16.7   *K27*   Small community of Valle de las Palmas on right. The small cafe there has served us some excellent fruit pies.

19   *K30+*   Road west to Cerro Bolas 12 km. Road winds uphill and back toward northeast, following canyon. 25.5 K39 Top of grade, road now heading generally south. Watch downgrade.

31   *K49*   El Testorazo, a small farming community.

39   *K63*   Ejido Ignacio Zaragosa. Begin downgrade, steep in places and sharp turns. 25-35 mph.

(turn back to page 33)

TIJUANA - MEXICALI (from page 33)

47.7   *K107*   To south is Rancho Las Juntas, 5 km. An interesting building development among huge oaks and giant boulders. There is a running stream and small lake.

49   *K105*   Signed dirt road south is to Santa Veronica. Beyond about 40 miles, past a number of ranches, is old gold town of Rosa de Castilla, and then Ensenada-San Felipe highway.

52.2   *K99*   El Hongo. Largest of several *ejidos* along here, including Chula Vista and Baja California.

62.5   *K83*   El Condor — New Pemex station, several houses and little else. Dirt road south goes to Laguna Hanson and beyond. There is a better road ahead at K73.

(continued on page 37)

THE ROADS OF THE SIERRA JUAREZ

Of all of the regions of Baja that has been settled to one degree or another, the Sierra Juarez may have changed the least. The nearly mile-high tableland extending south of El Condor and La Rumerosa has many of the same paths, trails and roads that it had a generation or more ago. Some go back to the days of the Padres and explorers of the 18th century, others to the gold seekers of the 1880's. Many of the villages, mining camps or mission waystations of other centuries are now the *ranchos* that lie along these same trails.

Today some dirt roads south from Santa Veronica, El Condor or La Rumerosa toward Laguna Hanson and Mexico 3 are passable to standard cars, but weather conditions can cause drastic changes overnight. We recommend more rugged vehicles for the roads through the beautiful pine forests, broad grassy meadows and the sparkling lake that is a part of the Sierra Juarez. The region offers much to the hiker and camper.

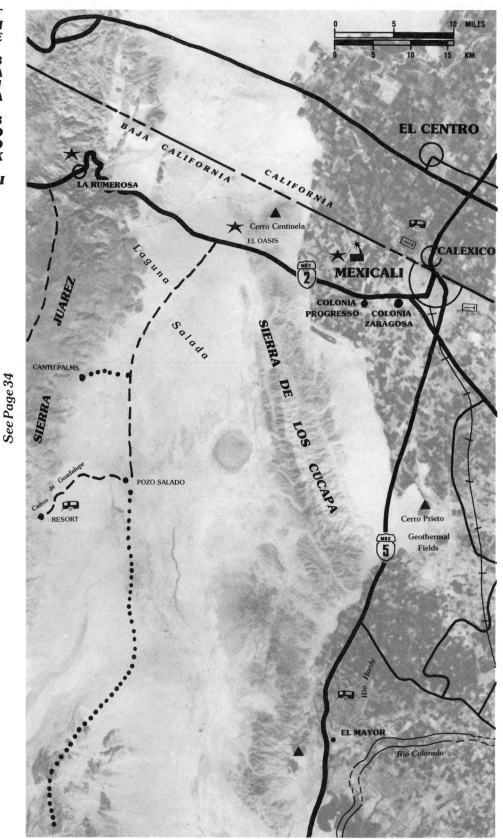

See Page 34

See Page 38

See Page 46

EL CENTRO

LA RUMEROSA

BAJA CALIFORNIA

CALIFORNIA

Cerro Centinela

EL OASIS

MEX 2

MEXICALI

CALEXICO

COLONIA PROGRESSO

COLONIA ZARAGOSA

Laguna

Salada

SIERRA JUAREZ

SIERRA DE LOS CUCAPA

CANTU PALMS

SIERRA

Cañon de Guadalupe

POZO SALADO

RESORT

Cerro Prieto

Geothermal Fields

MEX 5

Rio Hardy

EL MAYOR

Rio Colorado

72.7 **K68** After passing through area of various small mining operations, arrive at La Rumerosa (pg. 128), a small ranching and mining center.

74.5 **K65** Start twisting descent to desert floor down Cuesta La Rumerosa grade. Many sharp turns and spectacular views of Mexicali and Imperial Valleys, Salton Sea and Laguna Salada. Make sure brakes are in good order. Coming up the other direction, watch your temperature gauge.

89 **K42** The skeleton of a gas station is on north side just bottom of grade.

97.7 **K28** Marked road south along west side of Laguna Salada to Cañon Guadalupe and beyond. Cantú Palms is 19 mi., Cañon Guadalupe, 35 mi. (pg. 141).

100 **K24** Pemex station. Road south is to recreation area on shore of Laguna Salada. Incidently, the lake could disappear almost overnight, as it is very shallow and filled by overflow water from Colorado River delta. Proceed over low pass into Mexicali Valley.

112.5 **K4** A number of small *ejidos* and irrigated fields as you approach Mexicali. In Colonia Zaragosa, there is a small *charro* ring on south side of highway.

115 **K0** Intersection. Road straight ahead to downtown Mexicali (pg. 128). Road angling slightly to right intersects (4.7 mi.)with San Felipe highway, Mexico 5.
End of log...

MEXICALI — SAN FELIPE

0 **K0** Begin from border crossing in Mexicali, take diagonal road southeast through town past government building complex and out to signed Mexico 5 highway. (pg. 128).

5 **K8** Large traffic circle. When you get to other side take most westerly of two roads going generally south.

5.6 **K9** Mexico 2 comes in from right. To follow Mexico 2 east gets a little confusing...you have to go north about a half-mile to traffic circle mentioned above. Then take the easterly of the two roads...and on to San Luis and Guaymas.

15.6 **K25** Paved road east to the Cerro Prieto geothermal steam installation. It is the largest geothermal plant in North America.

23.5 **K38** Paved road east to Coahuilla, across bridge into Sonora, then Riito and on to El Golfo via Sonora Highway 40.

33.5 **K54** On the left is Campo Río Hardy, a trailer camp with rustic vacation homes for a number of Americans. The area boasts fine hunting for duck, quail, pheasant and dove, plus fishing in canals and river. Unfortunately the area is subject to flooding from the Colorado River overflow. 1 mile south is El Mayor, home for a number of Cucapa Indians, original inhabitants of the lower Colorado delta.

38.5 **K62** Enter alkalai flats of the Laguna Salada. In times past, the freeflowing Colorado River regularly flooded this region. Today the dams and irrigation systems hold back the water except during times of heavy flooding. The Laguna Salada basin extends about 50 miles to the northwest.

(continued on page 47)

T
H
E

B
A
J
A

B
O
O
K

III

See Page 36

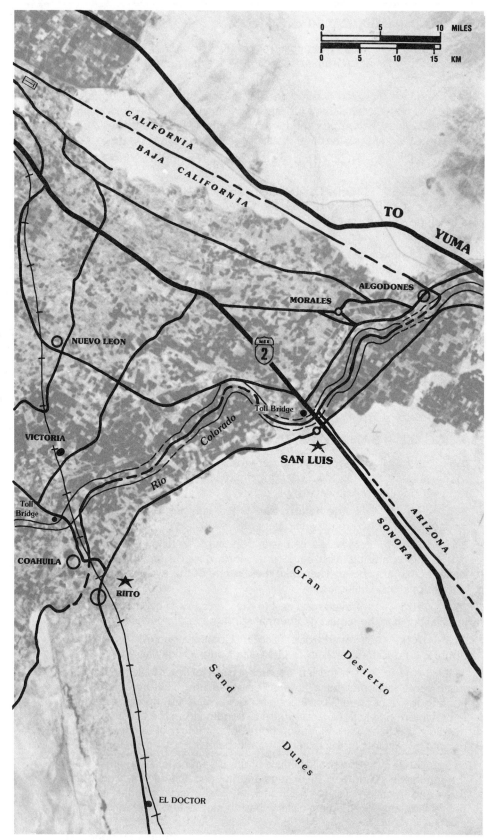

100 MILE SHORTCUT

The region east and south of Mexicali is the scene of extensive farming (seen on the map from 568 miles in space as tiny squares). Highway Mexico 2 passes through the many farms, across a toll bridge over the Río Colorado and into San Luís in the State of Sonora. The road south from San Luís is paved all the way to El Golfo de Santa Clara and follows along the bluffs that rise to the east of the Río Colorado.

Mexico 2 extends eastward from San Luís to meet Mexico 15, which is the main route for those driving to Guaymas, Mazatlán, and points south. Thus, Southern California motorists headed for Mexico's West Coast can save 100 miles.

A DUNE BUGGY PARADISE

Although it is actually in the State of Sonora the small town of El Golfo de Santa Clara should be mentioned for the benefit of the off-road buff.

Located 45 miles south of Riito, El Golfo is still lilghtly touched by the *norteamericano* traveler. Facilities are minimal and there is little to do unless you are equipped to travel along the beaches extending 40 miles to the southeast.

El Golfo's undisturbed beaches are a treasure trove of shells and clams. Behind the bluffs to the north and east of town are quantities of petrified ironwood, colorful jasper and agate. It is not advisable to travel this back country alone, however, as help is a long way off.

Limited camping facilities are found just above and below town, while several native restaurants serve fish and shrimp.

El Golfo is particularly popular with residents of Mexicali and San Luís during Easter and the June 1st *Dia de Marina* holiday when El Golfo takes on a carnival atmosphere.

THE WILL TO SURVIVE

The early Indians who lived along the Río Colorado below what is now Yuma regularly made pilgrimages across many miles of hostile desert in search of food. The ripening of the *piñon* pines would bring them across the Laguna Salada onto the mile-high plateaus of the Sierra Juarez. They also walked 75 or more miles through the barren salt flats to the beaches near San Felipe to gather clams and spear fish. Such trips required monumental endurance and emphasize the tremendous will to survive exhibited by these people.

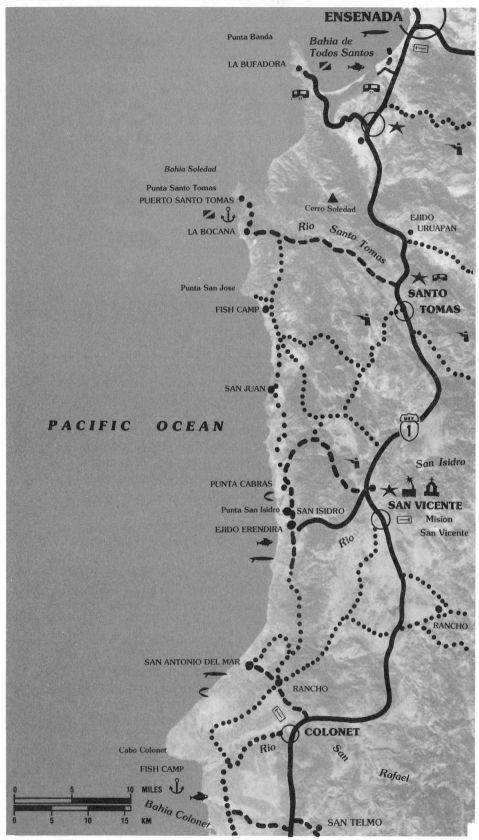

ENSENADA

Punta Banda
*Bahia de
Todos Santos*
LA BUFADORA

Bahia Soledad

Punta Santo Tomas
PUERTO SANTO TOMAS
Cerro Soledad
EJIDO
URUAPAN
LA BOCANA
Rio *Santo Tomas*

SANTO
TOMAS

Punta San Jose
FISH CAMP

SAN JUAN

PACIFIC OCEAN

MEX
1

San Isidro

PUNTA CABRAS
SAN VICENTE
Punta San Isidro SAN ISIDRO
*Mision
San Vicente*
EJIDO ERENDIRA
Rio

RANCHO

SAN ANTONIO DEL MAR

RANCHO

COLONET

Cabo Colonet
Rio *San*
FISH CAMP
Rafael

0   5   10 MILES
0   5   10   15 KM
Bahia Colonet
SAN TELMO

See Page 42

N

0 **K0** From signal at intersection of Azueta and Lazaro Cardenas turn south to skirt Ensenada's main business district on divided road. Harbor is on right until road turns left and rejoins Mexico 1 at 2.0 mi. (The highway kilometer marker reads 7 near here. Why, we don't know, because we couldn't find a "zero" marker. We accept the mystery, and go bravely forward!) Proceed south past El Cipres military camp.

7.2 **K15** Paved road right leads through Ejido Chapúltepec to Estero Beach Resort, left 2 mi., and Corona Beach campground right, 2 mi.

10.7 **K21+** Farming community of Maneadero (pg. 131). Road forks near center of town, right goes to Punta Banda, 8 mi., and La Bufadora 12.9 mi. (pg. 131). Left fork up a slight grade is Mexico 1.

11.7 **K23** Site of *"Migracion"* check point. It has been recently reopened on an intermittent basis. You should have your tourist permit validated here. (pg. 14) Proceed slowly past small office and stop if they appear open. Continues southeast up arroyo. Watch speed, many curves next 8 miles.

23.5 **K41+** Ejido Uruapan to left. An oak-shaded picnic ground is just below north side of road.

25.7 **K45** Begin descent into Santo Tomás Valley. Steep and sharp turns — speed 30 mph.

26.5 **K48** Road to La Bocana, Puerto Santo Tomás (pg. 132).

28.4 **K51** Pass El Palomar Resort and Campground, through Santo Tomás (pg. 131) and follow valley floor 5 miles, then begin ascent on south side of arroyo.

45.2 **K78** Paved road right to Ejido Erendira 12 mi. (pg. 132) and beach. First 10 miles through arroyo is paved. Surfing, fishing, shelling, camping, etc.

52 **K89** Enter San Vicente (pg. 132) Gasoline, several stores, small restaurants. 1 mi. South of town is new El Camino motel.

58 **K96+** Rancho Santa Marta on right. Beyond is rich, rolling Valle Llano Colorado and many grapes, olives and other crops. Begin winding South through hills.

73 **K124** Panadería Carmen on right above highway. This is the famous "purple panadería" that the many editions of **The Baja Book** (since 1974) has brought so much business that the overworked baker has moved twice and painted the building different colors at least a dozen times trying to hide! His bolillos and pan dulces are superb. The ovens are heated with firewood in the centuries-old manner. Now, with **The Baja Book III** he will have to redouble his efforts...to either bake or hide.

75 **K126+** Cross bridge and enter Colonet (pg. 132). Road right just before bridge goes northwest past old Johnson Ranch to San Antonio del Mar, 7.1 mi.

(continued on page 49)

Islas de Todos Santos... provide some protection for Bahia Todos Santos and city of Ensenada. On lee side are several anchorages, on windward side at isthmus, a good surfing spot. They are popular with locally-based sportfishing boats and yachtsmen from the U.S. An interesting island, but watch out for the flies — they're persistent — and they bite.

T
H
E

B
A
J
A

B
O
O
K

III

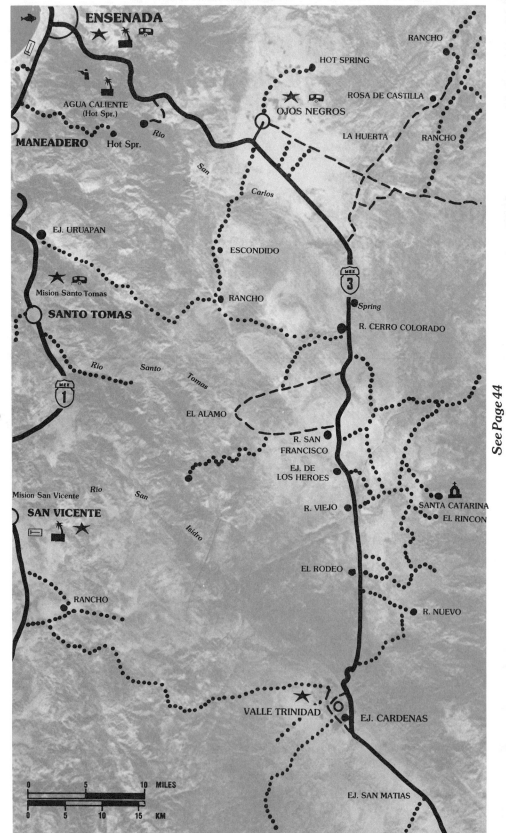

ENSENADA

RANCHO

HOT SPRING

AGUA CALIENTE
(Hot Spr.)

ROSA DE CASTILLA

OJOS NEGROS

MANEADERO   Rio
        Hot Spr.

LA HUERTA   RANCHO

San

Carlos

EJ. URUAPAN

ESCONDIDO

Mision Santo Tomas

RANCHO

SANTO TOMAS

Spring

R. CERRO COLORADO

Rio   Santo

Tomas

MEX
1

EL ALAMO

R. SAN
FRANCISCO

EJ. DE
LOS HEROES

Mision San Vicente   Rio   San

SAN VICENTE

R. VIEJO

SANTA CATARINA
        EL RINCON

Isidro

EL RODEO

RANCHO

R. NUEVO

VALLE TRINIDAD

EJ. CARDENAS

MILES

KM

EJ. SAN MATIAS

MEX
3

See Page 40

See Page 44

N

ENSENADA — SAN FELIPE HIGHWAY

0   *K0*   Leave Ensenada on Calzada Cortez, Mexico 3, near Benito Juarez Monument just south of main business district (pg. 130). Head east past a number of stores and homes and then bear left into rolling hills. Wind up a gentle, but constant grade past municipal dump and several *ranchos*.

8   *K13*   A good view of Bahia Todos Santos and islands to west. Continue upward on winding road with several sharp curves.

9   *K14+*   Watch for very large green frog along north side of highway.

16.2   *K26*   Dirt road to right is to Agua Caliente Resort. Located in a beautiful little valley it was once a popular hot springs, motel, campground and restaurant complex. Lately it has fallen on hard times but we hope it makes a fast recovery. Mexico 3 continues to wind upward before descending into Ojos Negros Valley. Watch for several well-marked sharp curves.

24.5   *K39+*   Paved road left goes to Ojos Negros and to several dirt roads leading north and east into mountains.

34   *K55*   Graded road left leads north past some cultivated land, a small *rancho* and on to Laguna Hanson, 19 mi. Our road continues southeast through several valleys past a number of ranches and small farming colonies. Vegetation is typical of high plains — chaparral, mesquite, manzanita and some cacti.

46   *K73+*   Very good small spring on east side of road. Bubbling right out of side of small hill, it is popular with passersby.

53.7   *K86*   Side road west is to El Alamo (pg. 132), 15 km.

57.5   *K92*   Ejido Heroes de la Independencia is to right. About 500 people live here. Gas and limited supplies available. Continue through few scattered signs of habitation, including El Rodeo, K103.

79.2   *K115*   Signed road into Valle Trinidad. It also gives distances to Leonardo Valle, 18 km; Cieneguita, 28 km; and Tepi, 35. Highway then turns east and skirts along north edge of this large agricultural settlement.

82.8   *K121*   Another road into valley, to Ejido Lázaro Cardenas. Gas (emergency only), stores and cafe.

86.5   *K138+*   Road right goes south into San Pedro Martír mountains and Mike's Sky Ranch, 21 mi. This is direct route to an interesting area, but not recommended for standard cars. Continue past small farm area and a number of houses.

(continued on page 45)

SCREECH
OWL

See Page 42

See Page 46

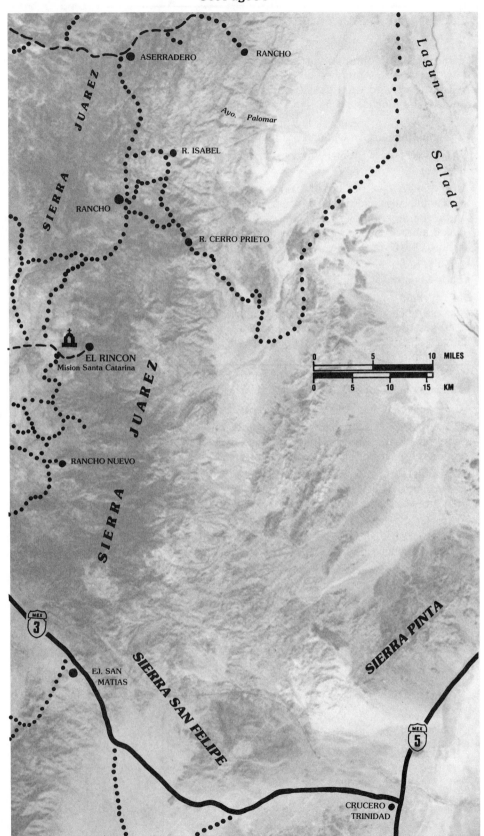

T H E   B A J A   B O O K   III

ASERRADERO

RANCHO

Laguna

Salada

Ayo.   Palomar

R. ISABEL

SIERRA   JUAREZ

RANCHO

R. CERRO PRIETO

EL RINCON
Mision Santa Catarina

SIERRA   JUAREZ

RANCHO NUEVO

| 0 | | 5 | | 10 | MILES |

| 0 | 5 | 10 | 15 | KM |

MEX 3

EJ. SAN
MATIAS

SIERRA SAN FELIPE

SIERRA PINTA

MEX 5

CRUCERO
TRINIDAD

92.5 **K148** Enter winding area along rocky south side of *arroyo*. Several sharp curves ahead. At bottom of *arroyo* a hard-to-find dirt road right goes through dry lake bed and dunes to San Felipe, 46 mi. 4-WD or dune buggy-types only are advised. Continue due east.

99 **K158** All around are many varieties of desert plants. In distance to south is Picacho del Diablo (10,156 ft.). Continue in easterly direction through *vados* (dips). Gradually drop in altitude.

108.9 **K174** The Sea of Cortez is barely visible on horizon past wide salt flats. Follow paved road through more shallow *vados*.

122.5 **K196** Reach Mexico 5 at Crucero Trinidad. San Felipe is to south 31 miles. See log page 53.
End of log...

BARREL CACTUS OR BIZNAGA

LAND OF CONTRASTS

A flight over the plateau portion of the Sierra Juarez shows an even more rugged landscape than seen from the Ensenada-San Felipe highway. Here and there are sparkling lakes or streams, verdant little meadows and huge jumbles of granitic rocks that stand out of the bush and tree-covered land. Occasionally a tiny ranchhouse will show in the middle of a small clearing. Closer inspection shows a well and a few cattle.

A wide variety of shrubs, cacti and annuals respond to the warming days of late spring with a bewildering array of color. Deer, coyote and skunks are among the many species foraging through head-high manzanita, scrub oak, piñon pine and sage. As you proceed south and east toward the pass leading onto the San Felipe plain, numerous varieties of cactus gradually replace the manzanita, piñon and chapparal.

A good supply of underground water has allowed the ranchers of Valle Trinidad to raise large crops of peaches, plums, almonds and potatoes. Originally the challenge was not so much in raising the crop but in trucking it out of the valley over the dirt roads without damage. Now with the paved road, Mexico 3, more of the valley is under cultivation.

*T
H
E

B
A
J
A

B
O
O
K

III*

45

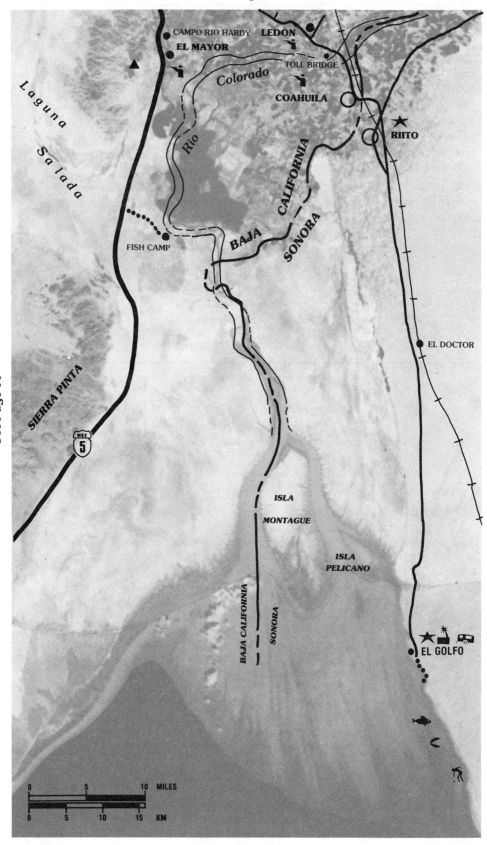

CAMPO RIO HARDY
EL MAYOR
LEDON

TOLL BRIDGE

Colorado

COAHUILA

Rio

★ **RIITO**

Laguna

Salada

BAJA

CALIFORNIA

SONORA

FISH CAMP

● EL DOCTOR

SIERRA PINTA

MEX **5**

ISLA

MONTAGUE

ISLA
PELICANO

BAJA CALIFORNIA

SONORA

★ 🌴 🚐
● **EL GOLFO**

0   5   10   MILES

0   5   10   15   KM

N

MEXICALI — SAN FELIPE (from page 37)

53.5   *K86*   On both sides of highway are dunes and excellent examples of native vegetation. After a rainy winter we have literally wallowed in the bounty of wildflowers, particularly desert primrose and verbena. Road winds somewhat, then straightens past more salt flats.

65   *K105*   La Ventana, a small gas station and *cantina*. Not a likely place for much else.

82   *K132*   Ahead to east is the black volcanic hill, El Chinero. It was named for a group of Chinese who were put off a ship by an unscrupulous captain near San Felipe. They got this far before dying of thirst.

(continued on page 53)

WATCH THOSE HIGH TIDES

Make sure your activities in the North portion of the Cortez are done with an eye on the tide for the forces that create tidal surges on the world's oceans cause special conditions in the Sea of Cortez.

The three foot variation from high to low tide at Cabo San Lucas is transformed into a sometimes-raging surge of nearly thirty feet at the mouth of the Río Colorado, some 600 miles to the north.

As the waters move past the Midriff Islands of the Cortez, currents develop that may hinder the progress of a boat, or speed it unexpectedly along its way.

The gently sloping beaches near San Felipe and El Golfo de Santa Clara are often exposed for more than a half-mile on a low tide, affording opportunities for the shell collector and clammer.

In these areas of big tides more than one boatsman has watched his craft floating merrily out to sea, unattended, because he went away from his boat for just a few minutes. He has also had his craft left high and dry hundreds of yards from the water after only a few hours.

The University of Arizona in Tucson has a tide table available for the regions around San Felipe. Copies may be obtained from the Printing & Reproduction Department, University of Arizona, Tucson, AZ 85721.

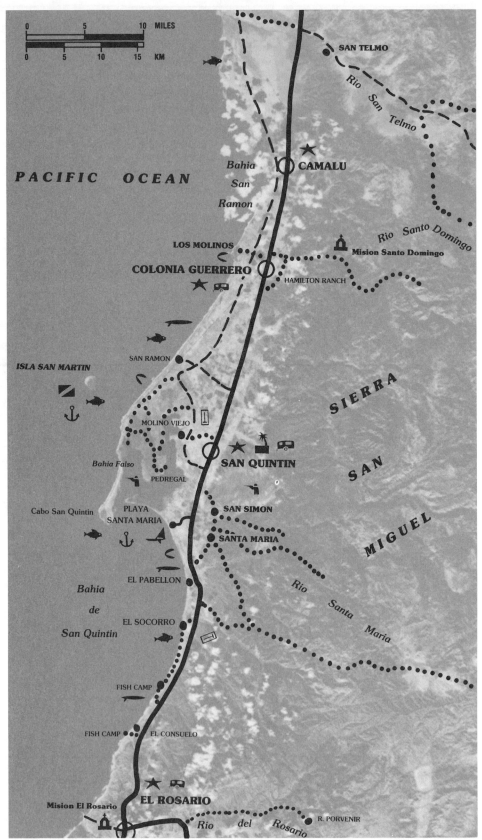

THE BAJA BOOK III

PACIFIC OCEAN

0 5 10 MILES
0 5 10 15 KM

SAN TELMO

Rio San Telmo

Bahia
San
Ramon

CAMALU

Rio Santo Domingo

Mision Santo Domingo

LOS MOLINOS

COLONIA GUERRERO

HAMILTON RANCH

SAN RAMON

ISLA SAN MARTIN

MOLINO VIEJO

Bahia Falso

PEDREGAL

SIERRA

SAN QUINTIN

SAN SIMON

SANTA MARIA

MIGUEL

SAN

Cabo San Quintin

PLAYA
SANTA MARIA

EL PABELLON

Rio Santa Maria

Bahia
de
San Quintin

EL SOCORRO

FISH CAMP

FISH CAMP EL CONSUELO

EL ROSARIO

Mision El Rosario

Rio del Rosario

R. PORVENIR

See Page 50

83.7   K140+   Road left to San Telmo (8 km), Meling Ranch (50 km) and *Parque Nacionál San Pedro Martir* and telescope (100 km). Mexico 1 continues south through farmlands with a number of sideroads to ocean.

94   K157   Camalu. Small farming settlement. To west are several fine fishing, camping and clamming beaches.

101.4   K169   Enter Colonia Guerrero (pg. 133). Just below is bridge over Río Santo Domingo. At K172+ is road right to Posada Don Diego and don Pepe campgrounds. Beyond about 2 miles is good beach. Continue South past many, many fields of tomatoes, strawberries, broccoli, etc.

114.4   K190   Enter San Quintín proper (pg. 133). On left is Pemex station with unleaded gas. Pass numerous small stores (ice plant on right just past Pemex station) with wide variety of supplies, several restaurants. Then comes a military camp and the School of the Americas.

118   K196   You are just past town. New roadlog begins here. See below.
End of log...

> **Isla San Geronimo**...a barren 1/4 by 3/4 mile pile of bird lime about ten miles south of Punta Baja and five miles offshore. Area for lobster, abalone and fishing, mostly by long-range boats.
>
> **(see page 54)**

SAN QUINTIN — PARADOR PUNTA PRIETA

0   K0   Continue south on Mexico 1 through more developing farming country.

2.5   K4   Road right is marked to Muelle Viejo Restaurant. It is also best road to Old Mill Motel (Molino Viejo). Main road continues south, swinging SE at K6 over a new bridge over Río Santa María floodplain.

6.2   K10   Paved road right 3 mi. to Hotel La Pinta and Cielito Lindo Motel and campground. A broad expanse of beach in front of both. Good surf fishing at times and plenty of sand dollars.

9   K14   Junction with old road, to rear on right.

10   K16   Dirt road right to Honey's Trailer Park and El Pabellón beach.

15.6   K25   Road right to El Soccoro ranch. Bluffs above road are full of fossil shells. Near water is a growing group of American weekend homes. Landing strip. Good fishing and camping. To south are a number unimproved campsites on small coves. A personal favorite.

26   K41+   Dirt road toward water is old Rancho El Consuelo. Good fishing. Many abalone are near beach, good fishing. Road turns inland up arroyo. Watch speed and sharp curves.

32.3   K52   After crossing plateau past several houses, begin descent toward Arroyo El Rosario.

34.7   K55+   Arrive in El Rosario (pg. 133). Gas, meals and supplies. Esponosa's Place is at corner across from market. Road right follows north side of *arroyo* to ocean, 7 mi.; straight across *arroyo* goes to Punta Baja, 9 mi.; paved road left continues down peninsula. In fall and winter you often see red chilis drying on south-facing hillsides along here.

(continued on page 55)

T
H
E

B
A
J
A

B
O
O
K

III

T H E

B A J A

B O O K

III

See Page 48

See Page 52

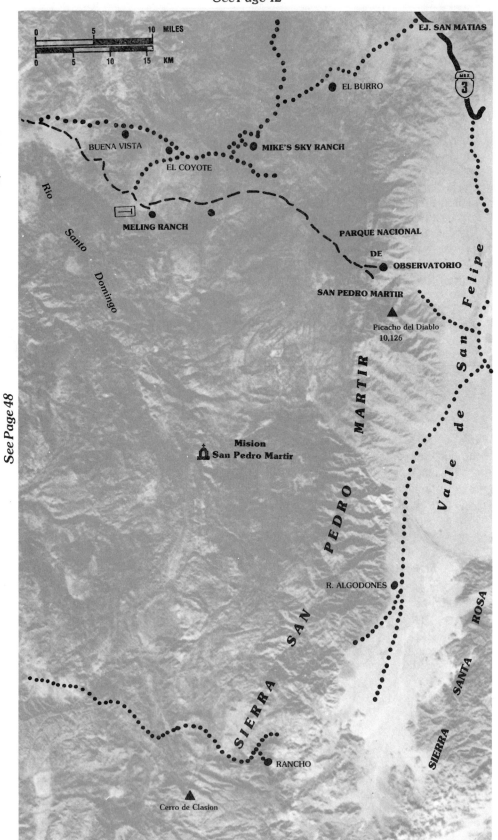

EJ. SAN MATIAS

MEX 3

EL BURRO

BUENA VISTA

MIKE'S SKY RANCH

EL COYOTE

Rio

Santo

Domingo

MELING RANCH

PARQUE NACIONAL

DE

OBSERVATORIO

SAN PEDRO MARTIR

Picacho del Diablo
10,126

Valle de San Felipe

Mision
San Pedro Martir

M A R T I R

P E D R O

R. ALGODONES

S A N

S I E R R A

SIERRA SANTA ROSA

RANCHO

Cerro de Clasion

N

TWO-MILE HIGH MOUNTAINS

The mountainous backbone of Baja California reaches its greatest heights in the *Sierra de San Pedro Martír*. A rocky, forested tableland nearly 75 miles in length, it contrasts sharply with the regions surrounding it.

To the east, it drops precipitously over 6000 feet onto the San Felipe Plain and the Sea of Cortez. Into this dry, lea side of the *sierras* are tucked a number of rocky, palm-dotted canyons that served as refuges for the nomadic Indians of the region. The small streams provided them moisture and served as gathering spots to much of what they hunted — deer, bighorn sheep and rabbits.

The six to nine thousand foot plateau that makes up the central portion of the *San Pedro Martír* is well forested and contains abundant wildlife near springs and the year-round streams winding through alpine meadows. It is here that a species of trout found nowhere else is still believed to exist. (see Meling Ranch, page 132).

Dominating the entire range is the 10,126-foot mountain, *Picacho del Diablo*. A formidable challenge a generation ago, El Diablo is now a popular target for mountain climbers. Its sometimes-snowy escarpments may be seen from both the Cortez and the Pacific.

Just to the northwest the Mexican government has built an observatory boasting the clearest air of any in the world. To insure a minimum of nightlight interference they have even tried to limit the amount of outdoor lighting near the town of San Felipe, 40 miles to the southeast.

Each winter the high plateaus of both the Martír and Juarez ranges are visited by deep snows and travel during this time is not recommended. The balance of the year, however, many forests and meadows offer great recreation to the hiker and back packer.

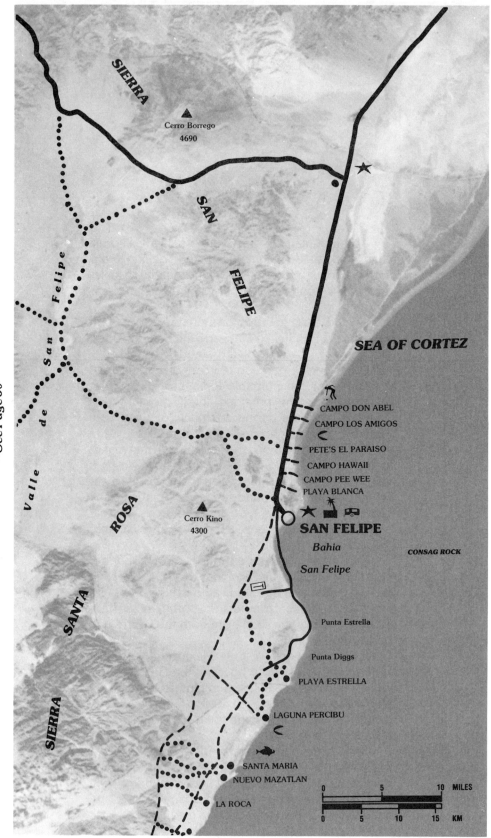

52

THE BAJA BOOK III

See Page 50

SIERRA

Cerro Borrego
4690

SAN

FELIPE

SEA OF CORTEZ

CAMPO DON ABEL

CAMPO LOS AMIGOS

PETE'S EL PARAISO

CAMPO HAWAII

CAMPO PEE WEE

PLAYA BLANCA

Valle de San Felipe

ROSA

Cerro Kino
4300

SAN FELIPE

Bahia

San Felipe

CONSAG ROCK

Punta Estrella

Punta Diggs

PLAYA ESTRELLA

SANTA

LAGUNA PERCIBU

SIERRA

SANTA MARIA

NUEVO MAZATLAN

LA ROCA

0		5		10	MILES

0	5	10	15	KM

N

MEXICALI — SAN FELIPE (from page 47)

87   K140   Paved road coming in from West is Highway 3 from Ensenada (see log pg. 45). Just past is small trading post with gas pump. Road south is straight, very straight. Toward mountains are a number of small *arroyos* with *mesquite*, ironwood and *palo verde* trees.

106.5   K172   Campo don Abel, first of about 15 roads to Cortez beaches and campgrounds over the next 9 miles. All are of varying quality and services and, as they change from season to season, we refrain from rating them ... except that we have watched Campo Hawaii, Pee Wee's Camp and Playa Blanca retain their balance over the years.

110   K179   San Felipe Zoo. An imaginative woodcarver has created his "zoo" out of ironwood. He has some nice carvings, better than most of the "Seri Indian" carvings coming out of the factories around Kino, Sonora.

118.7   K193   Pass the large arch at the entrance into San Felipe. (pg. 130) At about 0.5 mi., paved road south goes past breakwater, airport, then to Punta Estrella. Eventually this will be main road to Puertecitos, Bahía Gonzaga, etc. Today the preferred way to Puertecitos is via the dirt road which begins 1 mi. below intersection.
End of log...

Note: As there are no permanent kilometer markers set on the route of the following roadlog, for this section we will use our old mileage (marked "M") format.

SAN FELIPE — MEXICO 1 AT CHAPALA

We've two choices of roads between San Felipe and Puertecitos. The "improved" new road along the coast past Punta Estrella, and the shorter, old inland road. We're logging the old road, as it currently is easier on car and occupants. If the government does complete the paving of the new road it will be reflected in our next printing.

0   M0   Head south on paved road about 0.5 mi. east of center of town. After 1 mile take dirt road angling slightly to right. Continue past several houses and a pumping station.

6   M6   Road left comes in from airport. The airport is paved, has a tower, offices and communications facilities, etc. but has yet to be officially opened. Continue through several shallow, sandy *arroyos*.

(continued on page 59)

LOVE IN THE AFTERNOON

It is nothing new for Baja California and the Sea of Cortez to be unique...and here in the northern Cortez we have the only place in the world where a fish comes ashore on sandy beaches to lay its eggs in broad daylight!

This relative to what Southern Californians know as grunion, are found as far south as Guaymas in the State of Sonora and Bahia de Los Angeles, Baja California between January to June. Though it is hardly X-rated it is interesting to observe thousands of beached females and males go through their egg-laying and fertilizing dances. Watch for them in the late afternoons a few days following a new and full moon. Gulf grunion are excellent as bait, but only fair eating, even when scaled, dipped in egg, rolled in bread crumbs and deep fried.

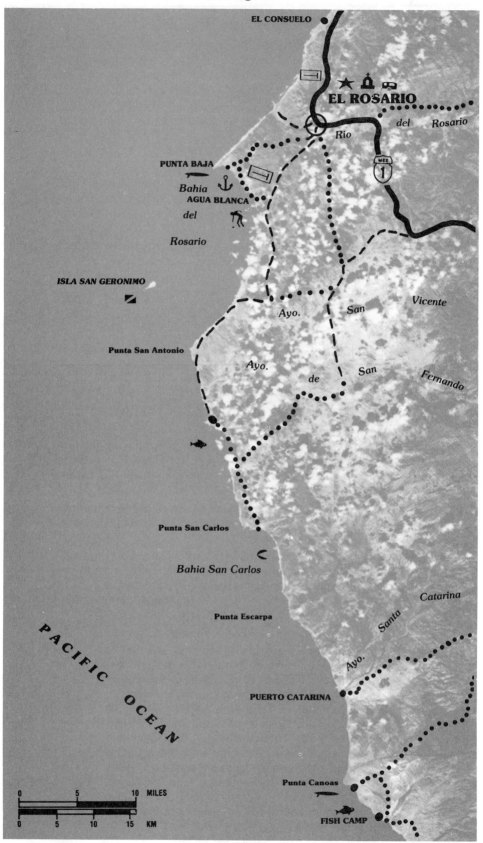

EL CONSUELO

EL ROSARIO

Rio *del* *Rosario*

MEX 1

PUNTA BAJA

Bahia
AGUA BLANCA

del

Rosario

ISLA SAN GERONIMO

Ayo. San *Vicente*

Punta San Antonio

Ayo.

de San *Fernando*

Punta San Carlos

Bahia San Carlos

Catarina

Punta Escarpa

Santa

Ayo.

PACIFIC OCEAN

PUERTO CATARINA

Punta Canoas

FISH CAMP

| 0 | | 5 | | 10 | MILES |
| 0 | 5 | | 10 | | 15 | KM |

N

38.7   *K62*   Highway crosses arroyo on new bridge and climbs into hills. A dirt road continues up north side of valley to several *ranchos.*

46.8   *K75*   You are coming into stands of cirio or boojum trees and large cardon cactus. You will see many more before leaving Baja. Watch for opposing traffic as road is narrow. Road often follows along tops of ridges.

48.7   *K78*   Signed, graded road south to Puerto San Carlos, 60km. Some fine surf fishing and several tiny coves where infaltable boat or cartop might be launched. Beware of winds, especially in spring and summer.

(continued on page 57)

THE BAFFLING BOOJUM

One of the most fascinating plants of Baja is the cirio, or boojum tree, *Idria columnaris.* A relative of the ocotillo, it occurs in a 150 mile wide east-west corridor from just below El Rosario to north of Guerrero Negro. It is a tree of rare distinction, for not only does it survive in one of the harshest climates in the world but it provides, in its endless odd shapes, a natural subject for the photographer.

When small the cirio is a roundish stubby plant that slowly elongates as it extends skyward, looking much like a carrot that is growing upside-down. Larger specimens often develop branches that look like wildly waving arms, which led botanist Godfrey Sykes to liken them to a fanciful desert dwelling creature called a "boojum" in Lewis Carroll's story "The Hunting of the Snark". Oddly, the name appears to have stuck.

Tiny leaves appear after a good rain, but they quickly die to leave barren thorny stalks. In summer bracts of small creamy white flowers appear on the tips of the branches.

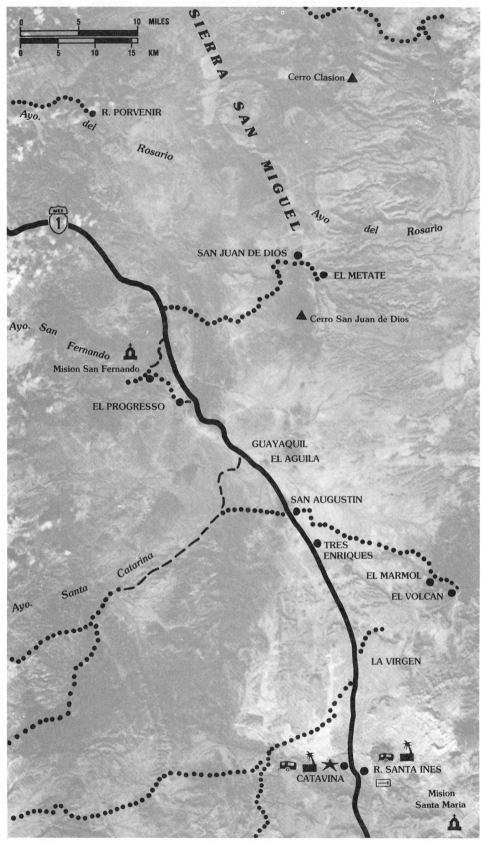

SIERRA SAN MIGUEL

0   5   10   MILES
0   5   10   15   KM

Cerro Clasion ▲

Ayo. del Rosario

● R. PORVENIR

Ayo del Rosario

SAN JUAN DE DIOS ●
EL METATE ●

▲ Cerro San Juan de Dios

Ayo. San Fernando
Mision San Fernando

EL PROGRESSO

GUAYAQUIL
EL AGUILA

SAN AUGUSTIN ●

TRES
ENRIQUES ●

EL MARMOL ●
EL VOLCAN ●

Catarina

Ayo. Santa

LA VIRGEN

R. SANTA INES
CATAVINA ★ ●

Mision
Santa Maria

See Page 54

See Page 58

55.6   *K88+*   Down hill to south is La Turquesa, a working turquoise mine. Some fine stones have come from here. The area is usually closed to visitors. Continue winding through low hills.

71.7   *K114*   Dirt road right leads to ruins of Misión San Fernando (pg. 166). Nearby is small *rancho*; 0.5 mi beyond are petroglyphs on canyon wall.

73.1   *K116+*   Rancho El Progresso just off highway to south. The ranch has been part of Baja's lore for many years. Restaurant has fine breakfasts. Just beyond is Rancho Santa Cecilia.

80.4   *K128*   Signed, graded road south to tiny fishing village at Puerto Santa Catarina. By taking left fork about 22 miles in (2.5 miles past Rancho Santa Catarina), roads meanders south past a few ranchos and many beaches for over 100 miles. No services and subject to weather closures. 4-WD vehicles recommended. Opposite dirt road (north) is to several prosperous-looking farms, Guayacuil and El Aguila.

87.7   *K140+*   San Augustín. Formerly a road maintenance and gas/camping stop, is virtually deserted.

89.9   *K143+*   Signed road left to El Marmol (see below). Just beyond is Tres Enriques restaurant. Another kilometer brings us to Rancho Sonora cafe.

96.5   *K154*   Have been seeing a white burro in here for many years. Lots of interesting cactus and other plants. A small spring is just ahead on left.

101.2   *K161+*   This region is known as Las Virgenes — an area of spectacular rock formations and many varieties of cactus and other desert vegatation. To right on huge boulder is a painting of the Virgin of Guadalupe. Several trees have been planted nearby. If you have extra water, the trees would appreciate it.

106.3   *K170*   Dip into arroyo with water running across road. Blue palms and other plants abound.

109   *K174+*   Arrive Cataviña and Hotel La Pinta. Unleaded fuel available at hotel. Leaded is across highway.

(continued on page 65)

THE HOME OF THE ONYX ELEPHANTS

Just past the road-maintenance camp at K140, a graded road leads to El Marmól, site of a large onyx quarry. For years the onyx was removed in heavy slabs and hauled 50 miles over makeshift roads to Puerto Santa Catarina to be loaded on waiting ships. In Tijuana artisans carved and polished bookends, chessmen and elephants, etc. In the 1920's and 30's their endeavors included bathtubs and sinks for palatial homes in the Los Angeles area.

Once the home of several hundred people, El Marmól is now deserted. A few slabs and fragments of the quarried rock are scattered about. Still standing is a small building built of onyx that served as a schoolhouse.

A trail leads three miles northeast to El Volcán, where you can literally watch onyx being made. Here, in these soda springs on the side of the arroyo onyx is being formed at the rate of a few inches each thousand years.

From El Marmól a poor road winds southward to Highway 1 near La Virgen.

THE
BAJA
BOOK
III

See Page 56

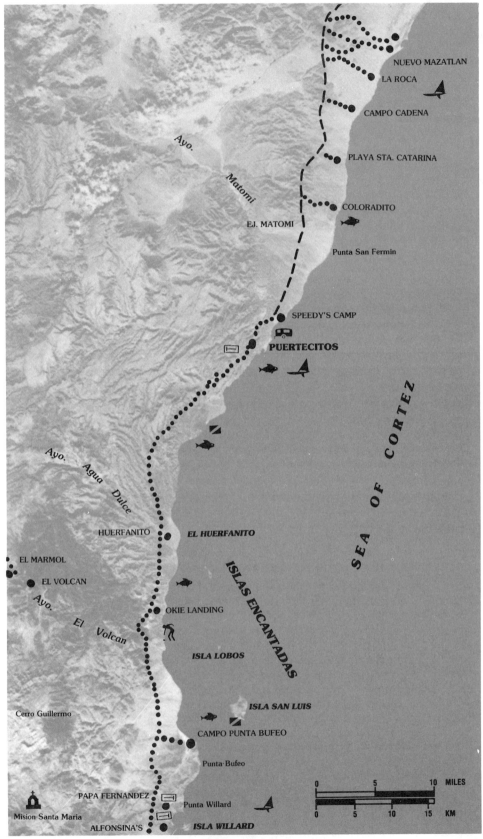

NUEVO MAZATLAN

LA ROCA

CAMPO CADENA

PLAYA STA. CATARINA

COLORADITO

EJ. MATOMI

Punta San Fermin

Ayo.

Matomi

SPEEDY'S CAMP

PUERTECITOS

SEA OF CORTEZ

Ayo.

Agua

Dulce

HUERFANITO   EL HUERFANITO

EL MARMOL

EL VOLCAN

Ayo.

El   Volcan

OKIE LANDING

ISLAS ENCANTADAS

ISLA LOBOS

ISLA SAN LUIS

Cerro Guillermo

CAMPO PUNTA BUFEO

Punta Bufeo

PAPA FERNANDEZ   Punta Willard

Mision Santa Maria

ALFONSINA'S   ISLA WILLARD

0		5		10	MILES

0	5	10	15	KM

N

14   *M8*   Intersection with road east to Laguna Percibu, a popular camping and vacation home area near an interesting tidal estuary.

21   *M7*   Small stand where you can usually purchase *refrescos*. Road east goes over to the coastal road, along which there are numbers of camps and a few clusters of *norteamericano* vacation homes.

22   *M1*   Sulfur mines. A good place to pick up a chunk of almost pure sulfur, if you have a need.

35+   *M8*   Rejoin washboarded coastal road. When and if the coastal road is paved, this is where the two logs will join. It will be nearly 40 miles to this point via the coastal road.

40   *M4+*   Rancho San Rafaél. To west is road into *arroyo*. Extending about 35 miles, it is a great adventure for offroading, but don't go alone.

49   *M9*   Speedy's Camp and several other camping areas.

51   *M2*   Puertecitos (pg. 134). Road below is even tougher on vehicles. Be very sure of your rig and driving skills before proceeding farther.

56+   *M5+*   Small camp near water. In years past we've had good fishing, including a yellowtail or two, from rocky points in the area. Road turns inland to skirt the *cuestas* (pg. 63) which for many years were the bane of all vehicles to pass this direction. The new road is much better and someday may even be paved!

69   *M12+*   El Huerfanito and Nacho's camp, a small collection of vacation homes. There is good fishing in the area, including halibut. Continue south past several sideroads leading to beaches and up arroyo. To east are a number of small islands.

81   *M12*   Short road east to water and tiny camp. It was uninhabited when last visited. Islands are just offshore.

88   *M7*   First of several roads serving several primitive camps around Punta Bufeó. The region has a remote beauty which almost defies description. The beaches, the rocky point, the adjoining sea, and all of the life which flys and swims through here give out very good vibes. A beautiful place which does not deserve motorcycles or dunebuggies roaring past.

(continued on page 63)

Las Islas Encantadas...are a group of six small islands scattered over a distance of about 15 miles. Separated from shore by a channel, several serve as rookeries for pelicans, cormorants and seagulls. Within the chain are several pinnacles coming to within 50 feet or so of the surface. Those who know their exact location are usually in for some good cabrilla and grouper fishing. The largest, Isla San Luís, offers some shelter around its southern point, where a shallow reef extends nearly a mile. Another, Isla Pomo, is almost entirely of pumice. As pumice floats, pieces of Pomo are seen throughout the northern portions of the Sea of Cortez, from El Golfo to well below Bahía de Los Ángeles. We have a piece as a door stop in our yard. As big as a basketball, it weighes little more than 5 pounds! Inside from here is Oakie's Camp, a now-abandoned fishing camp which in the 50's and early 60's yielded a lot of fish for the few who risked their rigs on the terrible road from San Felipe.

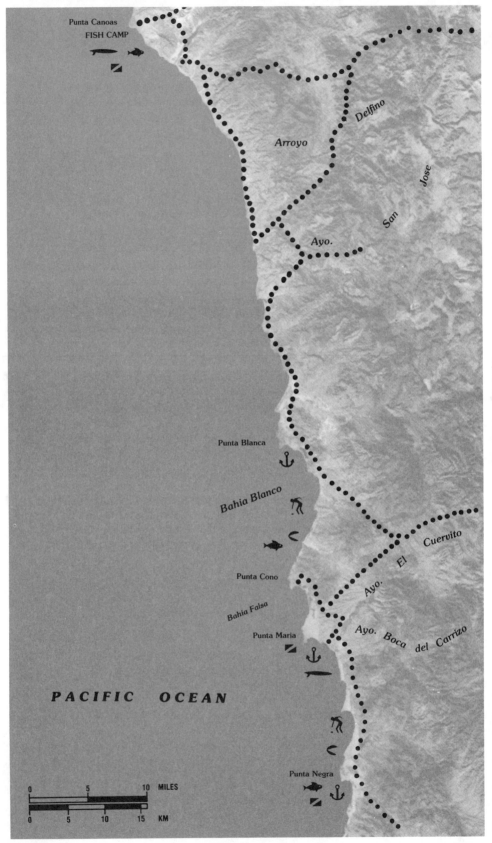

Punta Canoas
FISH CAMP

Arroyo

Delfino

San

Jose

Ayo.

Punta Blanca

Bahia Blanco

Punta Cono

El

Cuervito

Ayo.

Bahia Falsa

Punta Maria

Ayo. Boca del Carrizo

PACIFIC OCEAN

Punta Negra

0   5   10 MILES

0   5   10   15 KM

N

SEA ELEPHANT

ISLA GUADALUPE...early accounts described the island as rich in flowers, birds and trees, in short, a naturalist's dream. Its remoteness (160 miles to the nearest landfall) has led to the evolution of flora and fauna found nowhere else in the world. For example, the Guadalupe oak has an acorn fully two inches in diameter.

Cypress, pine, palm and oak groves covered much of the northwest portion of Guadalupe, where they thrive in a moist, foggy environment. The birdlife was reported to be so tame that most could be picked up with ease, and annual plants and shrubs proliferated.

Almost as the reports were being written the scene was changing, for these same expeditions loosed goats, cats and mice onto the island. Over the years their decendents have all but cleaned out Guadalupe. Today an awareness of the problem is prompting efforts to control feral populations.

While 19th century fur and oil hunters decimated Guadalupe's huge rookeries, today fur and elephant seals are back and registering healthy increases. Though growing numbers of scientists and passenger ships come to see the rookeries, the pinnipeds show little interest. Visitors also include fishermen who come for seasonal catches of yellowtail, albacore, bluefin and yellowfin tuna. A few abalone and lobster fishermen live on the island along with a small military garrison.

See Page 60

See Page 66

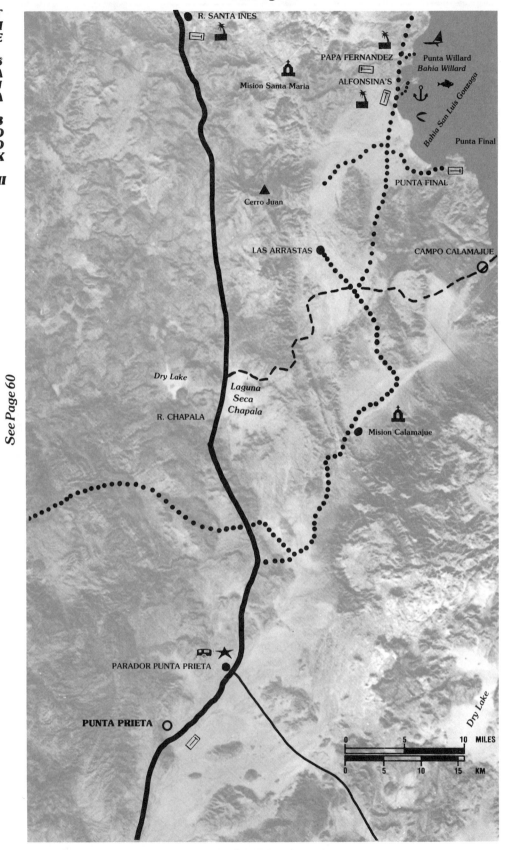

R. SANTA INES

Mision Santa Maria

PAPA FERNANDEZ

ALFONSINA'S

Punta Willard
Bahia Willard

Bahia San Luis Gonzaga

Punta Final

PUNTA FINAL

Cerro Juan

LAS ARRASTAS

CAMPO CALAMAJUE

Dry Lake

*Laguna
Seca
Chapala*

R. CHAPALA

Mision Calamajue

PARADOR PUNTA PRIETA

PUNTA PRIETA

Dry Lake

| 0 | | 5 | | 10 | MILES |
| 0 | 5 | 10 | 15 | KM | |

N

Note: The lack of permanent kilometer markers along this road causes us to use our old mileage (marked "M") format.

95   M7   Entrance into Papa Fernandez Resort, 1 mi. Camping, meals, sometimes gasoline, boats for rent and a nice beach. It has changed little since first visited in late 1960's. The place was one of John Wayne's favorite retreats. The rocks around Punta Willard on the lowtides are interesting for a wide variety of sea animals, shells, etc.

98+   M3   Road left to Alfonsinas, 2 miles around *estero and* landing strip. Popular with boaters and dunebuggy crowd. Camping, meals, some supplies, including gas from drums. To south are the sandy beaches of Ensenada de San Francisquito.

104   M5+   Road right used to go to Las Arrastas, but latest report is that it is no longer passable. Left is to Punta Final, 3.7 mi. where a number of homes are along a beautiful northfacing beach. Good fishing for small species from shore; yellowtail, cabrilla, corvina and whiteseabass over the many reefs in area. New graded road south joins up with Calamajúe road.

116+   M12+   Junction with Calamajué road. 16+ mi. east is fishcamp and small *ejido* on a nice beach. In a recent October we launched an inflatable here and took cabrilla and sierra mackerel both north and south of beach. East of junction 1.5 mi. is road through Arroyo de Calamajué and eventually Mexico 1 at El Crucero, 25 mi. Follow graded road west. The *arroyo* is the site of Mision Calamajué (pg. 166) and later a gold stamping mill. The road south crosses a little stream many times. Heavily mineralized at the bottom, the water becomes almost potable by the time you leave the *arroyo*.

119+   M3   Road right goes to Las Arrastas, about 4 miles. Once an ore processing center, there is a good well, abandoned (Apr, '86) house and several large trees. Past well on old road are several turquoise and gold mines. Continue east on graded road. We have found it to be generally well maintained and were able to make good time over to Mexico 1 at Laguna Chapala.

133   M13+   Intersect with Mexico 1 at K229.
End of log...

THE INFAMOUS CUESTAS

Until the recent realignment of the road beginning 11 miles below Puertecitos (Log, pg. 59) much of the development of the coast below here was held up by three terrible *cuestas* which were pure torture for both vehicle and driver. Sharp, broken, shalelike rocks intersperced with tire-grabbing holes deep enough to require a jack to extricate the undercarriage, combined to damage many transmissions, oil pans, etc.

A look over the side on the steep portions of the *cuestas* revealed a graveyard of all manner of vehicles. In 1978 there were 11 wrecks visible from one vantage point on the second grade. Those scarred hills hold memories for many a Baja traveler. Hopefully they will not have to be traversed again by any of us. We have paid our dues.

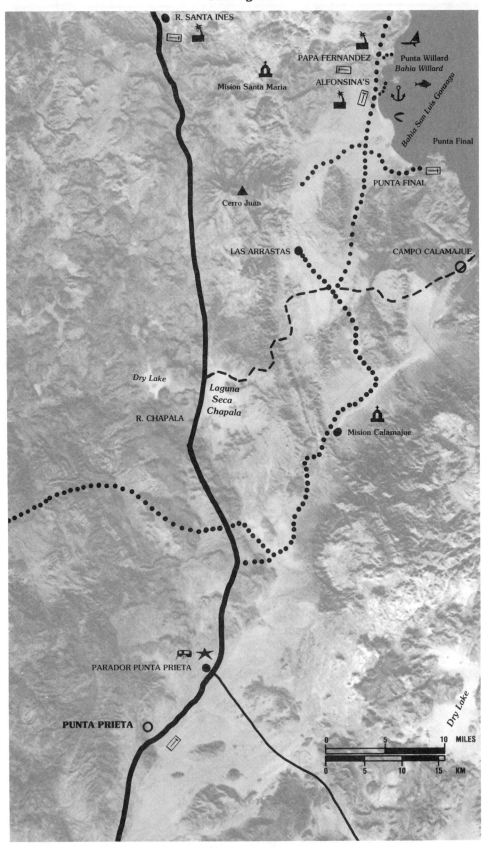

R. SANTA INES

PAPA FERNANDEZ

Punta Willard
Bahia Willard

Mision Santa Maria

ALFONSINA'S

Bahia San Luis Gonzaga

Punta Final

PUNTA FINAL

Cerro Juan

LAS ARRASTAS

CAMPO CALAMAJUE

Dry Lake

*Laguna
Seca
Chapala*

R. CHAPALA

Mision Calamajue

Dry Lake

PARADOR PUNTA PRIETA

PUNTA PRIETA

0   5   10 MILES
0   5   10   15 KM

109.7   *K176*   After crossing arroyo, paved road left leads to Rancho Santa Ines, 1 mi. Friendly atmosphere and fine ranch-style food. Road then heads ESE through stands of elephant trees.

116.5   *K187*   Rancho San Ignacito restaurant. Good food. Whole family can cook, but it's best when mama's there. It was here that Mexico 1 was officially completed. Plaque is across road.

119   *K191*   Rancho Jaraguáy off to left. Begin steep climb onto plateau. Road on top is easy driving, good visibility.

139   *K223*   In distance is Laguna Chapala, a dry lake bed, except following rare heavy rains.

142.7   *K229*   Graded road east skirting north edge of Laguna Chapala is to Bahía San Luís Gonzaga and points north (pgs. 53, 59, 63). Beyond at K230+ is restaurant, Rancho Nuevo Chapala (pg. 134) Road continues through sparse growths of cirio, cardon, yucca and cholla.

160.7   *K258*   El Crucero, where trail from left comes into highway. This is the old Gulf road through Arroyo Calamajué (pgs. 53, 59, 60) from San Felipe and Bahía Gonzaga. A number of high mesas are visible on both sides of road. Altitude 1500'.

174.4   *K280*   Parador Punta Prieta. Gasoline on occasions. Restaurant has been open of late, and the food was good, but it may not last. As with the rest of the paradors, the dream never came to be. Paved road east leads to Bahía de Los Ángeles, 41 miles (pg. 75).
End of log...

PARADOR PUNTA PRIETA — PARALLELO 28

0   *K0*   Continue south from intersection with LA Bay road.

8.1   *K13*   Enter small ranch community of Punta Prieta. There is a large unused airstrip NE of town. Why, is a long story. Road maintenance camp off to west of highway.

(continued on page 73)

THE NOPAL

Called *nopal* by the locals, wherever it is found in Baja it yields two opportunities to harvest some fine eating. In spring when the new leaves, *nopalitos*, are developing, and later in the summer when the fruit, *tuna*, is ripe. Either way its preparation requires effort, but some find it worthwhile.

   Remove the soft spines of the *nopalitos* with a knife and slice into thin strips. Parboil briefly, rinse and drain. Serve sauted with small pieces of pork and chopped onions. When the fruit becomes ripe we've removed them with tongs, split them with a knife and scooped out the insides. The red meat has a thirst-quenching tart-sweet flavor. We found this process more trouble than it is worth.

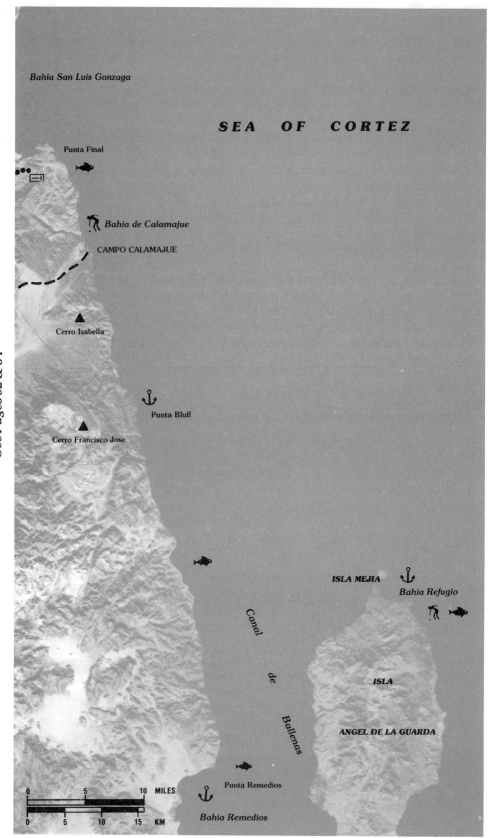

Bahia San Luis Gonzaga

SEA   OF   CORTEZ

Punta Final

Bahia de Calamajue

CAMPO CALAMAJUE

Cerro Isabella

Punta Bluff

Cerro Francisco Jose

ISLA MEJIA

Bahia Refugio

Canal

de

Ballenas

ISLA

ANGEL DE LA GUARDA

Punta Remedios

Bahia Remedios

| 0 | 5 | 10 | MILES |
| 0 | 5 | 10 | 15 | KM |

NAMING THE SEA OF CORTEZ

YOUNG
CARDON

The body of water which separates the Baja California peninsula from the Mexican mainland has had many names since it was first visited by the Spaniards in 1537.

That year, Francisco de Ulloa led three ships the entire length of the gulf. They charted many of the landmarks from Acapulco north to the mouth of the Rio Colorado, around Cabo San Lucas and up to the giant bay now known as Bahia Magdalina.

Ulloa named it *Golfo de Cortés* or *Mar de Cortés* after his captain Hernan Cortés. On most charts the name was short lived, being replaced by *Mar Vermiglion, Mar Rojo* and *Mar Vermijo*.

The last names refer to the reddish color of the water, probably due to the immense numbers of pelagic red crabs that periodically cover the surface in the southern half of the Sea.

After Padre Eusebio Kino walked the gulf's perimeter in 1700 it was known as *Mar Laurentaño*, after the Virgin of Loreto, patroness of the California missions, as well as *Seño California* and *Mar California*.

Jesuit maps of 1730 and 1772 documented it as *Golfo de California* and this name remained prominent until recently when there has been a movement to go to the anglicized, *Sea of Cortez*.

Whatever its name, this body of water is one of great interest to the marine biologist and angler, as it contains over eight hundred species of fish and thousands of other forms of sealife, many of which are found nowhere else on earth.

The islands in the Cortez offer naturalists opportunities to observe a wide variety of seabirds in their rookeries, plus a number of rare reptiles and plants.

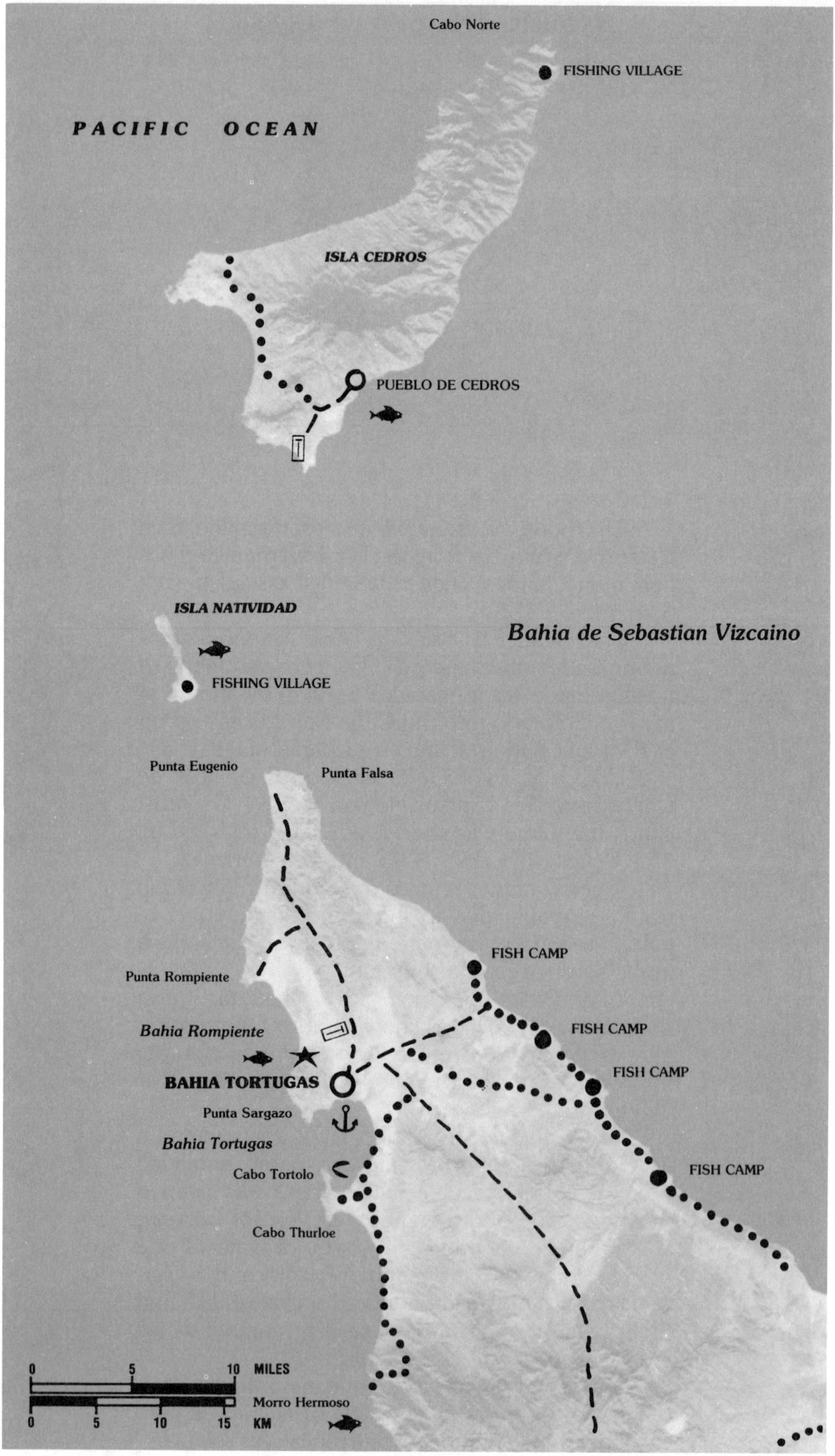

Cabo Norte

FISHING VILLAGE

PACIFIC OCEAN

ISLA CEDROS

PUEBLO DE CEDROS

ISLA NATIVIDAD

Bahia de Sebastian Vizcaino

FISHING VILLAGE

Punta Eugenio

Punta Falsa

FISH CAMP

Punta Rompiente

FISH CAMP

Bahia Rompiente

FISH CAMP

BAHIA TORTUGAS

Punta Sargazo

Bahia Tortugas

FISH CAMP

Cabo Tortolo

Cabo Thurloe

0		5		10	**MILES**

Morro Hermoso

0	5	10	15	**KM**

See Page 70

See Page 78

N

BAHIA TORTUGAS...nearly 100 miles from the nearest paved road, this fishing village of 3800 is one of the most remote settlements on the peninsula. Access is by boat, plane or via the newly graded and graveled *ramal,* or access road. It is a busy town — thanks to a thriving fishing industry. A well protected anchorage is popular with visiting yachts, and sandy beaches yield clams and surf fish. The climate is cool and windy much of the time, with lots of fog between March and July.

Water is critically scarce. It comes from small, outlying wells via tank trucks and a desalinization plant. Recent rumors say that ample water is coming soon — and there is a pipeline under construction to the east — but it will probably be a long time before anything changes here, such is the scarcity of water in the Vizcaino.

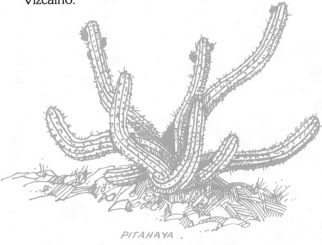

PITAHAYA .

ISLA CEDROS...is located about 12 miles northwest of Punta Eugenia. Its original inhabitants were Indians who would would occasionally float over to the mainland on rafts to gather clams and berries. It seems like a tough way to get a clam, and many Indians must have perished in the effort.

The coastal explorers of the 16th century logged its existence several times. Later pirates hid here and at nearby San Benitos awaiting the rich Manila galleons. The good spring, and goats descended from ones place on the island by the pirates, helped provision 19th century whalers. Accounts of abundant goats on Cedros were in Captain Scammon's log.

The small community near the south end of Cedros is principally involved in offloading and loading the 6+ million tons of salt produced by the Exportadora de Sal operation at Guerrero Negro. Brought over on barges from the shallows of Scammon's Lagoon, it is transferred onto large ships from all over the world.

There are also fish, lobster and abalone taken commercially. A rudimentry dirt strip allows airplanes from Ensenada to service the area. On the north end of the island is a small abandoned copper mine.

The region is popular with the private yachts and sportfishing boats out of San Diego.

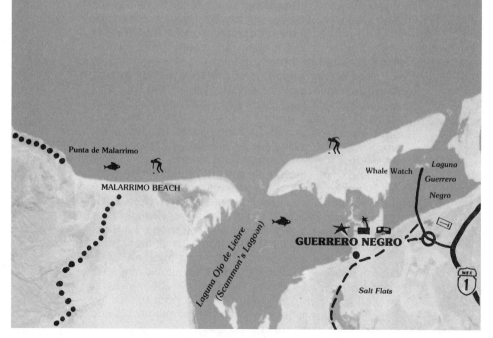

PACIFIC OCEAN

Bahia

de

Sebastian

Vizcaino

Punta de Malarrimo

MALARRIMO BEACH

Whale Watch

Laguna
Guerrero
Negro

Laguna Ojo de Liebre
(Scammon's Lagoon)

GUERRERO NEGRO

Salt Flats

MEX 1

See Page 68

See Page 72

See Page 80

THE BEARDED DESERT

TREE YUCCA

The coastal regions around Bahía de Sebastián Vizcanio are dominated by a strong, cool shoreward air movement. Much of the year, the nights and mornings are foggy, often for miles inland.

Although the region is rarely visited by major rainstorms — average annual rainfall is less than 3 inches — many desert plants are festooned with Spanish moss, a plant usually associated with regions of high humidity. The cirios and ocotillos in particular take on a bizarre appearance because of the long "beards" supplied by the grey-green moss.

Another plant common to this portion of Baja is the tree yucca. Although related to the joshua trees of the high desert north of Los Angeles, they are generally more slender and less branching. The Baja California yucca blooms during the summer, displaying masses of white blossoms in contrast to the springtime appearance of creamy flowers on the joshua tree.

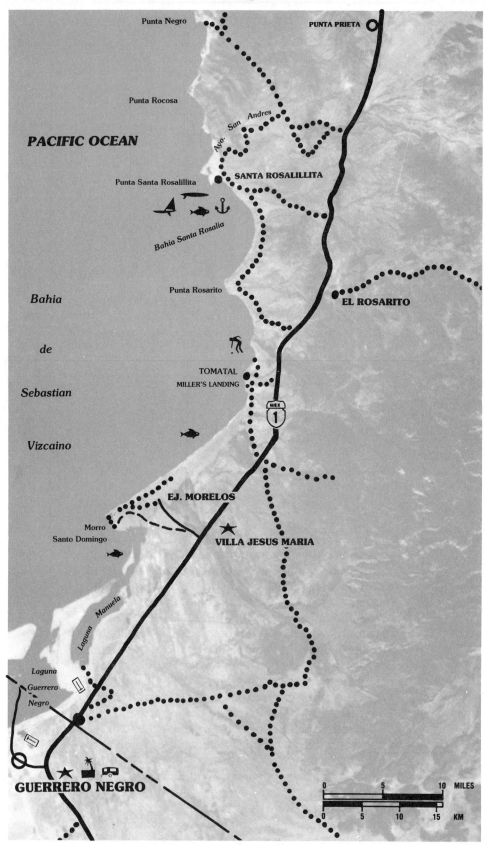

Punta Negro

PUNTA PRIETA

Punta Rocosa

Arroyo San Andres

PACIFIC OCEAN

SANTA ROSALILLITA

Punta Santa Rosalillita

Bahia Santa Rosalia

Bahia

Punta Rosarito

EL ROSARITO

de

Sebastian

TOMATAL
MILLER'S LANDING

MEX 1

Vizcaino

EJ. MORELOS

Morro
Santo Domingo

VILLA JESUS MARIA

Laguna Manuela

Laguna Guerrero Negro

GUERRERO NEGRO

0   5   10   MILES

0   5   10   15   KM

See Page 70

See Page 74

14.4   K25   Many of the *cirios* here have Spanish moss grow-ing on them. Ahead begins a steep, winding ascent to a ridge. Follow along top for about 2 miles, then down into valley. Watch sharp curves on downgrade.

21.8   K35   Road straightens and passes through *vados*, or dips.

24   K38+   New graded road right is to fishing village of Santa Rosalillita, 10 mi. Surfers are ecstatic about the area. They say they can get as much as a mile and a half ride with a good southwest swell. Large black butte is to left of highway.

31.6   K51   Small town to east is El Rosarito. A rather forlorn little town, a road out of east side leads to Misión San Borja (pg. 135). Leave town down attractive *arroyo* holding some marsh grasses and boulders.

39   K63   Dirt road west leads to Punta Rosarito, about 4 miles, then follows beach north to Santa Rosalillita. Good camping, fishing and surfing.

43.1   K69   Semigraded road right leads to El Tomatál beach and fish camp. At 2 mi. trail south to Miller's Landing, about 2 mi. From intersection it is another mile to beach. At one time, onyx from a small deposit in mountains, El Marmolito, was shipped out of Miller's. There are still a few pieces lying around.

59.7   K95+   Pemex station in Villa Jesus María. Paved road west leads to Ejido Morelos and Laguna Manuela/ Morro Santo Domingo. For Manuela, take graded road left 1 mile in from highway then, 5.5mi. to ocean. Excellent camping and fishing. Continue south with dunes of Laguna Manuela in distance.

78   K125   Paved road right leads to large landing field. It was origi-nally intended to be a refueling stop for transpacific passenger flights, but the scheme never happened. Now it serves occasionally as a drag strip. Just past west end is small beach on south end of Laguna Manuela.

80   K128   The 28th Parallel is the boundary between Baja Cali-fornia and Baja California Sur, and is adorned with a huge stylized eagle (pg. 135). The hotel La Pinta is on Baja Sur side.
End of log...

CHOLLA

PARALELO 28 — SANTA ROSALÍA

Note: The kilometer markers in the southern half of the peninsula run south to north, so our logs in Baja California Sur will begin with high kilometer values and decrease as we go south. (It may be confusing, but we couldn't get the road engineers to change the signs.)

0   K220   Leave hotel at Paralelo 28 and head south.

2   K217   Main road curves left at intersection with paved road into Guerrero Negro, 2.5 miles (pgs. 81 & 135). Mexico 1 turns ESE through low dunes with a sparse covering of brush.

(continued on page 83)

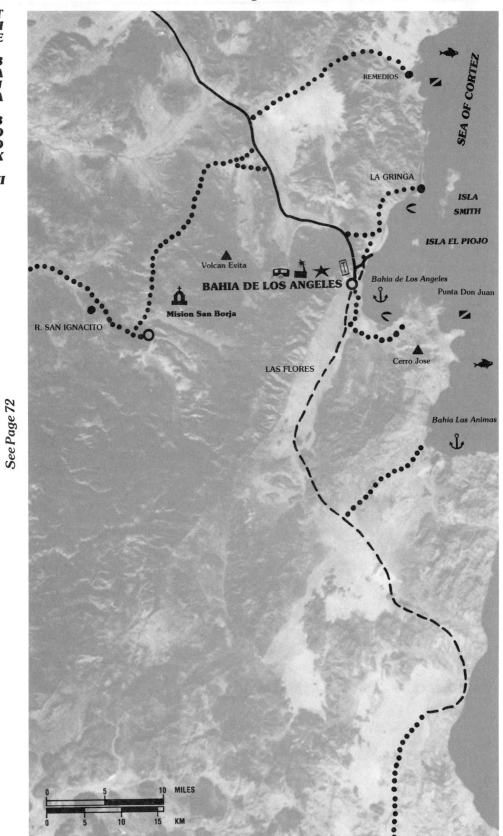

See Page 72

See Page 76

REMEDIOS

SEA OF CORTEZ

LA GRINGA

ISLA SMITH

ISLA EL PIOJO

Volcan Evita

BAHIA DE LOS ANGELES

Mision San Borja

Bahia de Los Angeles

Punta Don Juan

R. SAN IGNACITO

LAS FLORES

Cerro Jose

Bahia Las Animas

0   5   10 MILES

0   5   10 15 KM

BLACK MUREX

BAHÍA de LOS ÁNGELES...is a beautiful island-studded bay bordered by miles of fine beaches. My first trip to L.A. Bay was by private plane in early 60's,. The next time six of our eight vacation days were spent going and coming in dunebuggys. The area finally hit its stride after 1976 when the 43-mile road in from Mexico 1 was paved.

Today two motels, several launching ramps, campgrounds and restaurants make it seem almost as though its earlier remoteness was imagined.

The best fishing is from mid-April through October. During these times the reefs around the islands often become jammed with all manner of private boats looking for the current "hotspot" for yellowtail, cabrilla or grouper. The channel separating *Isla Angel de La Guarda* and the peninsula often hosts large pods of porpoise and finback whales. In times past the Bahía was a productive turtle fishing region, but over-harvesting has made it a rarity today.

The 41-mile paved road from Parador Punta Prieta into Bahía de Los Ángeles brings to the traveler one of the most interesting and accessible recreation areas in Baja. Rewards for visitors are many. Besides excellent fishing, shelling and clamming, diving and windsailing are popular pastimes. There are old mining sites to be explored, 4-WD roads to follow and trips to the adjoining islands.

The Villa Vitta and Casa Diaz motels have creature comforts, while camping areas offer lots of choices. Restaurant meals, especially seafood, are good and reasonably priced. Several small stores have limited supplies. Gasoline, water and ice can be scarce, so try and bring what you will need.

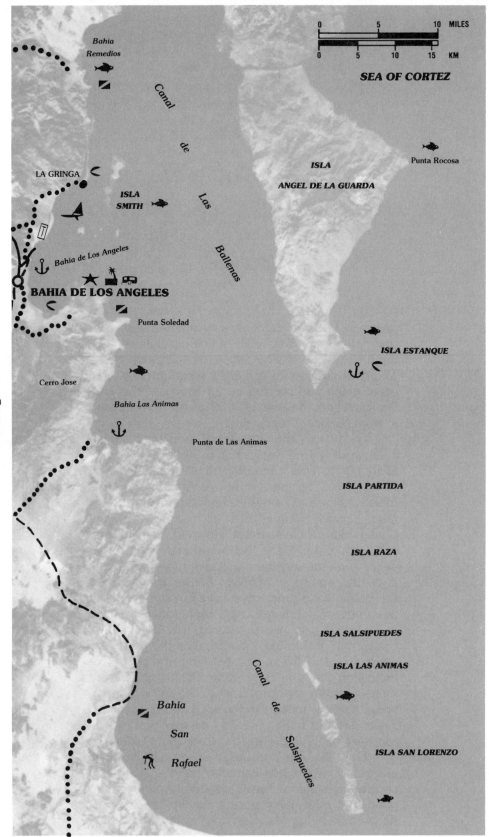

Bahia
Remedios

Canal

de

Las

Ballenas

SEA OF CORTEZ

0   5   10 MILES
0   5   10   15 KM

Punta Rocosa

ISLA
ANGEL DE LA GUARDA

LA GRINGA

ISLA
SMITH

Bahia de Los Angeles

BAHIA DE LOS ANGELES

Punta Soledad

ISLA ESTANQUE

Cerro Jose

Bahia Las Animas

Punta de Las Animas

ISLA PARTIDA

ISLA RAZA

ISLA SALSIPUEDES

ISLA LAS ANIMAS

Canal

de

Salsipuedes

Bahia

San

Rafael

ISLA SAN LORENZO

N

ISLA ANGEL de LA GUARDA...is the largest island close adjoining the Baja mainland (Tíburon on the eastern side of the Midriff is the largest island in the Sea of Cortez.) It's 4000-foot plus mountains and 42 mile length makes it a prominent landmark whether boating of flying in the vicinity. The largely barren surface supports a few coyotes and rodents, plus abundant numbers of lizards and rattlesnakes. Several seal rockeries are found along the north-eastern coast. Many schools of fish patrol the rocky reefs and coves of La Guarda Ángel.

The highlight of a visit to the island must be exploring the almost-surrealistic Bahía Refugio at the north end of the island. Here you will see pinnacles of white and black rocks jutting from the water's surface, high cliffs of reds, browns, greys and whites. Many coves and lees afford protection in any weather, thus the name, Refugio. Several of the small islands forming the bay also serve as early summer nesting grounds for the California brown pelican, or pelicano. Later, in September, sealions drop their pups, affording many opportunities for pictures.

Snorkeling the shallow coves reveals a veritable smorgasbord of sealife, much of which is edible.

Once, while fishing on a boat out of San Felipe, we spent several days in Refugio waiting out gale force winds that whipped the surrounding gulf to a froth. We experienced only a little wind and, at the same time, had almost nonstop yellowtail fishing. Everywhere a lure went in the water the yellows were waiting. We almost collapsed from exhaustion. (Also see page 66)

ISLA LA RAZA...is barely one-third of a square mile, but is of prime interest to naturalists as it is the only known breeding place for the beautiful elegant tern. In 1964, this low island was designated by President Lopez Mateos as a wildlife preserve. Currently, several biologists live on La Raza from March to July when they study and protect the nesting birds and their hatchlings. Though visitors are discouraged, permission can sometimes be obtained by hailing one of the biologists. (A frosty soda or *cerveza* sometimes helps get their attention.)

Once there you will experience an inteminal cacophany of shrieks, squeeks and squawks as the thousands of birds vie for their place on La Raza.

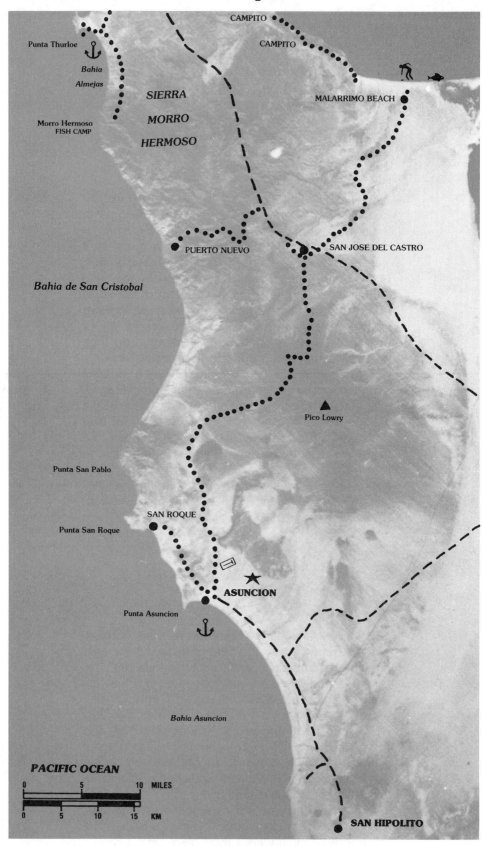

CAMPITO

CAMPITO

Punta Thurloe

Bahia
Almejas

MALARRIMO BEACH

SIERRA

Morro Hermoso
FISH CAMP

MORRO

HERMOSO

PUERTO NUEVO

SAN JOSE DEL CASTRO

Bahia de San Cristobal

Pico Lowry

Punta San Pablo

SAN ROQUE

Punta San Roque

ASUNCION

Punta Asuncion

Bahia Asuncion

PACIFIC OCEAN

| 0 | 5 | 10 | MILES |

| 0 | 5 | 10 | 15 | KM |

SAN HIPOLITO

See Page 80

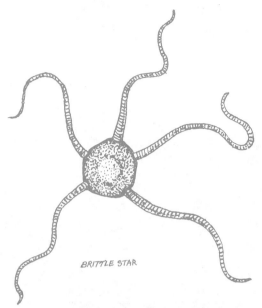

BRITTLE STAR

ISLA NATIVIDÁD...is a low, rather barren island almost four miles long by a mile wide. It lies four miles west of Punta San Eugenio with a small fishing village on the southern end. It was discovered recently by surfers and has been featured in at least one magazine.

ISLAS SAN BENITO...is a popular destination for anglers. The small fish camp on the westernmost island usually has a good supply of lobster and abalone. Once, on a long range trip, we placed our order for "bugs" and "abs," only to be told that they would have to get them. Several of us even went ashore, chatted with the townspeople and explored the tidepools. Others fished the nearby kelp beds. Finally the men returned with our *mariscos*, looking as though they had just run a 4-minute mile. We learned as we left that the abalones had been in a nearby shed all the time, while the lobsters were in a receiver in the next cove. They just wanted company.

Some of the region's best yellowtail fishing is off the reefs around these islands.

BAHÍA ASUNCIÓN...is similar to Bahía Tortugas. Its residents take and process abalone, lobster and fish. The beaches south of town afford excellent fishing and clamming, while offshore reefs yield many gamefish. Limited supplies are available. Water is precious, and comes from scattered wells or the reverse osmosis plant. (In the past much of it was brought in from Cedros Island by tanker.) As along most of the Vizcaino coast, it is windy much of the year.

See Page 78

See Page 82

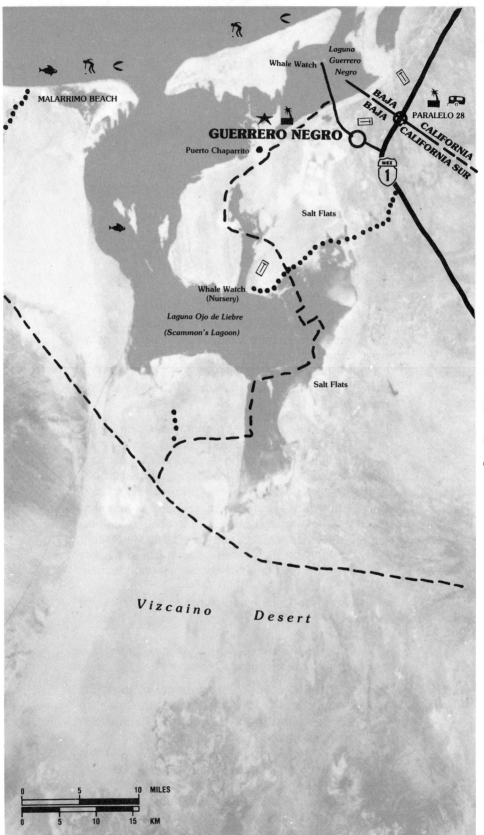

MALARRIMO BEACH

Whale Watch

Laguna Guerrero Negro

BAJA
BAJA
BAJA
CALIFORNIA
CALIFORNIA SUR

PARALELO 28

GUERRERO NEGRO

Puerto Chaparrito

MEX 1

Salt Flats

Whale Watch
(Nursery)

Laguna Ojo de Liebre

(Scammon's Lagoon)

Salt Flats

Vizcaino   Desert

| 0 | | 5 | | 10 | MILES |

| 0 | 5 | | 10 | | 15 | KM |

N

THE WHALES OF SCAMMON's LAGOON

Each year, from January through mid-March, an estimated 17,000 California gray whales, *Eschrichtius gibbosus*, turn Scammon's Lagoon, San Ignacio Lagoon and many miles of protected waterways in Magdalena Bay into the world's biggest nursery.

The food-rich Arctic and Bering seas are the homes of these fifty-foot giants until fall when they begin the longest migration of any mammal to their winter calving and mating grounds in Mexico.

Fifteen feet long and 1000 pounds when born, these "babies" consume up to 50 gallons of milk daily and put on nearly 100 pounds of weight per day for several months before heading north to their summer feeding grounds.

A popular whalewatching spot is the old salt loading dock north of town. Another is at the "nursery," 15 miles south of town on a dirt road. Turnoff is at **K208**.

Captain Charles Scammon discovered the entrance to the lagoon in the 1850's and proceeded to slaughter the giant beasts by the hundreds for their valuable oil. Others uncovered his secret and within a few decades the gray whale was nearly exterminated. Later, around 1915, another slaughter took place.

From the estimated 300 whales thought to be remaining in 1937, the California gray whale has made a remarkable comeback.

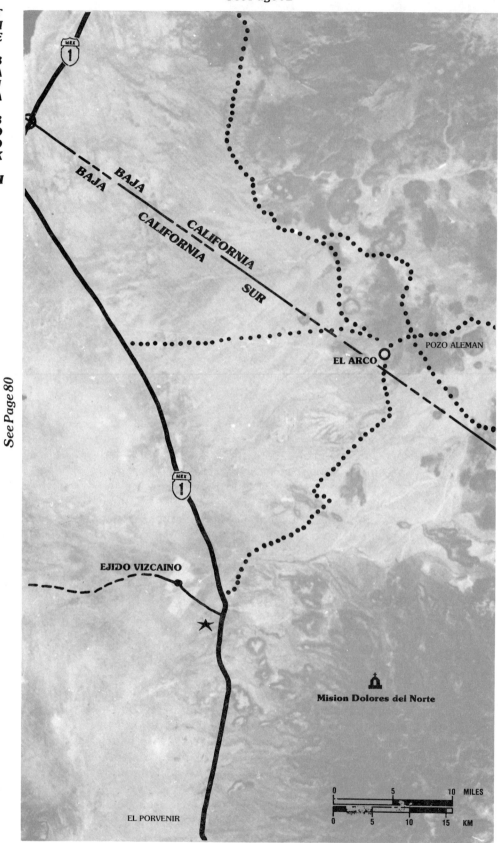

BAJA CALIFORNIA SUR

BAJA CALIFORNIA

MEX 1

POZO ALEMAN

EL ARCO

MEX 1

EJIDO VIZCAINO

Mision Dolores del Norte

EL PORVENIR

See Page 80

See Page 84

0		5		10	MILES

0	5	10	15	KM

7.7   K208   Signed road right goes to Scammon's Lagoon at spot called the "nursery" because of the many gray whales (pg. 81) found from January through March.

19.3   K189+   Paved-appearing road left leads to El Arco, 26 mi. It was thinly paved in 1973 just before the Baja highway opened. Within months it began falling apart. Now it is a disaster; potholes, washboards, rocks, loose chunks of paving, etc. If you have to go to El Arco, the dirt trails paralleling "roadbed" are generally passable.

25.5   K179+   Recently settled farming community of Ejido Lagunero.

47.5   K144   Intersection. Pemex station, several restaurants and store nearby. Paved west past Ejido Vizcaino goes about 5 miles before turning into graded dirt. This is one entry into Vizcaino Desert (pg. 89).

60.6   K123+   Well kept, modern Rancho Los Ángeles on south side of highway. The dips, or *vados*, found throughout here can flood easily during a storm. Be very careful when crossing if there is water running.

(continued on page 91)

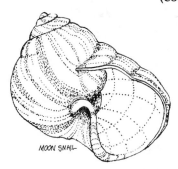

MOON SNAIL

THE FOSSIL WATERS OF BAJA

As you drive through the flatlands southeast of Guerrero Negro, you will see large tracts of cleared desert land. The area was originally pioneered by the government to determine the most effective way to grow cropw in this incredibly rich, but parched desert land. It began at Ejido Vizcanio — below Guerrero Negro and three miles west of the highway at **K144** — in the late 60's with the installation of drip irrigation systems. Today a wide variety of crops are to be found in the area. At times, at the gas station some farmers will be seen selling some of their produce.

Of particular interest is that the water used for farming here is many, many thousands of years old! It is not from the rains of recent times, but rather water which percolated into the substrata during an age when water was plentiful, probably well before the last ice age.

Like oil and coal deposits, once it is gone it cannot be replaced. Thus the size of the resource dictates the success of the project. Preliminary tests indicate sufficient reserves for many years if water conservation practices are heeded.

THE
BAJA
BOOK
III

See Page 82

See Page 86

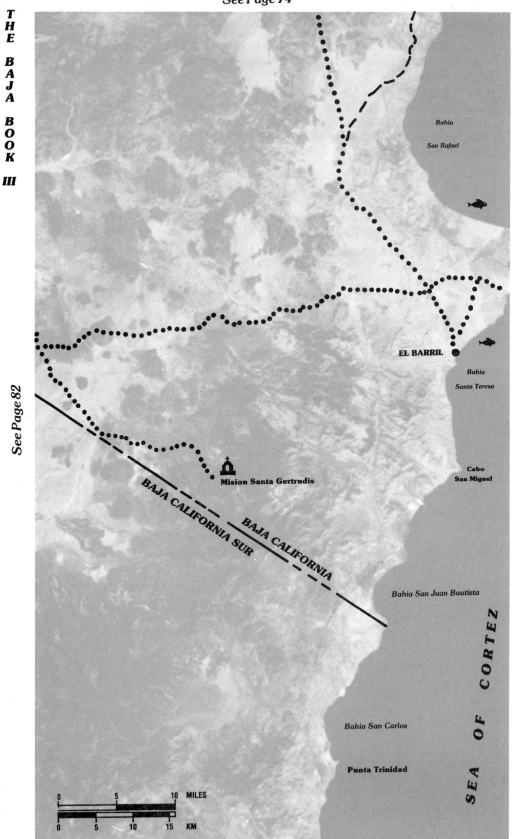

Bahia

San Rafael

EL BARRIL

Bahia

Santa Teresa

Cabo
San Miguel

Mision Santa Gertrudis

BAJA CALIFORNIA SUR

BAJA CALIFORNIA

Bahia San Juan Bautista

Bahia San Carlos

Punta Trinidad

SEA   OF   CORTEZ

0	5	10	MILES

0	5	10	15	KM

N

BROWN PELICAN

THE PELICAN WATCHERS

Those who have enjoyed the antics of the relatively few pelicans found along our Pacific shores will be especially happy to see the many long flights of the awkward-looking *pelícano*, or *alcatráz*, throughout the Sea of Cortez and Baja's Pacific side.

Pelican rookeries abound on many of the smaller islands of the Cortez. The adults are a good harbinger of where to toss a lure when they begin their wheeling, hellbent dives for baitfish pushed to the surface by larger game fish. At such a moment any angler's heart will skip a few beats and his fingers will likely flub even the simplest cast.

When watching a flight of pelicans you might count how many are flying together. Most of the time it will be an even number. This bit of trivia might be worth a *cerveza* wager on an otherwise quiet day. (If you can find someone who does not have a copy of **The Baja Book III**.

For some years the U.S. Fish and Wildlife Service marked young pelicans on their Cortez nesting grounds in order to study their movements. From this they have learned that a number traverse the mountainous Baja peninsula to patrol the Pacific shores as far north as San Francisco.

See Page 84

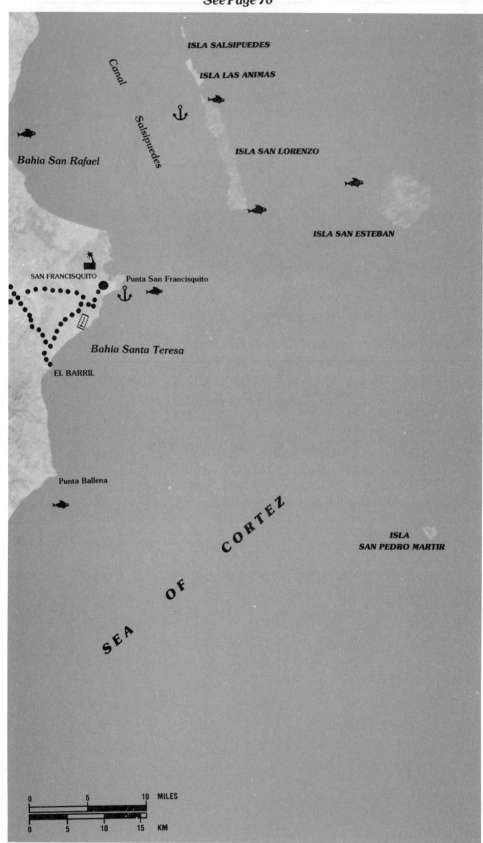

ISLA SALSIPUEDES

ISLA LAS ANIMAS

Canal

ISLA SAN LORENZO

Salsipuedes

Bahia San Rafael

ISLA SAN ESTEBAN

SAN FRANCISQUITO

Punta San Francisquito

Bahia Santa Teresa

EL BARRIL

Punta Ballena

CORTEZ

ISLA
SAN PEDRO MARTIR

SEA

OF

| 0 | 5 | 10 | MILES |
| 0 | 5 | 10 | 15 | KM |

N

ISLA SAN LORENZO...is at the bottom of a closely situated narrow chain of three islands that comprise the southernmost of what is popularly known as the Midriff Islands. There are two fine anchorages on the top one, Isla Salsipuedes, the balance offer little shelter from the prevailings. At the north end of Isla Las Animas a small sandy beach offers protection from southerly winds.

Incidentally, *salsipuedes* in Spanish means "get out if you can," and whenever this name is attached to a location it indicates there is a reason to take extra care. In this instance, it is the currents which at times of great tidal change can exceed 6 knots and create giant upwellings.

Fishing on both sides of the islands is generally good. Ashore there is little of interest, except for a few rattlers and lizards.

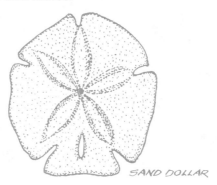

SAND DOLLAR

BAHÍA SAN FRANCISQUITO...is a tough 25 miles from the highway to El Arco, and then a tougher 50 miles more to Bahia San Francisquito and El Barril, but well worth the effort for anyone with a good offroad vehicle. Those who make it to this region during the hot months of May through October will find yellow-tail often congregated just offshore in great numbers. Not only do anglers in boats get the action but a if you watch for baitfish being driven close to shore you could well hang a yellow to 25 pounds right from the beach.

March, April and May are good months for white seabass over the reefs south of the point, while sierra appear in July, August and September.

A small, rather primitive fly-in resort is on the beach at San Francisquito. They are not overly friendly to campers, but on occasion can provide a bunk and a meal at a stiff price.

Mounds of pearl oyster shells are seen along the shore near the small bay. Some date back to the days of the Spaniards. but today the pearl oyster is a rare find. There is a fair supply of clams, scallops and conchs awaiting the skilled diver.

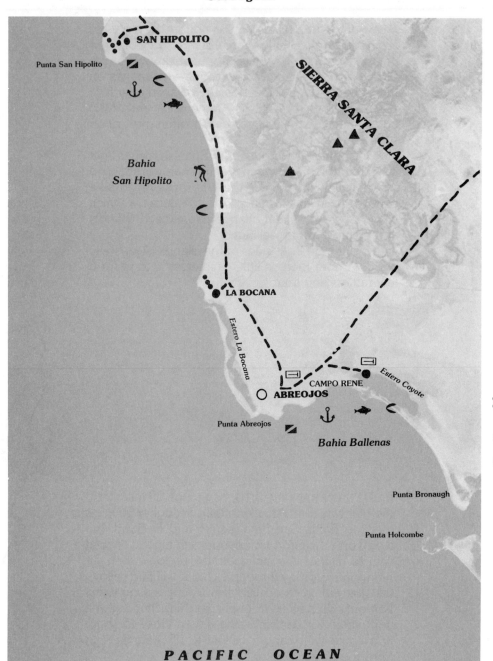

See Page 90

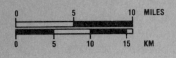

PUNTA ABREOJOS...has great potential to become the hub of a region centered around marine activities. Nearby Laguna San Ignacio is a major calving spot for gray whales, fishing and clamming abound, waterfowl are plentiful. Unfortunately, there is little water, except that generated by a so-so saltwater conversion plant. All else must be trucked in. Here too plans are afoot for water piped in from afar, but it is some years off.

THE VIZCAINO EXPERIENCE

As man's influence has spread over the Baja California peninsula one major region remains much as it was in the days of the first padres, the Vizcaino peninsula. Other than a few fishing villages along its margains and a scattered rancho or two, it has changed little.

If you are equipped to handle poor roads, enjoy virgin beaches and friendly fishing villages, and really want to get away from it all, then this is for you. But we recommend that you don't go alone.

Beginning from the turnoff from Mexico 1, 15 miles northwest of San Ignacio at **K98**, the first leg is through desolate terrain that includes sand dunes, salt flats and more sand. It is 47 mi. to the turnoff to Estero Coyote and Campo René. Though not like it was, good numbers of corvina, cabrilla and croaker still patrol the entrance to the bay.

At 54 mi. enter Abreojos (pg. 89). Many nearby beaches hold large numbers of pismo and other clams, along with quantities of surf fish, rays and small sharks. The offshore rocks are regularly worked for commercial quantities of abalone and lobster. Some of the warm water species such as the triggerfish, corvina and grouper are taken near Abreojos and to the north.

All of the water in this region must be trucked in. Fuel and limited groceries are available. The graded road closely follows the coastline beyond La Bocana (12 mi.) northward past San Hipolito (35 mi.) and Punta Prieta (40 mi.). At mile 52 a signed road goes northeast to join Ejido Vizcaino-Tortugas road (22 mi.). Continue 8 miles to Asunción where a side road leads up the coast to San Roque (8 mi.).

All along this stretch are more inviting beaches than you can count, many within walking distance.

Though the fall can be especially beautiful, carry warm clothing in case of fog and wind.

Once past Asunción, the road turns inland for about 36 miles to a large ranch, San José de Castro. Built around a well of good water, it is a welcome sight after crossing the barren Sierra Pintada.

Despite the fact that much of the "good" flotsam and jetsam of the Pacific has been gleaned from its beaches, Malarrimo still holds a fascination for many Baja travelers. Though the road is not a good one, it may be entered by going a few hundred yards east on the Tortuga-Vizcaino road to a rough and sandy 4-WD trail leading 26 miles to Malarrimo Beach.

Though a few treasures still exist — look in the (continued on page 91)

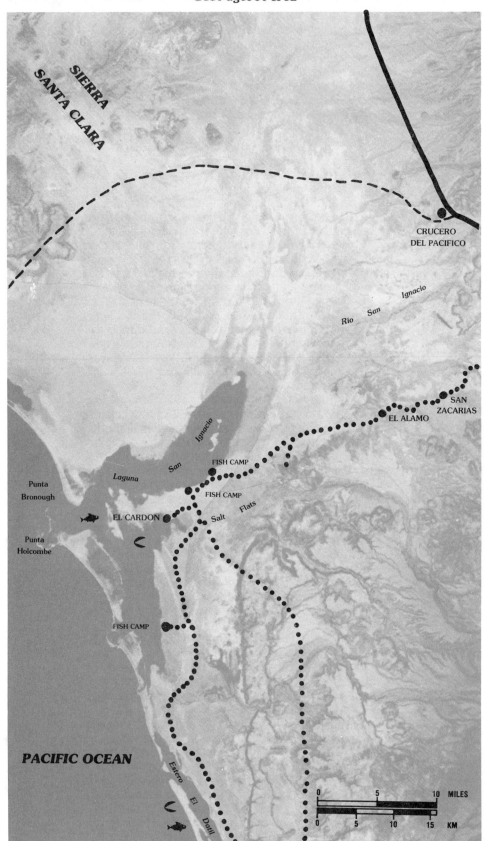

See Page 88

See Page 92

SIERRA
SANTA CLARA

CRUCERO
DEL PACIFICO

Ignacio

Rio   San

SAN
ZACARIAS

EL ALAMO

San   Ignacio

FISH CAMP

Laguna

Punta
Bronough

FISH CAMP

EL CARDON

Salt   Flats

Punta
Holcombe

FISH CAMP

PACIFIC OCEAN

Estero   El   Datil

MILES

0   5   10

0   5   10   15
KM

N

THE VIZCAINO EXPERIENCE (from page 89)

dunes directly behind the beach — unfortunately most of the booty will be in the form of styrafoam floats, coffee cups and Big-Mac wrappers, plus plastic bottles by the thousands (pg 142).

Leave San José de Castro and go northwest 30 mi. to Bahia Tortugas (page 69). Just before town there's an interesting turnoff west to Cabo Tortolo — camping, fishing, beachcombing.

The roads north and west of town go to lobster camps and fine fishing beaches. The north road can take you along the coast nearly to Malarrimo if you have 4-wheel drive.

YOUR OWN BAJA 1000 CHALLENGE

Several times on the route of the Baja 1000 races, the road leading out of San Ignacio past the cemetery, the south side of Laguna San Ignacio and on to Villa Insurgentes is one of adventure. Passing through a desolate, waterless plain past a tiny believe-it-or-not winery (San Zachariás), it is one of the least traveled roads in Baja.

Continuing, and taking the coastal trail, you pass Estero El Datíl (77 mi.), and the surfing spot of San Juanico (112 mi.) to eventually connect with the road across the Sierra Giganta to La Purisima before the intersection (142 mi.). Farther south comes the Las Barracas turnoff (155 mi.) and finally La Poza Grande at 183 miles. Twenty miles later you are on the way to Villa Insurgentes over a paved road.

PARALELO 28 — SANTA ROSALIÁ (from page 83)

76.4   K98   Grade road west just past several small buildings (one of which is Fischer's Restaurant) leads to Abreojos and other fishing villages along Pacific side of Vizcaino Desert. The area is only lightly touched by the visitor. Some locations, such as Campo René and Abreojos are experiencing some visitations, but the 45 miles of washboraded road discourages most (pgs. 89, 91).

(continued on page 93)

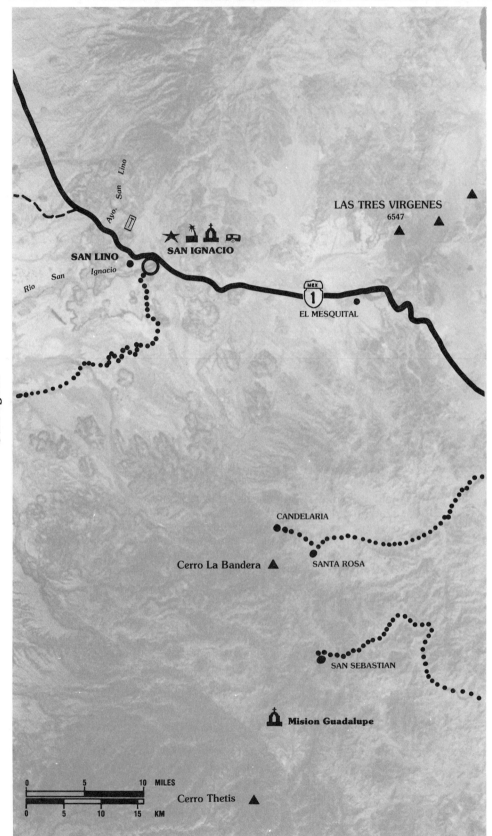

LAS TRES VIRGENES

6547

San Lino

Ayo.

SAN IGNACIO

SAN LINO

Rio   San   Ignacio

MEX 1

EL MESQUITAL

CANDELARIA

Cerro La Bandera ▲

SANTA ROSA

SAN SEBASTIAN

Misíon Guadalupe

| 0 | | 5 | | 10 | MILES |
| 0 | 5 | | 10 | 15 | KM |

Cerro Thetis   ▲

N

88.5   *K78+*   Signed road left to paved landing strip.

89.1   *K77+*   Agricultural inspection station which stops all vehicles going north. Quichule Restaurant across street.

91.3   *K74*   On left is gas station and trailer park, road right leads into San Ignacio, 1.5 mi. (pgs. 136, 167). As you continue east there are several small clusters of houses and a restaurant.

92.5   *K72*   To south is upper end of this truly remarkable desert oasis. Road winds through hills, watch for oncoming traffic on the curves.

100   *K60*   Signed, graded road left to Santa Martha 30 km. and El Carricito, 20 km. This road leads into the mountains near several painted caves. While most require mules and guides, there are several here within walking distance.

104.3   *K53*   Ejido Alfredo Bonfíl, a new community perched out in the middle of nowhere. What their main purpose might be, we have no idea.

113   *K39*   Rancho El Mesquitál. A restaurant specializing in *machaca*. Very good. Then road begins winding, watch speed. Ahead on left are three tall volcanic mountains, Los Tres Vírgenes.

(continued on page 95)

IGLESIA SANTA ROSALÍA

Shortly after Santa Rosalía was settled in 1885 the French owners of this copper-rich town received a prefabricated church consisting of large sheets of galvanized iron. Its architect, Alexandre Eiffel, also designed the Eiffel Tower in Paris!

Just what path it took to get to Santa Rosalía is lost in time, but records show that it did serve as a display at the Columbia World's Fair in the 1890's.

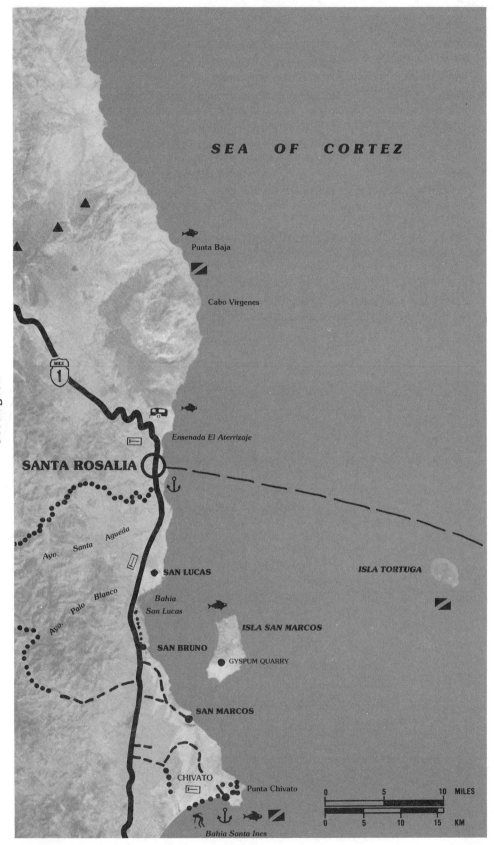

See Page 92

SEA OF CORTEZ

Punta Baja

Cabo Virgenes

MEX 1

Ensenada El Aterrizaje

SANTA ROSALIA

Ayo. Santa Agueda

SAN LUCAS

Bahia
San Lucas

ISLA TORTUGA

Ayo. Palo Blanco

ISLA SAN MARCOS

SAN BRUNO

GYSPUM QUARRY

SAN MARCOS

CHIVATO

Punta Chivato

Bahia Santa Ines

0 5 10 MILES
0 5 10 15 KM

118   K31   Small rancho north of highway with one windmill. Continue downhill.

125.5   K19   Your first view of the Sea of Cortez. A half-mile further, begin descent from 1500′ to 300′ in less than 4 miles. Road is steep, narrow and winding with no turnoffs. Use caution and you'll do fine. Heavy rigs should use low gear. Watch for slow vehicles, and don't overheat when coming up from other direction.

132.4   K7+   Bottom of hills. Sea of Cortez is right in front of you. Unimproved camping is just to north along beach. We've seen yellowtail feeding right along shore here during months of November-February. If you see 'em, cast a chrome Krocodile at 'em.

137   K0   Just past array of smelter buildings and a couple of fish processing plants. Turn up arroyo into Santa Rosalia (pg. 136). Ferry office is just beyond street into town. If you plan to take the ferry to Guaymas we suggest you purchase your tickets at least one day in advance. It doesn't mean that you have to wait in line — take some time to look around town, and the beaches to the north and south.
End of log...

SANTA ROSALÍA — LORETO

0   K197   Leave town past ferry building and gas station.

1.2   K195   El Morro Motel overlooking water. We have found lots of small shells — coweries, clams, snails, etc. — on beach. Look right below hotel and to the south a few hundred yards.

4.6   K189+   On left is new state prison. Most assuredly they will not be turning these inmates out to work in town during the day as they used to in Mulege in the years before there were roads into the region.

5.1   K188+   Graded road west to Agua Agueda, 12 km. Beyond on rough road are several small *ranchos* and cave painting sites. The trip is an all-day affair, but a rewarding one if you can take the time.

9.1   K182   Entrance to San Lucas Trailer Park and beautiful San Lucas Cove. Palm shaded, sandy beach with good fishing. The bay is shallow and usually quite calm. A good place for the kids and small boats. Good clamming and shelling across the lagoon.

21.6   K162   To east of highway the government is working (Feb, '87) on an international airport for the Mulege area.

25.3   K156   Graded road left past houses leads to Punta Chivato, 20 km. (pg. 136).

(continued on page 101)

ISLA SAN MARCOS...is an important source of gypsum to mainland Mexico and users in the United States. One of the world's largest deposits is located on the south end. A joint venture between Mexican and American corporations, it supports about 700 people in a small village just south of the mine. When the Spaniards first arrived, there was a small colony of Indians living on San Marcos. They were removed to Mulegé by the Jesuit missionaries but they were unable to adjust and all died very soon after.

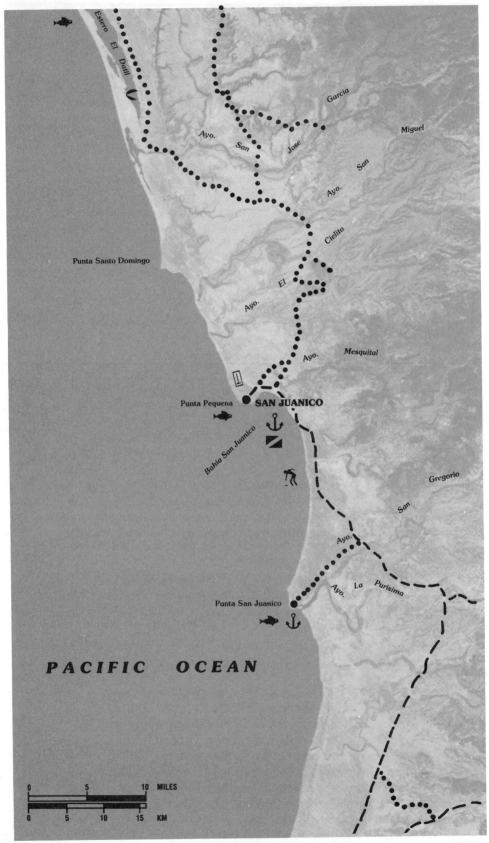

Estero El Datil

Garcia

Miguel

Ayo.

San

Jose

San

Ayo.

Cielito

Punta Santo Domingo

El

Ayo.

Ayo.

Mesquital

Punta Pequena

SAN JUANICO

Bahia San Juanico

Gregorio

San

Ayo.

Ayo.

La

Purisima

Punta San Juanico

PACIFIC   OCEAN

0   5   10   MILES

0   5   10   15   KM

See Page 98

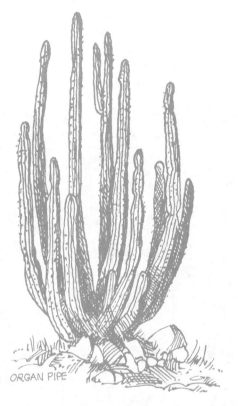

ORGAN PIPE

THE 800 MILE CACTUS GARDEN

As the *cirio*, or boojum, might be considered the plant that best symbolizes Baja California, the cactus family must be considered the group of plants that best represents this magnificent peninsula.

Botanists have identified over one hundred species of cactus living in Baja California and fully three-quarters of these are found nowhere else.

Baja is truly an 800-mile-long cactus garden that boasts the largest cactus in the world — the 60ft. cardon — and some of the smallest. Several are barely an inch high when fully grown.

EL COYOTE

He is everywhere...he can be heard at night almost anywhere in Baja...yet rarely seen. *El Coyote* is an everpresent shadow and companion to those who take to the backroads. His ability to adapt is well known, but nowhere is he more sorely tested than in Baja. From dead seals and fish to lizards, mice and beetles, he eats them all.

His size and color varies with the region in which he lives. There is hardly a square mile of Baja that does not have its share of coyotes.

See Page 96

See Page 100

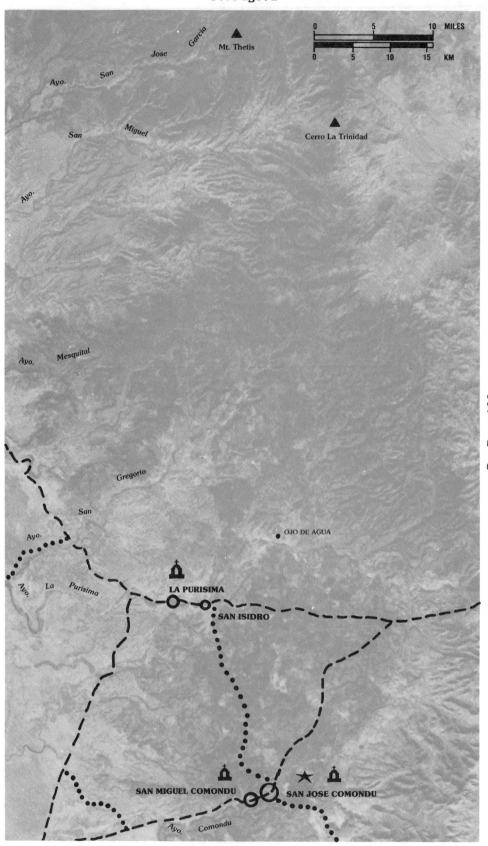

Ayo.

San

Jose

Garcia

Mt. Thetis

Cerro La Trinidad

San

Miguel

Ayo.

Ayo.

Mesquital

Gregorio

San

Ayo.

OJO DE AGUA

Ayo.

La

Purisima

LA PURISIMA

SAN ISIDRO

SAN MIGUEL COMONDU

SAN JOSE COMONDU

Ayo.

Comondu

0   5   10 MILES

0   5   10   15 KM

A MATTER OF SURVIVAL

When the Spainards first saw an elephant tree, or *torote*, they must have wondered why such a short tree would have such a thick trunk and heavy limbs. They may even have thought it dead, for it rarely has leaves.

Some specimens, such as near San Ignacio, have a trunk over 3 feet in diameter, yet reach a height of only 10 or 12 feet. The branches extend but a few feet and may still measure 18 inches at the base.

The heavy trunk acts as a water reservoir for the months and sometimes years that pass without rain. Yet within days of a good rainstorm, the *torote* bursts forth with a mass of small green leaves. During its few weeks of greening, it does all of its growing — until the next rain.

Blooms come during the summer when the leaves are usually gone, creating a weird scene of pink blossoms on an otherwise dead-looking plant.

There are at least 4 separate species, from 2 different families, yet all share very similar physical characteristics...it is a matter of survival.

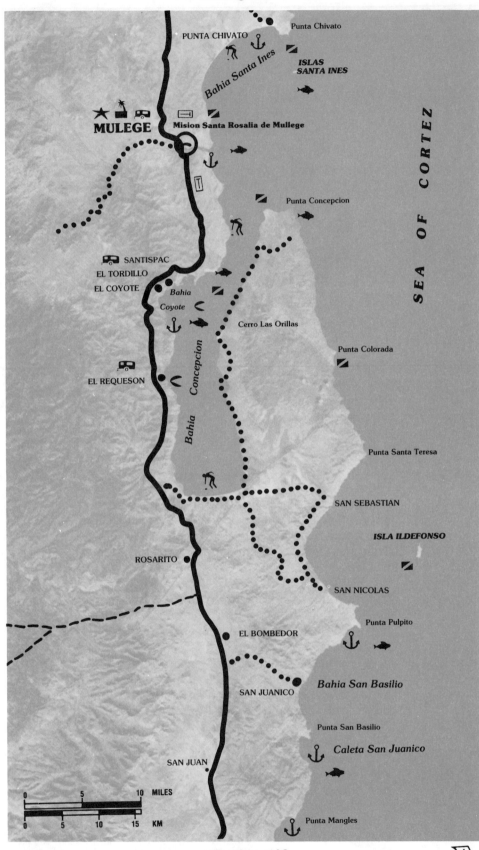

PUNTA CHIVATO

Punta Chivato

Bahia Santa Ines

ISLAS SANTA INES

★ 🌴 🚐 **MULEGE**

Mision Santa Rosalia de Mullege

Punta Concepcion

🚐 SANTISPAC
EL TORDILLO
EL COYOTE

Bahia Coyote

Cerro Las Orillas

Punta Colorada

🚐 EL REQUESON

Bahia Concepcion

Punta Santa Teresa

SAN SEBASTIAN

ISLA ILDEFONSO

ROSARITO

SAN NICOLAS

Punta Pulpito

EL BOMBEDOR

Bahia San Basilio

SAN JUANICO

Punta San Basilio

Caleta San Juanico

SAN JUAN

Punta Mangles

S E A   O F   C O R T E Z

0	5	10	MILES

0	5	10	15	KM

SANTA ROSALIA-LORETO (from page 95)

33 **K143** Begin winding upgrade. Watch for slow traffic, and your own speed on upcoming downgrade.

37.7 **K135+** Road east into Mulegé (pg. 137). Several hotels, restaurants, gas and markets make this a good place to stop. A word of caution — the streets are narrow and a source of frustration for motorhomers and those towing trailers.

38 **K135** Cross bridge over Rio Santa Rosalía and continue past a number of turnoffs into trailer parks and restaurants.

40.2 **K131** Turnoff east into Hotel Serenidad and several parking/camping areas.

42.5 **K126+** View of sand dunes and Bahía Concepción. Just beyond is a road to a sandy beach.

47 **K119** To left of highway is a large stone corral, then road to secluded Playa Punta Arena.

50 **K114+** On left is Playa Santispác. Popular with campers, windsailers and boaters. Limited facilities, but a lady named Ana has a fine bakery and restaurant on east end of beach.

52 **K112** Bahía Tordilla and Posada Concepción. Now almost all spaces have been converted into permanent sites, but there are some overnight spaces. Beyond are several more developing camping areas on small coves.

54.5 **K108** Bahía Coyote. Good public beach with some services, a few permanent homes. Best beach south is over short rough road along bay. Watch it at high tide.

64 **K92+** Road left is to Playa Requesón. Good clamming and snorkeling on sand bar and outside island. Begin climbing over low hill shortly after passing turnoff. On left there are several views of the old road. (It doesn't take much to imagine the challenge the old road presented.) After climbing out of Concepción basin wind past many large *cardon* cactus.

74 **K76** Bottom of Bahía Concepción. Poor road east forks several times to a number of beaches and small ranchos.

(continued on page 109)

Isla Coronado...located just north of Loreto, is one and one-half miles offshore. A terrific spot to spend a day lazing around on a dazzling white beach, gathering clams or fishing for a beach barbeque. The crystal water is ideal for snorkeling. Once we trailed a 20-pound-plus *dorado* as it cruised near shore in only 3 feet of water. Isla Coronado is a personal favorite. *Fantastico!*

Isla Carmen...one of the largest islands in the Sea of Cortez. At 7 to 10 miles offshore, it provides some protection for Loreto in all but the heaviest storms. The numerous coves and anchorages get a lot of play from boats out of Puerto Escondido. It offers spectacular grottos, great fishing around the reefs and many opportunities for diving and swimming. Fishing and sightseeing trips can be arranged through the hotels or Alfredo's Sportfishing in Loreto. You might also check around the new docks at Puerto Escondido. On the east side of the 17-mile island is a fair-sized evaporative salt works employing several dozen families.

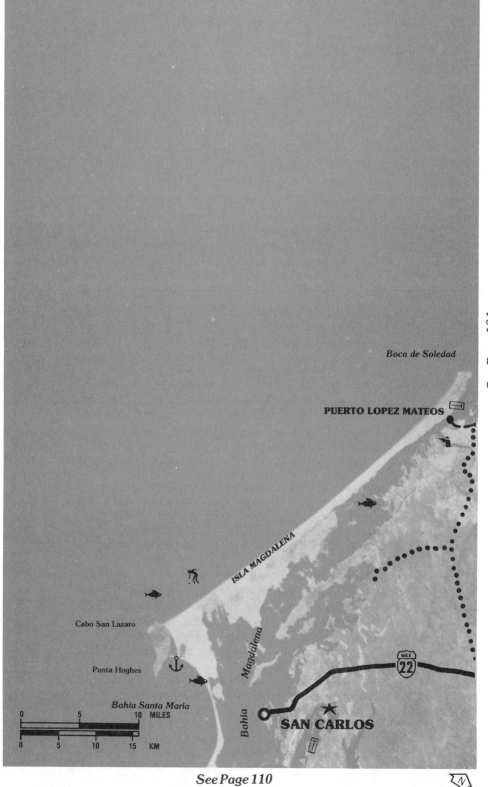

Boca de Soledad

PUERTO LOPEZ MATEOS

ISLA MAGDALENA

Cabo San Lazaro

Punta Hughes

Magdalena

Bahia Santa Maria

Bahia

SAN CARLOS

MEX
22

0   5   10 MILES

0   5   10   15   KM

See Page 104

See Page 110

BUSH PILOT AIRSTRIPS

Scattered throughout Baja Calfiornia are numerous small clearings which are used by a special breed of private pilot. These dirt landing strips are located on ranches, by old mining claims and along remote beaches. They afford a special "getaway" opportunity for a surprising number of pilots and their families.

The condition of these strips must be checked very carefully before attempting a landing, for once down you are likely to be completely alone. Such adventures are not for the inexperienced pilot, nor should they be attempted without notifying someone where you plan to go.

EL BERRENDO, IS HE COMING BACK?

The dim past provides us with ample evidence that there were once large herds of pronghorn antelope, or *berrendo*, ranging over the Baja Peninsula and Southern California. Then came the rifle, fences and the *coyote*. Together they destroyed herd after herd until they were believed to be extinct.

Then...from the Vizcaino came a few scattered, unconfirmed reports. Someone had a picture...a trained observer saw a small herd...a rancher found a recent skeleton. *El Berrendo* has survived! In fact, the 1986 census counted 97 individuals, up from only two years earlier.

Mexico has assigned several scientists to observe and protect the pronghorn, and with care and patience they may once again be counted in the thousands. The effort is also being supported by the Foundation for Field Research, 787 S. Grade Rd., Alpine, CA 92001. Write for more information.

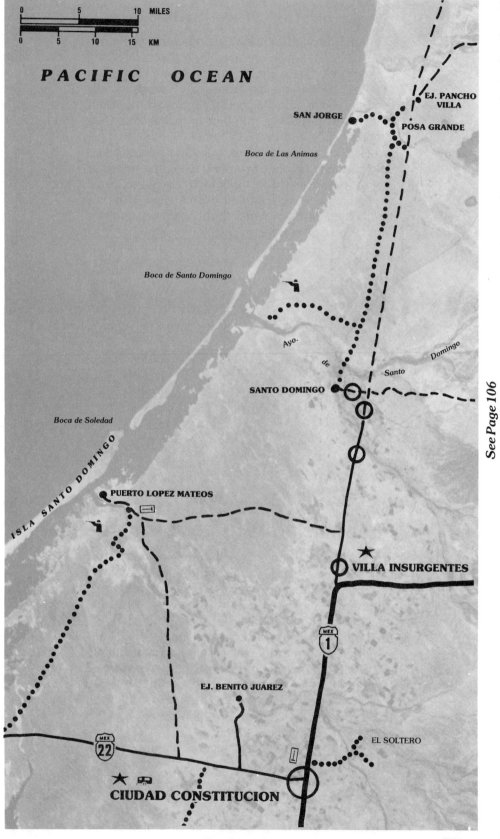

PACIFIC OCEAN

EJ. PANCHO VILLA

SAN JORGE

POSA GRANDE

Boca de Las Animas

Boca de Santo Domingo

Ayo.

de

Santo

Domingo

SANTO DOMINGO

Boca de Soledad

ISLA SANTO DOMINGO

PUERTO LOPEZ MATEOS

VILLA INSURGENTES

MEX 1

EJ. BENITO JUAREZ

EL SOLTERO

MEX 22

CIUDAD CONSTITUCION

MILES

KM

0   **K236**   Intersection. Turn south and continue toward La Paz past numerous farms and small *ejidos*.

13   **K215+**   Large cotton gin is on east side of road.

15.5   **K213**   Enter Ciudad Constitución. Pemex station on right, just beyond is paved road west to Puerto San Carlos (35 miles). The hub for a growing numbers of farms, it has little to show the tourist, but supplies are relatively plentiful. Most complete supermercado is at north end of town.

(continued on page 113)

BAKING OVEN

NEW FARMS FROM OLD WATER

The many small rectanglular shapes which show on the Baja Spacemaps around Villa Insurgentes and Ciudad Constitucion show the considerable amount of land under cultivation.

Here, as in the Vizcaino Desert, "fossil water" is a primary source of what's needed to make this rain-parched desert produce. It gives life to great quantities of cotton, grain, citrus, tomatoes and peppers. A number of cotton gins are seen as you drive through the countryside.

Through much of the year the climate is modified by an onshore flow of moist air from the adjacent Bahía Magdalena and Pacific Ocean. If camping in this region, do not be surprised at the amount of dew that collects on everything during the night. The fossil water is also an important factor for the fish processing plants located on Bahía Magdalena at San Carlos and Puerto Lopez Mateos.

As the underground water supply for the Magdalena plain is a finite amount, much as you must consider the amount of oil in a field, the future of this portion of the Baja peninsula depends greatly how well the farmers husband their precious water. Only time will tell how well they do.

T
H
E

B
A
J
A

B
O
O
K

III

105

See Page 104

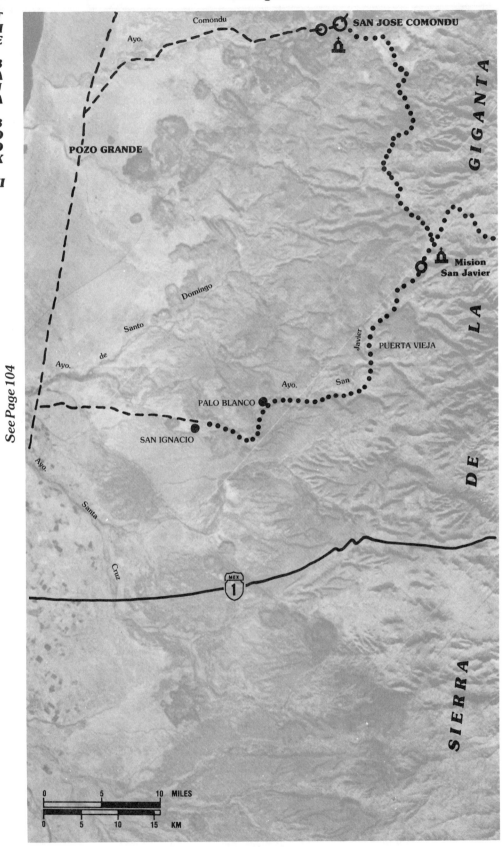

SAN JOSE COMONDU

Comondu

Ayo.

POZO GRANDE

GIGANTA

Mision
San Javier

LA

Domingo

Santo

Javier

PUERTA VIEJA

de

Ayo.

Ayo.

San

PALO BLANCO

SAN IGNACIO

DE

Ayo.

Santa

Cruz

MEX
1

SIERRA

0   5   10 MILES

0   5   10   15   KM

30.5   *K70*   A microwave tower is on left. Tall peaks everywhere as road continues to wind through narrow valleys. Watch for cattle.

34.5   *K63+*   Graded road south to Agua Verde, 40km. We found last few kms very difficult even in 4-WD. Check road conditions.

44   *K48*   A deep canyon is on the south side as road continues along the edge of the mesa. Descent becomes more rapid.

49.5   *K39*   Leave mountains and follow straight path in SW direction across gently sloping plain and past growing numbers of farms. Deep well irrigated, they are proving to be very productive.

73.7   *K0*   Intersection. To north 1 mi. is Ciudad Insurgentes and unpaved road along Pacific. To the south, Ciudad Constitución and La Paz (236 km.)
End of Log ...

SIGNS OF THE TIMES

As you drive south on Mexico 1 below Guerrero Negro you will begin seeing a series of steel towers perched atop hills. Identified as *microondas,* microwave relay stations, they and orbiting satellites have brought a new way of life to the Bajacaliforniano.

Television is now an everyday fact of life, not a fuzzy curiosity as it was a few years ago. All over Baja telephones are ringing. The Lopez family in Ciudad Constitucion can now talk with their *primos,* or cousins, in Mexico City any time they wish. And the *norteamericano* who wants to get away from it all? His options have narrowed.

You may now confirm reservations personally, or get an on-the-spot fishing report. And emergencies are better dealt with, thanks to new waves of electronic magic.

T
H
E

B
A
J
A

B
O
O
K

III

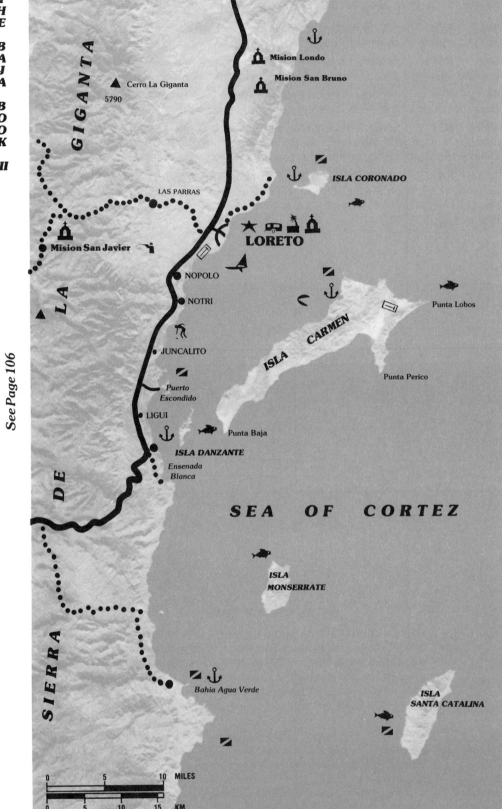

GIGANTA

▲ Cerro La Giganta
5790

LAS PARRAS

✝ Mision San Javier

NOPOLO

NOTRI

JUNCALITO

Puerto
Escondido

LIGUI

ISLA DANZANTE

Ensenada
Blanca

SIERRA

DE

LA

⚓ Mision Londo
✝ Mision San Bruno

ISLA CORONADO

★ LORETO

ISLA CARMEN

Punta Lobos

Punta Perico

Punta Baja

SEA OF CORTEZ

ISLA
MONSERRATE

Bahia Agua Verde

ISLA
SANTA CATALINA

0   5   10   MILES

0   5   10   15   KM

N

SANTA ROSALÍA — LORETO (from page 101)

83.5   *K62*   Rancho Rosarito is to right. Beyond, at K59+, road west goes to the Comondu villages (39 mi.) and La Purísima (38 mi.). Signed San Isidro, it is for high clearance cars. The area is fascinating (pg. 137).

92.2   *K48*   Road east to Playa San Juanico, 12 km. Had a good day of fishing there recently.

105   *K27*   Road right goes into a beautiful little tree-filled arroyo. Highway 1 climbs out of arroyo and onto plain. Shortly it becomes more winding.

118   *K6+*   A fine view of Loreto and Isla Carmen before descending into valley.

122   *K0*   Paved road to left 2 miles to Loreto (pg. 137).
End of Log...

LORETO — INSURGENTES

0   *K119*   Leave intersection with Loreto (above) and go south.

1   *K118*   Road west leads to Misión San Javíer (pg. 169), 21.5 mi. past several picturesque ranchos. Road has been improved as part of mission restoration program. Inquire in Loreto before attempting in passenger car.

1.5   *K117*   Road to airport.

5   *K111*   Nópolo. Site of El Presidente Hotel and infrastructure for more hotels, convention center, housing, etc. Camping on sandy beach at south end near large rock. Good fishing here at times.

10   *K102*   Rancho Notri. Ranch house to right. To left is beach where many species of fish come in close to shore. Someday someone will build something here. If you camp, watch for biting insects.

13.7   *K97+*   After winding up and down, entry to Juncalito is at bottom of grade. Camping on southern end. Fishing.

15.7   *K94+*   Paved road on left is to Puerto Escondido (1.5 mi.) and Tripui trailer park. Well worth a visit. The region abounds with fish and other sea life. A major touristic development is underway here. (pg. 138)

22   *K84+*   Liguí is a small group of houses back from sea. Beyond about 1 mi. is Ensenada Blanca fish camp and camping beach.

23   *K83*   Turn inland and up into pass leading through Sierra de La Giganta and onto Magdalena Plain. Watch for interesting remnants of old road.

25.5   *K77*   The worst of the grade is behind you.

(turn back to page 107)

Isla Monserate...measures two by four miles and is about halfway between Isla Santa Catalina and the mainland. Its reefs and coves are well visited by boaters from Puerto Escondido. There's not much else to say about it.

Isla Danzante...provides some protection to Bahía Escondido, 2.5 miles to the west. Danzante has long been a favorite of fishermen, divers and beachcombers. Several Indian middens have been discovered in the arroyos, but today it is uninhabited, except for occasional temporary fishcamps.

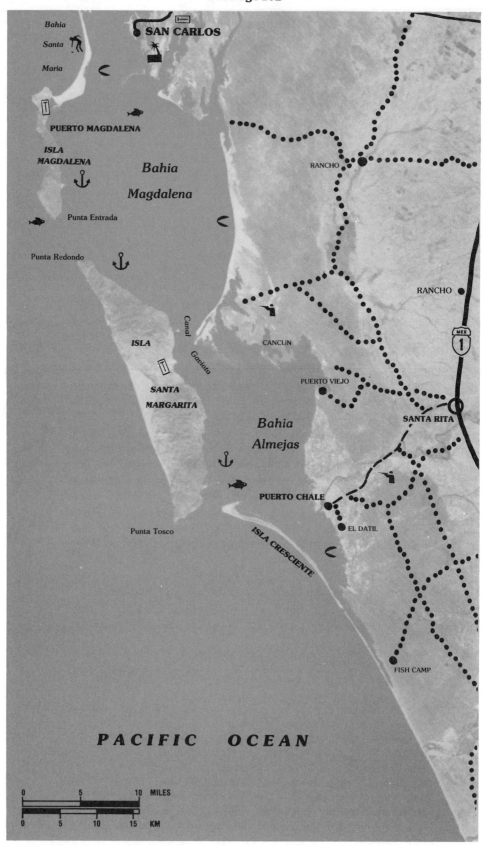

See Page 112

Bahia
Santa
Maria

SAN CARLOS

PUERTO MAGDALENA

ISLA
MAGDALENA

Bahia
Magdalena

RANCHO

RANCHO

Punta Entrada

Punta Redondo

Canal
Gaviota

CANCUN

MEX
1

ISLA

SANTA
MARGARITA

PUERTO VIEJO

Bahia
Almejas

SANTA RITA

PUERTO CHALE

EL DATIL

Punta Tosco

ISLA CRESCIENTE

FISH CAMP

PACIFIC   OCEAN

0   5   10 MILES

0   5   10   15   KM

N

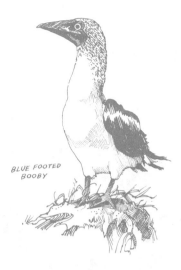

BLUE FOOTED
BOOBY

THE WATER WILDERNESS

With a shallow draft boat Bahia Magdalena and its interconnected waterways offer literally hundreds of miles of bays, mangrove-lined channels and inlets to explore. It is easy to get lost here. Fishing is not what it used to be, yet there are "pockets" of activity tucked among the channels, along the numerous beaches and off the rocky headlands at the entrance. Snook (rarely taken today), snappers, halibut, cabrilla, grouper, various members of the jack and croaker families are all likely catches in "Mag Bay".

The many beaches and coves make fine boat camping areas, with fish and clams as a bonus.

Great flights of ducks and other migrating waterfowl come from both north and south to winter, or summer in this rich region. The miles of mangrove swamps are nesting places for numerous species of insect-eating songbirds. Mag Bay literally jumps with life, yet there are few people to enjoy it.

The port towns of San Carlos and Lopez Mateos total about 6000 people — add 1000 more for scattered fish camps and ranchos...that's it. The only paved road to the bay is from Constitución to San Carlos, 35 miles. This and a few scattered dirt trails are all there is.

Nights are often foggy, and unless protected, everything you have will get soaked. Bugs, too, can be pesky around the mangroves, but a good repellent (we like Muskol) makes it bearable.

With hundreds of miles of waterways to follow the possibilities for the small boater are almost unlimited. It is not a fact today, but watch for several launching ramps to be built in the next few years. Currently the only public ramp is about a mile south of San Carlos at the site of the old Flying Sportsman resort.

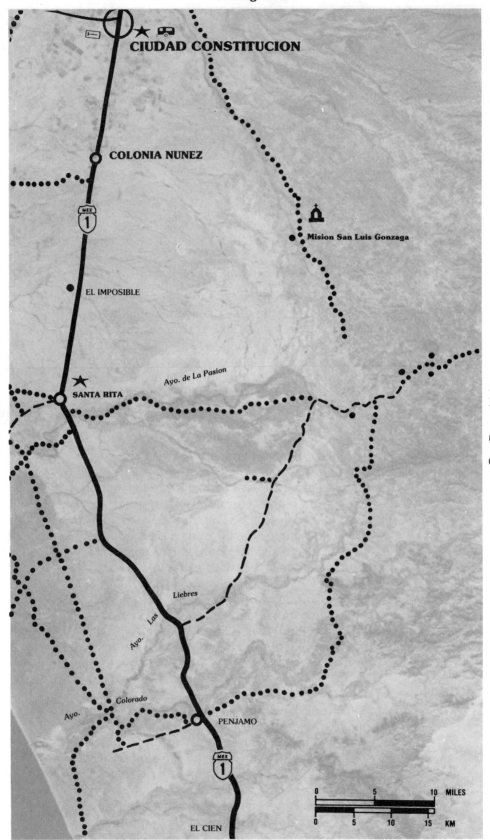

CIUDAD CONSTITUCION

COLONIA NUNEZ

Mision San Luis Gonzaga

EL IMPOSIBLE

Ayo. de La Pasion

SANTA RITA

Liebres

Las

Ayo.

Colorado

Ayo.

PENJAMO

EL CIEN

15.5   *K213*   Enter Ciudad Constitución. Pemex station on right, just beyond is paved road west to Puerto San Carlos (35 miles). The hub for the growing numbers of farms, it has little to show the tourist, but supplies are relatively plentiful. *Supermercado* at north end of town is most complete.

17.5   *K210*   Radio tower on left. Leave town, continue southeast.

25.0   *K198*   Villa Morelos, a small, prosperous farm community.

22.5   *K185+*   Rancho El Coyote. Below here there used to be a sign — ''Rancho El Imposible'' — and boy, does the surrounding area look it. Soon road will turn slightly to east.

30   *K173*   Graded dirt road west leads to Cancun fish camp.

40   *K156+*   Santa Rita. An extra dry portion of a very dry desert — less than 2 inches of rain per year. Dirt road south and west is to Puerto Chale and El Datíl, about 15 miles. The road continues in long straight sections while slowly entering area of low hills.

68.5   *K110*   Road southeast to Santa Fe, 16 km. Santa Fe has the deepest talcum powder-like dust imaginable. It is a disaster to car engines and everything in it. If you do get there, there is nothing anyway. Avoid at all costs.

74.7   *K100*   Shortly after entering foothills you pass El Cién which is 100 km, or 62 miles, from La Paz. Road then climbs and for the next 20 miles meanders through increasingly heavy vegetation.

(continued on page 117)

VULTURE

CARDON

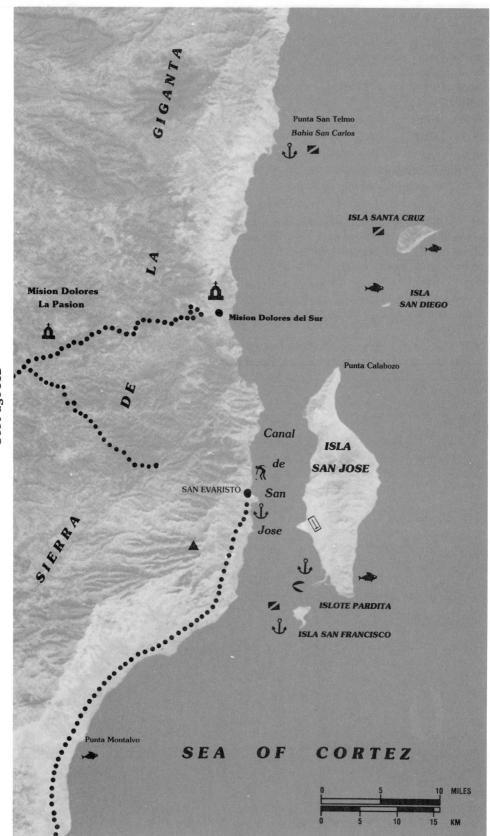

GIGANTA

Punta San Telmo
Bahia San Carlos

ISLA SANTA CRUZ

ISLA
SAN DIEGO

LA

Mision Dolores
La Pasion

Mision Dolores del Sur

Punta Calabozo

DE

Canal

de

ISLA
SAN JOSE

San

SAN EVARISTO

Jose

SIERRA

ISLOTE PARDITA

ISLA SAN FRANCISCO

Punta Montalvo

SEA   OF   CORTEZ

0   5   10   MILES

0   5   10   15   KM

Isla Santa Catalina...is an island of interest to the naturalist. It is the home of a rattleless rattlesnake and the largest *biznagas* (barrel cactus) in the gulf islands. It also has plants which, through centuries of isolation, changed their form slightly to better adapt to the island's harsh environment. The island has long been a campground for the itinerant *vagabundos* of the Sea of Cortez. Evidence of their visits may be found near the southern end. The snakes and lizards have the one-half by two mile island to themselves. The Mexican government is considering Catalina as a sanctuary (pg. 108).

Isla Santa Cruz...located about four miles north of Isla San Diego, it is a steep mass of rock, with only one small rocky landing located near the southwestern end. It is one of the most barren of the islands in the Sea of Cortez.

Isla San Diego...is a narrow mile-long island that juts to 722 feet above sea level. Its abundant sea population is contrasted to the few terrestial inhabitants — lizards, scorpions and rodents. There are no good landing spots, thus it is little visited.

Isla San José...lies parallel to the mainland and forms the eastern edge of the 5 to 7-mile wide Canál de San José. Measuring 16 miles by 4 miles average width, it is one of the most fertile of the islands in the Mar de Cortéz and harbors a good variety of plants and cacti — plus many birds, coyotes, rodents, and even a few deer. Several families work a small evaporative salt works near the southwest end. At Bahía Amortajada, the beach, nearby lagoon and connecting mangrove channel provide about everything needed for a good stay...clams in the shallows south of the mangroves, calm, crystal clear water and plenty of fish to watch or catch.

A pest found around mangroves can be here with a vengeance...the Mexicans call then *jejenes*, or *bobos*. We would call them no-seeums or gnats. When the wind dies, the *jejenes* come winging in, armed to the teeth, so to speak. Their bites aren't usually felt until well after they get you, and do they itch! Be ready in advance with Muskol or a similar product. If you're too late, try one of the first aid sprays or lime juice.

There is a small landing field on the southeast corner of the island. Skilled pilots do land here occasionally, usually just for a day's outing.

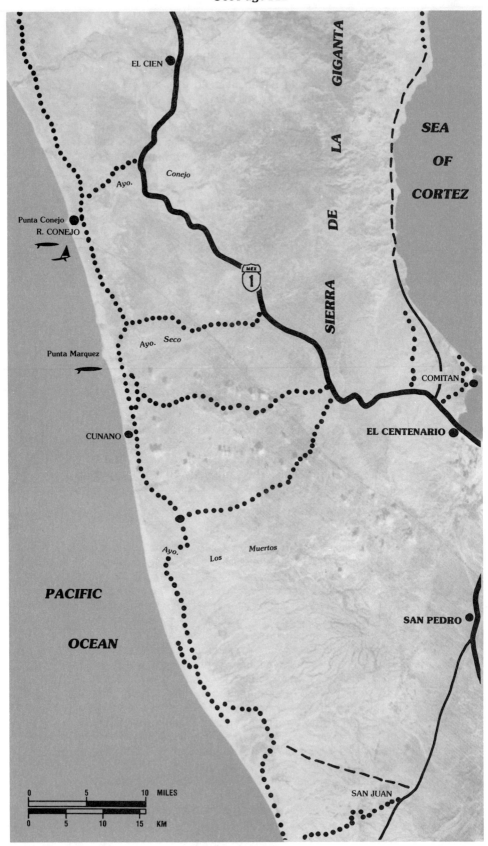

EL CIEN

SIERRA DE LA GIGANTA

Conejo

Ayo.

SEA

OF

CORTEZ

Punta Conejo
R. CONEJO

MEX 1

Ayo. *Seco*

Punta Marquez

COMITAN

EL CENTENARIO

CUNANO

Ayo. *Los* *Muertos*

PACIFIC

SAN PEDRO

OCEAN

See Page 118

| 0 | | 5 | | 10 | MILES |

| 0 | 5 | 10 | 15 | KM |

SAN JUAN

87   *K80*   Road right, 17 km, is popular surfing spot, El Conejo. Good rock clams here, also good fishing. From the point a road goes south along coast to Todos Santos, about 75 miles. There are lots of "untracked" beaches along here.

98.5   *K62*   On the right is a strange whitewashed cactus-shaped shrine. A longtime landmark, it is suffering with years, one arm is gone, and the other is getting wobbly. Soon it may be only a memory.

111   *K34+*   You are on the crest of the *cordillera* leading into the La Paz valley. Large white shrine is on right. On a "perfect" day when the sun is low in west you can see both the Cortez and the Pacific from a spot just above shrine. Winding downgrade next 4 km.

121.5   *K17*   Road (first 15 miles is paved) north is to San Juan de La Costa (25 mi.), site of a large phosphate deposit. A poor road continues to many small beaches and San Evaristo (about 70 mi.)

(continued on page 119)

Islote Pardita...would not be worth mentioning if you consider only its size (about an acre) were it not for the fact that 40 people live here! Located about a mile south of San José, it has about a dozen buildings — including a new schoolhouse! — perched on its lee side. The population began years ago when a fisherman and his family came to catch and process the abundant closeby sharks. All supplies, including water, are brought from the mainland.

They hosted a number of us one evening to a great turtle *(caguama)* stew, complete with tortillas and limes. Occasionally live bait may be obtained here if you give them notice. In the several times we have visited the island there has always been a garden...one scrawny tomato plant well protected from kids, chickens and dogs!.

Isla San Francisco...is popular with visiting yachtsmen and anglers. About one mile square, it has several good anchorages inside a hook-like arm on the south end. It has sparse vegetation and several brackish marshy areas. Occasionally worked by pearlers, it was the site of a one-man gold rush in the 1880's when a German uncovered enough metal to keep him busy for about five years (pg. 114).

Isla Espiritu Santo...along with nearby Isla Partida, does much to shelter Bahía de La Paz from the east. The eastern sides have many beautiful coves for swimming, diving, camping, etc. Their combined 12 by 5 mile area is of volcanic origin. The eastern escarpments show beautiful layers of red, pink, ochre, white and black in the high cliffs. The sandy beaches are white and clean. Like the other gulf islands, they yield fish, clams and other examples of a fertile marine environment (pg. 118).

T
H
E

B
A
J
A

B
O
O
K

III

See Page 116

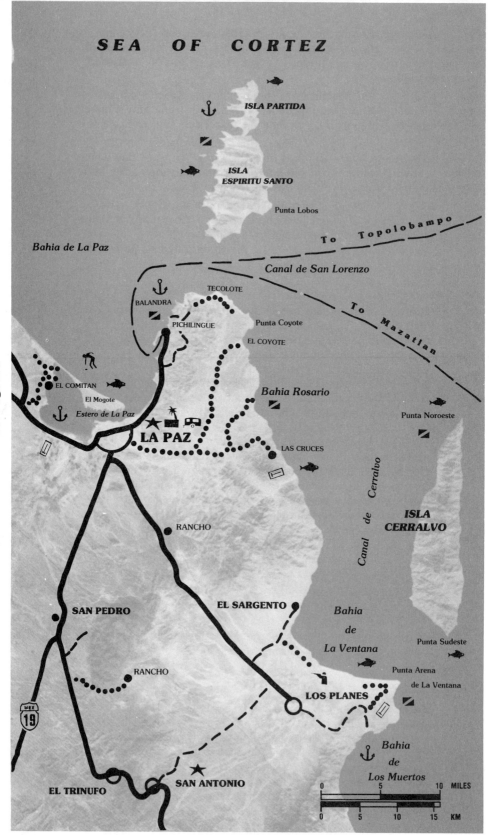

SEA OF CORTEZ

ISLA PARTIDA

ISLA
ESPIRITU SANTO

Punta Lobos

Bahia de La Paz

To Topolobampo

Canal de San Lorenzo

TECOLOTE

BALANDRA

PICHILINGUE

Punta Coyote

EL COYOTE

To Mazatlan

EL COMITAN

El Mogote

Estero de La Paz

Bahia Rosario

Punta Noroeste

★ **LA PAZ**

LAS CRUCES

Canal de Cerralbo

**ISLA
CERRALVO**

RANCHO

SAN PEDRO

EL SARGENTO

*Bahia
de
La Ventana*

Punta Sudeste

RANCHO

Punta Arena
de La Ventana

19

LOS PLANES

*Bahia
de
Los Muertos*

EL TRINUFO

★ **SAN ANTONIO**

| 0 | 5 | 10 | MILES |

| 0 | 5 | 10 | 15 | KM |

121.7   K16+   Just a few yards past the above paved road, the Comitan turnoff leads to edge of La Paz Bay. Several Americans have homes here.

123   K15   Trailer park on bay side of road. Area is known as El Centenario.

126.7   K9   Road south to La Paz International airport.

132.2   K0   Downtown La Paz (pg. 138). More specifically we are at Pemex station at corner of 5 de Febrero and Abasolo.
End of log...

LA PAZ — CABO SAN LUCAS

0   K213   From corner of 5 de Febrero and Isabél La Católica. From here bear west and south. (pg. 138)

1.2   K211   Road left to Los Planes (30 mi.) and Bahía de Los Muertos (42 mi.). A fine beach at Muertos. Facing south, it is protected during winter. Vegetation typical of region — cacti and tall brush. Lots of farming around Los Planes. Road north at 40 miles goes to Punta Arena de La Ventana (excellent fishing, camping) and Hotel Las Arenas.

13.7   K191   Enter small community of San Pedro. Ahead on right are the best *carnitas* anywhere in Baja. Called El Paraiso de San Pedro, it is worth a stop.

17.4   K185   Paved road to right leads to Todos Santos, Pescadero and, ultimately, Cabo San Lucas (pg. 121).

20   K181   Road right to Algodones. Livestock is common through here, so be cautious.

28   K168   El Aguajito. Site of small ore processing plant. Road beyond goes to a number of mines and ranches.

29.7   K165   Top of grade, excellent view of El Triunfo. Note well kept graveyard (panteon) on hill.

30.3   K164   Enter El Triunfo (pg. 139). Across bridge on right is a small basket shop. Items are made by the children of the town. Usually open M-F, 9:30-12:30 and 3:30-5:30. Across street, a small restaurant.

(continued on page 125)

Isla de Cerralvo...is the southernmost island in the Sea of Cortez. Sixteen miles by four in a north-south direction, it forms the eastern boundary of the Cerralvo Channel and is uninhabited. Though it appears short of vegetation, there is quite a bit in the arroyos. The waters around Cerralvo teem with fish, clams and scallops. It was a main source for the Baja pearls almost since its discovery in 1533. Here, as elsewhere in the gulf, pearling came to a virtual halt in the 1940's when a mysterious disease wiped out most of the oysters.

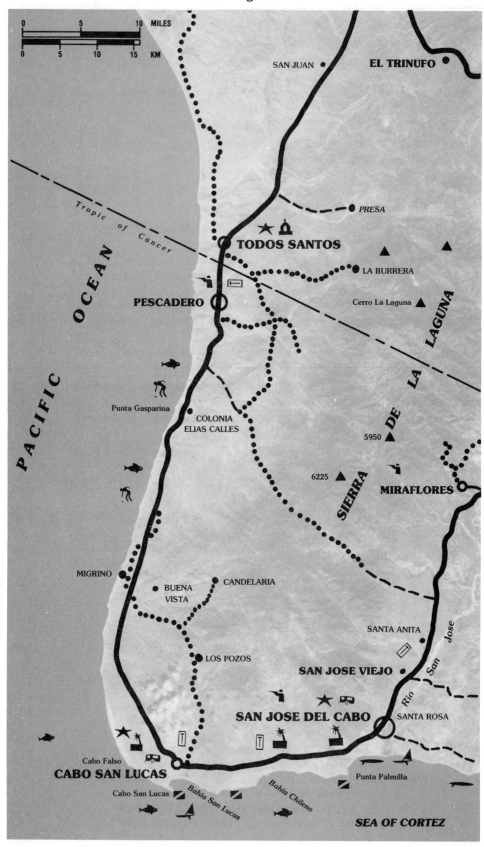

See Page 124

MEXICO 1 — CABO SAN LUCAS VIA TODOS SANTOS

Note: We begin this log at K185 of Mexico 1, 6 kilometers south of the town of San Pedro.

0   K0   Road heads almost due south through broad savannah of cactus, *palo blanco* and other small trees.

4.5   K7+   To west is semi-defunct Club Carrizál campground and family recreation center. Beyond are series of sideroads leading west toward Pacific. Some make it, others don't. The roads, that is.

16   K26   Heading west is signed road, Ramál Rancho Albanéz. This one does get to ocean.

19.2   K31   Road goes straight through rather level new farming area, Llano Carrizál.

33   K53   After passing a number of ranches, enter Todos Santos (pg. 140). Follow paved road through town. Pemex station is on unpaved street one block north. Santa Monica Restaurant is a good one. For next 5 miles there are a number of roads leading to beaches.

35   K56+   Playa San Pedrito. About 1.5 miles to beach. Many palms, lovely beach, small clearings for camping. Good fishing.

37.2   K60   Enter Pescadero (pg. 140). Rich farms abound around here. Center of town is off to east around a small hill. Supermarket on east side of highway has good selection. Continue south.

39.7   K64   Road toward Playa Los Cerritos, 1.6 mi., a beautiful beach protected on north end. Just below is abandoned trailer park (hurricane got it some years ago) and impromptu camping area. Several times we've enjoyed good luck for small gamefish near the rocks using small, shiny lures and white feathers.

42.8   K69   During rainy season a sizeable freshwater lake forms between road and sand dunes. In the early winter we've seen lots of ducks here.

44.7   K72+   Road west to southern end of same beach mentioned above. Watch for strong currents.

48.2   K78   Rancho Los Pinos, one of several ranches along road in this area.

50.5   K81+   Beautiful beach near road. Many small, interesting shells. Heavy surf and steep dropoff. Dangerous swimming, but good fishing. Cast lures past breaker line or use bait near rocks on north end. Road continues south, winding past small hills and arroyos.

61.5   K99   Begin curving downgrade with beautiful sandy beach in the distance. Soon you cross the bridge, Puente El Pastoral.

66.3   K107   Cross another bridge and begin long, gradual grade to top of last hill before you see the Sea of Cortez.

71.4   K115   Roads both to right and left near here, leading whence we know not.

74.5   K120+   Sign, Brisas del Pacifico land development. Though inland, this rapidly growing area enjoys cooling breezes off the Pacific while still offering good views of the Cortez and Cabo.

75.7   K122   Enter outskirts of Cabo San Lucas (pg. 140). New buildings seem to be going up daily as Cabo prospers.

79   K128   Intersection with Mexico 1 on east end of the business district of Cabo San Lucas.
End of log...

T
H
E

B
A
J
A

B
O
O
K

III

THE BAJA BOOK III

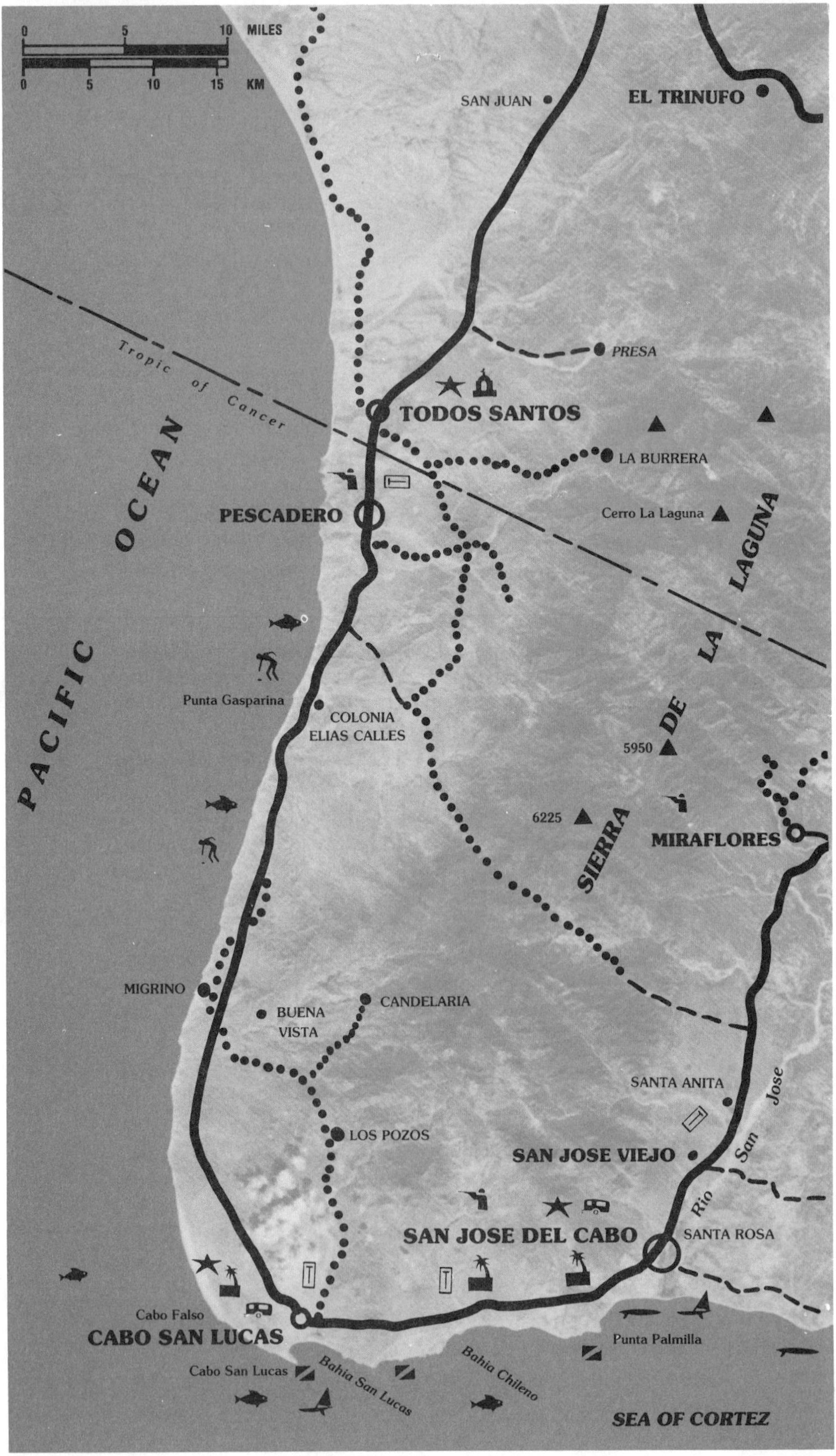

See Page 124

SCALE
0   5   10   MILES
0   5   10   15   KM

PACIFIC OCEAN

Tropic of Cancer

SAN JUAN

EL TRINUFO

PRESA

★ **TODOS SANTOS**

LA BURRERA

PESCADERO

Cerro La Laguna

DE LA LAGUNA

Punta Gasparina

COLONIA
ELIAS CALLES

5950

SIERRA

6225

MIRAFLORES

MIGRINO

BUENA
VISTA

CANDELARIA

SANTA ANITA

LOS POZOS

SAN JOSE VIEJO

Rio San Jose

SAN JOSE DEL CABO

SANTA ROSA

Cabo Falso

CABO SAN LUCAS

Cabo San Lucas

Bahia San Lucas

Bahia Chileno

Punta Palmilla

SEA OF CORTEZ

N

90.5   *K67* Road right to Caduaño, an agricultural *ejido*. The main portion is about 3 miles up the arroyo. The amount of trees, vegetable gardens, etc. is impressive. Lots of gentle winding roads coming up.

103.5   *K46+* Enter Santa Anita. This is one of several sleepy little towns that change but little, except along the side of Mexico 1 highway. Back a block they are the same as generations ago. Some Americans are discovering the charm, and are building homes among the locals.

105.5   *K43+* Paved road west to Los Cabos International Airport. They have recently completed a new, sterile, cement building. The friendly charm of the much smaller thatched terminal, even if it was hot and dusty at times, has succumbed to a battery of airconditioners. Unfortunately, that's progress...

108.3   *K39* San José Viejo, a long-established farming area. To the south are many fan palms, a few date palms, mango trees, bananas and papayas. You will also see fields of corn, chiles and beans.

11.4   *K33* Fork left to San José del Cabo (pg. 139). Pemex station at intersection. Mexico 1 continues toward ocean. Below town along the coast are a series of beachfront hotels, a golf course and a growing cadre of fairway homes.

113.4   *K30* Brisa del Mar trailer park on a beautiful beach. Open all year. Just past is the new La Jolla Los Cabos resort development. Then we pass a beach which is often crowded with surfers during the summer storm season. They are waiting for a tropical storm off Acapulco to generate a few good days of big waves. And between mid-June and October the storms cooperate very nicely.

115.5   *K26+* Turn left to Hotel Palmilla, the first major hotel in the Los Cabos area. It is beautifully landscaped; palms, hibiscus, coleus, etc.

122.5   *K14+* On left is Hotel Cabo San Lucas. An older, well maintained, fishing resort with lots of memories for the old timers. Winter visitors are often treated to pods of California gray whales cruising close in to the rocks here. Several people have even reported watching the whales feed on schools of small sardines.

127.8   *K6* Entrance to Cabo Baja Hotel. Next, a good view of Baja's famous arch "land's end," and the first of several trailer parks between here and Cabo San Lucas.

130.7   *K1+* Pemex station. Just beyond is road on right to Pacific side of peninsula and La Paz, via Todos Santos. See log on pg. 121.

131.5   *K0* You are now in Cabo San Lucas (pg. 140). To south are marina and ferry dock.
End of log...

**Congratulations, Amigo...
you have reached Land's End!**

See Pages 120 & 122

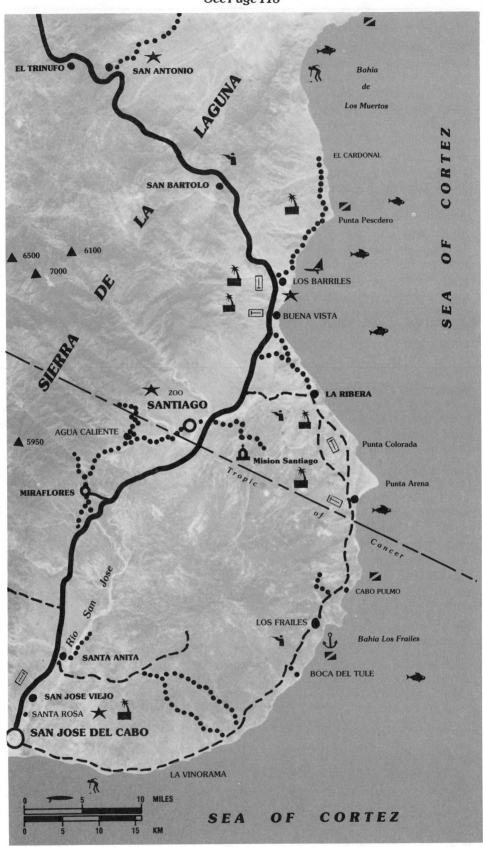

EL TRINUFO

SAN ANTONIO

Bahia de Los Muertos

SAN BARTOLO

EL CARDONAL

Punta Pescdero

LA LAGUNA DE LA SIERRA

6500   6100

7000

LOS BARRILES

BUENA VISTA

SEA OF CORTEZ

5950

ZOO

SANTIAGO

AGUA CALIENTE

LA RIBERA

Punta Colorada

Mision Santiago

Punta Arena

Tropic

MIRAFLORES

of

Cancer

CABO PULMO

Rio San Jose

LOS FRAILES

SANTA ANITA

Bahia Los Frailes

SAN JOSE VIEJO

BOCA DEL TULE

SANTA ROSA

SAN JOSE DEL CABO

LA VINORAMA

| 0 | | 5 | | 10 | MILES |
| 0 | 5 | 10 | 15 | KM |

SEA OF CORTEZ

33.1   **K159+**   After winding ascent, reach top of ridge and drop into San Antonio Valley. Many curves through here; suggest 30 mph.

35   **K156+**   San Antonio is on right (pg. 139). Mango trees and date palms are visible in canyon. Semi-graded road down canyon 14 miles intersects with La Paz-Los Planes road a few miles west of Los Planes. Continue past small Pemex station and begin climbing out of canyon almost immediately. Road winds sharply in places (30-35 mph). Shortly, you will have views of Sea of Cortez as you pass through area of many flowers (during rainy season).

40   **K148+**   Start down hill into arroyo.

51.8   **K129**   Enter San Bartolo. The narrow town has many picturesque little houses with thatched roofs nestled along sides of arroyo. Long famous as a garden spot. A good place to stock up on citrus fruits, mangoes and avocados. Hunters will find many dove throughout the region. The infamous *"topes"* or speed bumps, are gone, but take it easy anyway.

63.5   **K110+**   Road left to Palmas de Cortez and Playa Hermosa hotels (.4 and .9 miles respectively). Pemex station on right 1 mile further south. This graded dirt road, or *ramal,* continues northward along the coast past Hotel Punta Pescadero, the small settlement of El Cardonál, and eventually through to the Los Planes valley. The last portion of the road is not recommmened for the fainthearted or illequipped.

66   **K106+**   Road right to El Coro, 10 km., a few remote ranchos in sierras.

66.2   **K106**   Road left to Rancho Buena Vista resort about 1/2 mile. The area is experiencing a minor real estate boom of its own. A number of new homes are being built, others are being remodeled. A beautiful area.

67   **K105**   Cross bridge and left to Hotel Spa Buena Vista. Here too, people are leasing or building homes. Continue south through cacti, small trees and shrubs.

74.5   **K93**   Small village of Las Cuevas. Dirt road east is to La Ribera (8 mi.). Several small stores and Pemex station .7 mile south of town. Road continues south and east past Hotel Punta Colorada, 13 mi. (You need a high clearance vehicle beyond here.) Next comes El Rincón, 21 mi., El Pulmo and on to Los Frailes, 31 mi. A road continues around past several beaches and finally joins Mexico 1 at 80 mi., in San José del Cabo. Storm damage is common in this area so inquire locally before proceeding too far.

79.8   **K84+**   Road right to Santiago (pg. 139). Paved road winds sharply down into Arroyo de Santiago and across to town. A large stand of fan palms is along side of arroyo. Santiago has a nice plaza surrounded by stores and cantina. To south is El Palomar restaurant, a beautiful church and Baja's only zoo.

81.7   **K81+**   Monument in form of large cement sphere marks the Tropic of Cancer. Stand here at high noon on June 21st and you will have lost your shadow.

88   **K71**   Road right to Miraflores, 1.2 miles (pg. 139).

90.5   **K67**   Road right to Caduaño, an agricultural ejido.

(turn back to page 123)

T
H
E

B
A
J
A

B
O
O
K

III

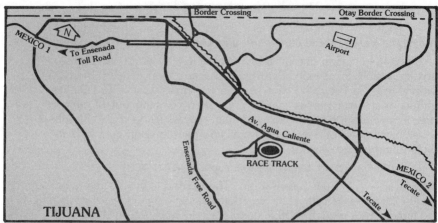

Tijuana...The prohibition era of the 20's and the wide-open gambling that survived well after repeal in 1933 spurred the growth of Tijuana. Formerly called *Tia Juana*, or Aunt Jane, it was a sleepy village of 600 people, around the time of the revolution of 1911. Now, as a sometimes-dazzling mass of about 1,400,000 people, it defies description. But however you look at it their lives are closely tied to their neighbor to the north.

Thousands of Mexicans daily cross the border to work in the fields, homes and factories around San Diego Bay. Thousands more are there waiting for their turn to cross the border under cover of darkness and hope to make it far enough north so they can work in jobs most Americans turn down. It is a tedious cycle...get to Tijuana...sneak across the border...get work...get caught...get deported...get to Tijuana, etc.

Many U.S. corporations have assembly plants in Tijuana to take advantage of favorable wage structures and special duty rates. The electronic and clothing industries especially have tapped the great labor reservoir only a few miles south of San Diego.

Most of the souvenirs presented to tourists as they walk through open stalls, or found on the arms of hucksters working the streets or lines of cars waiting to recross the border, are produced locally. Side streets are often crowded with the white, naked, plaster-of-Paris replicas, including "The Last Supper", "Snoopy," lionhead bookends and "Rambo".

In the suburbs sacks of empty tin cans are snipped, bent, hammered and painted into lamps, candle holders, bird cages and wall decorations. Onyx elephants, chess sets, ashtrays and statues are cut, ground, smoothed and polished in hundreds of garages throughout the city. In the outskirts, red clay pots are fashioned to the shape of the moment and often decorated with everything from so-called authenic Oaxacan designs to the faces of the latest rock stars.

Some of the more talented craftsmen are furtively chipping "genuine" carved statues out of stone brought from central Mexico. Upon completion, they are buried for several days in the back yard, resurrected and clandestinely palmed off on those visitors who, with a touch of larceny themselves, smuggle the "ancient" artifacts home.

The border crossing between Tijuana and San Ysidro on the U.S. side is the busiest in the world, with nearly 40 million people passing through customs annually. At times lines of cars extend well back awaiting the decision of the U.S. Customs officers as to whether to send you into "secondary" for a more thorough check, and perhaps search.

Most visitors to Baja California see little more than the shops and bars within a mile or two of the border. Many even hesitate to try the excellent food in the many restaurants in Tijuana and beyond. For this we suggest you refer to our book, **Eating Your Way Through Baja**.

Some will attend the Jai Ali games at the Frontón Palacio on Avenue Revolución, or the horse and dog races at the beautiful Agua Caliente Race Track. Others find the bull fights at the Plaza de Toros near the race track, or at the Plaza Monumentál to their liking. The latter overlooks the Pacific ocean and is the second largest bull ring in the world.

The number of dollars spent by Norteamericanos and its proximity to the United States attracts people from all over Mexico to Tijuana, and this onrush of humanity is presenting problems to Tijuana's city fathers that defy solution. However, during the last few years, a great effort has been made to bring adequate water, power and other services to Tijuana's citizens. Public housing is much in evidence. Health care facilities are expanding into many sections of the city. Numerous streets have been paved and trees planted. Civic pride is evident.

Tijuana will continue to depend on the tourist, but in the future, local industrial development in the fields of furniture, pharmaceuticals, electronics, paints, foods and others will assist in broadening the economic base. And don't forget this is still the best place in the west to get custom seat covers — tucked and rolled, as only the "TJ" vinyl artisans can.

And where else than in the world's largest Woolworth's can you buy Chanel No. 5 duty free, then one aisle over, sit down to a blue plate special of *chiles rellenos,* and a frosty *cerveza*?

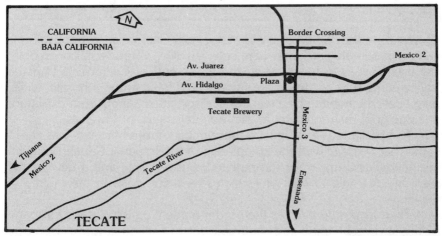

Tecate...A busy farming and business community on the border at 1600 feet elevation, it is surrounded by ever-increasing acreages of grapes, poultry and olives. Tecate is also part of the special industrial zone which allows duty-free assembly plants to be set up on Mexican soil. The climate is warm in the summer, cool in the winter.

Its population of 60,000 is rapidly becoming aware of tourism, as evidenced by its own version of the running of the bulls, ala Spain's *Pamplonada*. Held in August it attracts 50,000 or more visitors. Several bike races begin here, including the largest in the world, the Tecate-Ensenada (over 10,000 contestants!). And don't pass up the many small *taquerias* around the plaza. Rancho La Puerta, a noted health spa is located on a hilltop just west of town.

La Rumerosa...at an elevation of 4,370 feet atop the pass through the Sierra Juarez, serves as a summer destination for some Mexicali residents. Leading to the south are several roads which eventually link with the Ensenada to San Felipe highway. The roads, however, are not for light duty vehicles.

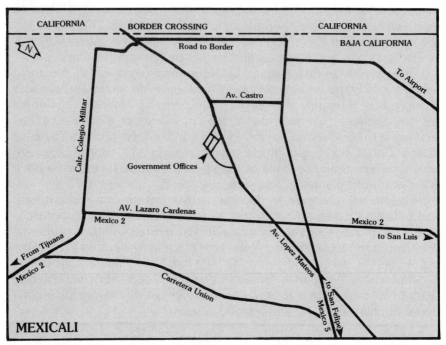

Mexicali...is the capitol of the State of Baja California. Its population is variously estimated at somewhere between 800,000 and a million people. Yet if you were to have visited the lower end of California's Imperial Valley at the turn of the century, you would have found a hostile, wind-swept desert inhabited by a few dozen disgruntled miners from El Alamo, a fading gold rush town set in the mountains east of Ensenada.

The precarious existence of these miners-turned-farmers was eased somewhat in 1902 with the completion of the Imperial Canal. But even the new water supply for the parched, but rich soil, and a new name, Mexicali, did little to change its status as a tiny oasis in the middle of nowhere.

Then its position across the border made it a hiding place for many of the lawless bands being squeezed out of California and Arizona by the law. In 1911, during the Mexican Revolution, Mexicali was occupied by dissidents and soldiers of fortune with designs on capturing portions of Mexico for their own gain. Order was reestablished in 1915 when Colonel Esteban Cantú became governor of the Northern District of Mexico. His rule of the region was autocratic, and virtually independent of what was going on in the rest of Mexico.

Agriculture expanded under the new governor. Cotton was planted over wide areas. Much of it was under the managementment of the American-owned Colorado Land Company. Many people came into the area, including thousands of Chinese — until new immigration restrictions were enacted in 1919. (It is interesting to note that their decendents are a powerful force in the economy of the Mexicali Valley.)

In the middle 30's Mexico's foreign-owned property was nationalized and the Colorado River Land Company was forced back across the border. In its place came the cooperative farms or *ejidos*, and a new land rush began.

With a strong labor force and abundant water from the Colorado river this new oasis in the desert had a bright future...until Boulder Dam was completed in the late 30's. Then the water supply was no longer purely a function of Mother Nature's whims. Now it was more a function of the United States bureaucracies whether, when and how much water was going to trickle down to Mexicali.

Finally, in 1954 the issue appeared settled when a treaty was signed guaranteeing Mexico a minimum 1,500,000-acre-foot share of Colorado River water. This treaty has not completely served its intended purpose, however, due to the practice, in some regions, of American farmers taking the water destined for Mexico and using it to leach the salts out of their land, and returning it to the river near the border! In addition, our Bureau of Land Management has repeatedly released huge amounts of water into Mexico, sometimes with little or no warning, causing widespread damage. Though nothing has yet been put on paper it appears that high level meetings are bringing about understandings to halt these practices.

Another side of Mexicali came in the 20's when prohibition in the United States prompted most border towns to permit liquor, gambling and prostitution. They were given legal status by state and city governments as the high taxes imposed on the profits helped finance roads and other civic improvements. Business flourished. Each day thousands of pleasuer-seeking Americans streamed across the border to find their particular brand of pleasure. The first automobile road connecting Mexicali and Tijuana was financed in this manner. Gambling and other practices were finally closed down, or went underground in 1935, with enactment of new Mexican national laws. Today, there is only a shadow of that part of Mexicali's bawdy past remaining.

Agriculture is still the main source of income in this part of Baja California although industrial employment centered, in part, about the establishment of assembly plants by American corporations is becoming more important. Tourism is not much of a factor here, though many residents living immediately across the border do cross the border regularly for the fine food offered in restaurants, and for bargains in some specialized commodities.

American sportsmen have long known Mexicali as the "Gateway to the Sea of Cortez," with San Felipe only 125 miles to the south over an excellent paved road. Here the first rendezvous with this wondrous sea begins. Accommodations in Mexicali tend more toward what would interest the businessman, not the tourist. Restaurants are numerous and many of are of top quality, especially those specializing in Chinese cuisine.

The climate is typical of that in the lower desert regions of the Southwest. Daytime temperatures during the winter months are usually pleasant, with chilly nights and occasional winds. The summer (June to September) are hot, tempered by occasional thunderstorms. Extreme temperatures in the summer will sometimes push the mercury above the 120 degree mark. Average rainfall for the year is about 3 inches.

San Felipe...though it has made great strides in the past dozen years it is still some distance from becoming the booming resort that seemed to be in its future. Still in its own way it is getting there. New homes are going up in several areas near town. There is even a traffic signal over the main intersection. The adobe and tarpaper houses that comprised the town of the early 1950's are gone, replaced by larger homes of block and wood. Following the completion of a graded road (built by the U.S. Government to service a radar station during World War 11), the town grew on its fishing and shrimping industries.

In the late 40's, American sportfishermen discovered the excellent *totuava* fishery and the town experienced a welcome burst of prosperity. By the late 60's, the totuava disappeared, due to heavy netting and the loss of spawning habitat in the Colorado River delta. It was then that San Felipe's warm and sunny winters, miles of beaches and vast desert inviting exploration, came to the attention of the *norteamericano*. Today tourism is a major portion of the economy of this town of 10,000-plus. Hotel rooms are plentiful — except during holiday periods — and there are enough restaurants to please almost everyone.

There is a spring run of white seabass in the vicinity of Consag Rock and small corvina may be caught close to shore. Interesting tidal flats are found both to the north and south, and a new breakwater and harbor is located below town. The road to Bahía Gonzaga and over to Mexico 1 has been recently been improved, even some paving, but portions are still on the rough side.

Guadalupe...In 1905, members of a religious sect called Molokan fled Russia and received permission to settle in Guadalupe. Excellent farmers, they raised grain, olives and grapes on the fertile land. For many years Russian was the mother language of the town. Even into the early 40's the town was characterized as being inhabited by blonde women and bearded men. Today it has all but disappeard as subsequent generations have intermarried or moved away. As recently as 1980 several of the old family bath houses could still be seen along the main street.

Rosarito...in the dim past, the local Rosarito Beach Hotel was a famous casino that even operated beyond the law for some years after gambling was outlawed in Mexico. Today hotels, condos, restaurants and trailer parks bring in far more income to the residents of this fast-growing small city. The beaches are broad and tranquil, the vistas, inviting. Few more reasons are needed to spend a few days, or a few months in Rosarito.

El Sauzal...is the site of several fish canneries. Be ready to roll up your windows when passing, as the odor can knock you out. A small harbor serves as an anchorage for commercial fishing boats.

Ensenada...is the third largest city on the peninsula. In less than a generation it has mushroomed more than 500%, to around 400,000 population. The climate is similar to San Diego's — a two hours drive to the north. Historically Ensenada has been the deepest point of penetration into Baja for most North American tourists. And while Ensenada does derive much of its income from the visitor, it does not resemble Tijuana in mood or appearance, for Ensenada is also a major seaport.

Its beautiful beaches, hotels and active sportfishing fleet draw hundreds of thousands of visitors annually. Shopping in the duty-free stores may turn up bargains in watches, cameras, perfumes, English woolens,

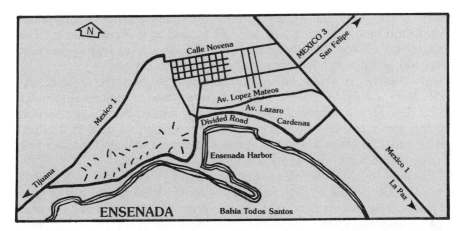

and other imports, for all of Baja is a duty-free zone. Custom-crafted wrought iron, furniture, leather items, and other native products of excellent quality from all over Mexico are to be found here.

The large well-protected bay was first discovered in 1542 by Juan Cabrillo, who named it San Mateo. Later, in 1602, Sebastian Vizcaino, not recognizing it, renamed it Bahia de Todos Santos. There is no evidence of any early native settlements, probably due to lack of water, although it was visited by inland tribes to catch fish and gather clams.

As the missions came northward from Loreto the bay came into use as a supply point but there were apparently no permanent residents until the after the gold strike in the foothills at Rosa de Castilla in 1870.

Some buildings in the older central portion of town date back before the turn of the century. One of these, *Hussong's Cantina*, has been a landmark for nearly a century. It still serves the best *Margaritas* in Ensenada, and a popular stop for some of the old timers. Today, however, today it is becoming more of a hangout for the college crowd.

Fishing and related businesses provide many jobs for residents. Several canneries process fish taken from all over Baja's Pacific shores. Fish reduction plants gobble up many thousands of tons of anchovies and other small fish to meet the demand for fishmeal for chicken food and fertilizer. Sportfishing is also an active industry with tens of thousands of passengers venturing forth for a wide variety of fish. Once famous for its seemingly inexhaustible supply of yellowtail, halibut and white seabass, the local grounds have suffered greatly from the lack of controls placed on commercial harvesting of the resources.

Ensenada's stores can supply almost everything you might need for driving on down the peninsula. Be sure you are well stocked before leaving town, as the selection — and supply — gets smaller as you go south. Of course such things as beers, sodas and many staples, including coffee and wearing apparel are inexpensive in Mexico.

Ensenada's sense of remoteness, yet being near to San Diego, gives the visitor a taste of the real Baja without having to venture too far from the border. There are many restaurants offering almost anything you might wish...from French to Chinese, Italian to classical Spanish. And of course specialty dishes from all over Mexico. Accommodations are many and varied, and the people are friendly. You find little hype and hustle here.

Is Ensenada a good spot to spend some time, particularly over short periods? You bet. We recommend it highly.

Maneadero...is a rapidly growing farm community just below Ensenada. Population here is bulging past 40,000, according to some sources. The "migracion" office is at the south end of town where open you must stop and attempt to have your tourist permits validated.

Punta Banda...is a principally-gringo community centered around several campgrounds and homesites. The paved road continues 12.5 miles to La Bufadora, a spectacular water spout generated by the wave action forcing water and air into a tidal cave, then through a vent in the top. Many beautiful coves are found in this scenic area. It would make a fine location for a hotel, but let's hope it stays the way it is.

El Alamo...in 1889 the place was jumping. El Alamo was a booming city of 8,000 people as gold fever hit its zenith. Widespread placer gold deposits drew miners from all over the West. Within months most of it was gone, and only the hardcore miners remained. Even these left when most operations halted by 1910. Today, El Alamo, 10 miles off the Ensenada-San Felipe highway, is practically deserted, but there are some old buildings and remnants of mine machinery to be seen. Gold is still mined on a small scale, and nearby ranches raise livestock.

Rosa de Castilla...a gold mining center in the mountains behind Ensenada. From 1870 into the early 20th century it produced some millions of dollars in gold. The first strike brought miners from all over North America. It was even the capitol for the Territory of Baja California between 1870 and 1882. Then the seat of government moved to Ensenada for a short while before finally settling in Mexicali.

La Bocana/Puerto Santo Tomás...La Bocana is at the outlet of the Río Santo Tomás to the ocean. Boats can be rented here through the Gomez family. Several Americans have built homes here.

A few miles north is Puerto Santo Tomás, where boats may also be rented. The water is usually clear and cold from an upwelling current. The area has coves reminiscent of our Monterey Peninsula.

Santo Tomás...an agricultural community of 1200 inhabitants that dates back to mission times. It was the original site for the famous Santo Tomás Winery that now stands in Ensenada. Some grapes are still grown here, along with many acres of olives. El Palomar Resort offers trailer sites, swimming pool and a store with limited supplies of groceries and curios.

Ejido Erendira...on the coast 11 miles west of the highway via a mostly-paved road. It is a farming and fishing community of a thousand-plus people. Just past town to the north are cabin and trailer sites around Castro's Camp. The region offers many isolated camping sites, fine surf fishing from rocky or sandy beaches and excellent offshore fishing.

Skiffs from Castro's Camp, will take you out for some of the finest rockcod fishing you have ever experienced. It is not unusual to catch 100 pounds of excellent-eating fish in a short time. In fall and winter, schools of yellowtail, white seabass and barracuda occasionally move in here. A few cabins are rented by the Castros.

San Vicente...is a farming center of growing importance. With more than 10,000 people this valley and adjoining Valle Llano Colorado raises fine crops of grapes, olives, chiles and barley. The site of the San Vicente mission, started by the Dominicans in 1780, is just out of town. After the collapse of the mission and withdrawal of the military garrison in 1849, the valley was virtually deserted until the 1940's, when ample water from deep wells was located.

Colonét...the site of a small hospital started by the Flying Samaritans — a group of doctors from the United States who at one time provided the majority of medical services south of Ensenada. Just past Bradley's a road right leads to a fishing and clamming area, San Antonio del Mar (7 mi.). Below bridge is road southwest leading to Punta Colonet (7.5 mi.).

San Telmo...main part of the village is 5 miles east of the highway is on the way to the Meling Ranch (50 km). The ranch, a working cattle operation (can accommodate a dozen or so guests at a time). Pool, horseback riding and trips into the tree-studded mountains are some of the activities.

A brief story points up the casual nature of the ranch:

A few years ago two guests were asked to pitch in around the ranch house because the help had just quit. The pair were "volunteered" into the kitchen and Aida Meling kept them hopping. After everyone was fed and the dishes washed the volunteers collapsed in Aida's office for a well-deserved breather. By way of making conversation she asked one of the men what kind of work he usually did. "Señora," he said, "I am your governor."

Beyond, at 62 miles (100 km) at the 9200-foot level of the Sierra San Pedro Martír, is the largest telescope in Mexico. In a marvelous alpine setting and offering a spectacular view of the desert and Sea of Cortes, it is worth a visit. This road should not be attempted with a standard car.

Colonia Guerrero...the changes that have taken place here in the past decade are legion. Whole sections of *chapparal* are now under intensive cultivation. Cauliflower, brussels sprouts, snowpeas, tomatoes, chiles and strawberries are found on the thousands of acres of irrigated land, much of which is raised for the American frozen food market. This new activity has brought many workers from southern Mexico and the Yucatan have come into the area, providing an interesting infusion of tropical culture into this sometimes chilly climate. Just south of the bridge over the Rio Santo Domingo at K172+ a road west leads to the Posada Don Diego Trailer Park. (Watch carefully, for it is not well marked.) Beyond Don Diego's about 1.5 miles, is a fine beach for fishing and clamming. Though not up to what it was a few years ago, there are still plenty of bowls of clam chowder here.

Bahía San Quintín...has yet to reach the popularity as a tourist destination that many believed was its destiny. Nonetheless there are numbers of Americans who have fallen in love with the area. There is plenty to do for the outdoor-oriented: the large bay has good numbers of ducks and black brant during the winter; the ocean-facing beaches have lots of pismo clams, perch, croaker and halibut. Tidal flats offer opportunities to observe wideranging marine ecosystems. The fall and winter months are usually temperate with little rain. Summers have a tendency to be cooler and windier than, for example, San Diego. Fishing in the outer bay and around Isla San Martín can be some of the best ever.

El Rosario...before the highway this fishing and agricultural village was the last outpost before plunging into the remote central portion of Baja. It has changed but little because of limited arable land and decreasing supplies of lobster, abalone and fish. For years, Espinosa's Place was the last chance to fill up on gas, food and cerveza. Their reputation as a place to stop continues, especially when it comes to Doña Anita's famous burritos, ranging from straight beans to exotic lobster and crab meat, they should not be missed. Breakfasts and other dishes also reflect her touch in the kitchen. Formerly a checkpoint for the Baja 1000, the back yard still has a few skeletons from the old days.

Some years ago, when asked about the effect of the highway on what was before one of the most remote areas in North America, Senora Espinosa, noting that for the first time they had found it necessary to put locks on their doors, said, "The bad road brought us good people, the good road has brought us bad people."

The climate is cooler than Ensenada, definitely windier, and with about half the rainfall. Punta Baja, eight miles south of town is a small fishing and lobstering community. The hospitality offered by the residents is great. There are lots of kids and many of them are happy to guide you around the tide pools or help in a search for rock clams.

Puertecitos...several hundred vacation homesites surround the small natural harbor. Boats launched here find good fishing only a few miles off shore. Toward the point is a series of warm spring-fed pools that afford comfortable bathing if the tide is not too high. Weather is hot in the summer, but pleasant at other times. Rainfall here is practically nil.

Bahía San Luis Gonzaga...for many the area represents the last frontier of life as it was before the Baja highway. Marginal roads and an also-marginal (at high tide) airstrip service the area. A number of trailers and small houses host a loyal cadre of visitors. The region is rich in sea life, from the tidal flats to the offshore islands. Winds can be nasty and care should be taken in venturing from shore. Spring tides to 20 feet set up strong currents and leave boats far from the water. Scenery is stark and beautiful. Boats are available to rent at both Alfonsina's and Papa Fernandez resorts. Shelling and clamming are also attractions.

Rancho Santa Inés...In the days of the old road, the Rancho was one of the rare way-stations where a meal, bed and sometimes gasoline could be obtained from the drums laboriously hauled over more than 250 miles of bad road between Santa Inés and Ensenada. It was necessary to filter all fuel through a chamois to remove dirt and water that accumulated in the drums. It was in Santa Inés that adventuresome groups going north and south would exchange stories about road conditions and as to where they might camp the next night. Mechanical problems were also discussed, sometimes parts were adapted or fabricated on the spot by the talented *mecanicos* who worked there.

Rancho Santa Inés still serves its famous *tacos, enchiladas* and breakfasts while back on the highway the Hotel La Pinta Cataviña provides rooms, gasoline and meals.

About 14 miles farther east over a very poor trail lie the ruins of Misión Santa María (See Mission Section).

Laguna Chapala...is a large and very dusty lake bed to the east of the highway...well remembered by everyone who attempted to conquer the Baja road in the days before the highway. If you were able to avoid getting the inside of your vehicle knee-deep in dust up to this point, your efforts were in vain. The depth and fineness of the *tereño,* or *polvo,* just north of the lake bed is unbelievable.

Nuevo Rancho Chapala...is owned by the Grosso family. The original ranch site was on the east side of Laguna Seca Chapala, but moved to the highway in 1973. The late Arturo Grosso's hospitality, and obvious optimism in this desert region where one cow is hard pressed to survive on five square miles of desert, was legendary. He fed almost anyone and everyone who came along, and even had cool cervezas when the refrigerator worked. He used to challenge anyone who came by to a foot race — and had few takers, even though he was in his 60's. Their small restaurant serves a fine breakfast.

Parador Punta Prieta...located about eight miles north of the town of Punta Prieta at the turnoff to Bahia de Los Angeles. Facilities are minimal, you'll find gas upon occasion and a sometimes-open restaurant. Despite its lack of most everything there usually is some traveler parked there who can pass on a hot tip on fishing, road conditions, etc.

Bahía de Los Ángeles...see page 75

San Borja...is a tiny, but charming, community of maybe a half-dozen families centered around the *Misión San Francisco de Borja*. Subsistence quantities of dates, olives, pomegranates and vegetables are raised here. Water is from several small springs and a well. The roads in and out from both south and north are a challenge, but OK for 4X4s and most pickups. Remarkably preserved, the daylong trip is worth it if you have the time and the proper vehicle.

Punta Prieta...a bleak-looking collection of old homes contrasting with the new buildings to the west of the community which have been built for road maintenance crews. Northeast of town is an enormous paved air strip. Planned as an alternate landing field for jets that were supposed to come into Guerrero Negro, it was never never used, but then neither was the one built at Guerrero Negro. It's a long story.

El Rosarito...a group of houses and *ranchitos* totaling maybe 300 people. Exactly how it survives is a mystery to us. Just below are several stands of small, but beautiful cirios, or boojums.

Paralelo 28...a small tourism complex located 2.5 miles north of the Guerrero Negro intersection. A 28-room La Pinta hotel is all that is left of an ambitious complex of trailer park, gas station, etc. The tall stylized eagle or *agila,* straddles the border between the states of Baja California and Baja California Sur. Just to the north is a large jetstrip presumably built to allow the refuelling of the large transoceanic jets going to the Orient, etc. It was never put into operation, and today serves for little more than an occasional drag race. It, too, is a long story.

Guerrero Negro...Here salt is the main commodity. Most of the nearly 10,000 residents work for the Exportadora de Sal, while others are involved in fishing and tourism. The vast regions of tidal flats of Scammon's Lagoon provide over 6,000,000 tons of salt each year for use in chemical processing throughout the world. Giant trucks shuttle the salt from the evaporating pens to the dock at Puerto V. Carranza, where it is loaded into barges and towed to Isla Cedros for trans-shipment to their ultimate destinations. Services in town include a Pemex station, two motels, several small supermercados and restaurants, including the Malarrimo. This restaurant is a special find, for the owner, Enrique Achoy, excels in the preparation of seafoods. The weather is often windy and foggy, especially during spring and early summer. (See page 69)

Ejido Vizcaino...a relatively new colony of about 4,000 and site of an agricultural experiment station where a wide variety of crops are being successfully grown in a desert environment and with limited water.

El Arco...was once the center of considerable mining activity; then it became a major way-station for those early adventurers driving the old road to Mulegé and points south. Mexico 1 by-passes El Arco and it has resumed its quiet ways, in fact it is nearly deserted.

Abreojos...see page 89.

Asunción...see page 79

Bahia Tortugas...see page 69

San Ignacio...is acclaimed by almost everyone who visits this palm-studded oasis as one of the beauty spots of Baja California. Here the Arroyo San Ignacio brings its underground water to the surface and supports 80,000 date palms, hundreds of citrus and fig trees, vinyards, flowers and gardens galore. More than 4000 lucky people call San Ignacio and adjoining San Lino home. It has a beauty and charm that is bound to make a stop here memorable.

The reconstruction of Misión San Ignacio was completed in 1976. Its chapel and outbuildings, overlooking the cool plaza lined with giant Indian laurel trees, provide a most worthwhile stop. Nestled among the date palms as you enter town is the La Pinta Hotel.

Though we see the town as having the potential of becoming a popular resort it has yet to catch on. The small lakes north of town contain fish and frogs (turtles too, we hear). The Sea of Cortez is only an hour away; Mulege just two hours. Closer, there are many Indian caves, hidden valleys and abundant varieties of cactus. Instead of being overrun with visitors it still lies there, a charming oasis, waiting to be discovered.

The late Frank Fischer was for years the salvation to many Baja travelers. His ability to repair anything mechanical is one of the legends of Baja. Since the opening of the highway his son Oscar operates a small motel, Posada San Ignacio, and takes people into the nearby Sierra San Francisco to look at the cave paintings.

Santa Rosalía...came into existence when copper was discovered in the nearby hills during the 1870's. In 1885, interests were consolidated under the French, Boleo Mining Company, and the large smelter they built began producing copper for Europe and the United States. Yaqui Indians were brought from Sonora to work in the mines while French engineers supervised the mining and smelting operations.

By 1953 the high grade ores were depleted and the Boleo cut down their operations. Later attempts to reopen the mines and import ore for the smelter also have failed. The central portion of this town of 12,000 has changed little over the years as turn-of-the-century houses, offices and stores still line the streets.

Vestiges of the original French company still remain in the architecture, an excellent bakery and in a very picturesque church. The church, designed by Alexandre Eiffel, was prefabricated in France for a display in the St. Louis world's fair. It then ended up in Santa Rosalía.

The terminus for the ferry to Guaymas is in Santa Rosalía. This modern air-conditioned building looks somewhat out of place among the older structures and the great sheds of the antiquated smelter. The town offers many subjects for the dedicated camera bug.

Summers in Santa Rosalía can be oppressive, as it is sheltered from the cooling breezes, yet it is open to strong winds during the winter. There are two hotels in the area, the historic Frances on the hill above the town and the El Morro, on the highway about a mile south.

Punta Chivato... 15 miles east of highway on the point forming the north end of Bahia Santa Inés. The area has seen changes during the past few years. The old hotel, Borrego de Oro, has been refurbished and is now open as the Hotel Punta Chivato. A number of homes have been built nearby, and a large trailer and tent camping area has been opened. The beaches to the west of the hotel are especially abundant with shells of many varieties. The shallow, rocky reefs are excellent for snorkeling and provide good fishing. A short distance away an international airport is under construction with regular flights scheduled to begin in 1988.

Mulegé... The population of 4,500 has increased but little since opening of the new road. To many this is a blessing, for they prefer Mulegé as it was, a small, friendly and beautiful town in an incomparable setting. Site of Misión Santa Rosalía de Mulegé (pg. 168) and the very unique old territorial prison, the town extends along the banks of the Río Santa Rosalía (also called Estero Mulegé), the only navigable river in Baja California. Thousands of fan and date palms and many flowering shrubs provide a tropical atmosphere that is almost unreal when compared to the brown dusty desert surrounding it. A fair number of *norteamericanos* have established part-time residences in the numerous trailer parks along the river and on the shores of Bahía Conceptión, and the demand for space is growing each year. July, August and September are very hot, particularly when the prevailing southeast breezes fail. Good fishing and several comfortable resorts are in the area.

The Comondús... refers to the two small adjoining settlements of San José Comondú and San Miguel Comondú (pg. 169). Going back to colonial times the nearly 1000 residents live a quiet life harvesting a wide variety of farm products and taking care of their livestock. Both mission sites, they are accessible from the east and the west. The towns offer limited supplies of fuel and groceries. A small, clean cafe serves a Mexican fare. Travel by standard cars through here is not recommended.

La Purísima... an old mission site (pg. 169), it is one of the better irriga-tated valleys of the region, with fields of grapes, corn, tomatoes, citrus and dates much in evidence. Its climate is tempered by sea breezes — cool in winter and pleasant during summer. They record only 2 inches of rainfall annually, usually in August and September. Nearly 2,000 pople live here and in adjacent Colonia San Isidro. The inhabitants have a tendancy to be a bit aloof, in part because of some unfortunate experi-ences with several groups of "hippies" in the early 70's. The springs and small lakes along the north side of the arroyo, plus the plush vegetation make this tiny settlement one of our favorite scenic treats in all of Baja.

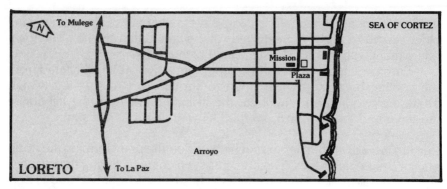

Loreto... is the oldest settlement in Baja California. For 132 years, 1697 to 1829, it was the capitol of the entire California territory — which included present day California as far north as San Francisco and all of the peninsula. Its reign ended abruptly when a hurricane virtually destroyed the town. The Misión de Nuestra Señora de Loreto, "Mother of the Missions" (pg. 169), has been restored and is worth a visit, as is the small museum.

The growth of the town was greatly accelerated when the government designated Loreto and adjoining areas to the south as a major tourist development. The many workers required to implement these projects has boomed the population to nearly treble of what it was a decade ago. The international airport, the Hotel El Presidente and adjoining support facilities at Nópolo cove, and now the ambitious marina and resort village program being built at Puerto Escondido all add to the economy of this suddenly-prosperous region.

Many see the announced development programs as being overly ambitious considering the amount of available water. They also cite the lack of conservation measures directed toward the region's main resource, the abundant schools of fish that visit the area.

Well-stocked markets, good hotels and restaurants, organized panga fishing fleets and friendly inhabitants will always make Loreto a favorite for many thousands of visitors.

Puerto Escondido... its name, hidden port, and its low profile in Baja tourism, hardly seems appropriate now. The reasons become obvious when looking at all the construction equipment busily reshaping this lovely natural harbor. Long a haven for American "yachties" the arrival of the transpeninsula highway brought trailerboats, campers and motorhomers in ever-increasing numbers. The first change came about in 1981 with the opening of the Tripui Trailer Park. Next a dock and a few slips brought in larger motor cruisers. Now a wide boat ramp, bulkheads, permanent slips and anchorages are on stream. Next comes more infrastructure, then a Mediterranean-styled village complete with red tiled roofs, white walls and narrow winding walkways. The effect should be stunning, and it's progress is being followed carefully by boat owners.

Ciudad Constitución... is the commercial hub of Magdalena Plain farming operations. Many of the nearly 40,000 residents work servicing the region's expanding agriculture. Thirty-four miles to the west is the shipping and fishing port of Puerto San Carlos. Here wide-ranging ocean fishing boats unload their catch, and the area's cotton and grain production is sent to the Mexican mainland.

La Paz...contrary to its name (The Peace), La Paz's history is one of the most violent of all the cities on the peninsula. Site of the first Spanish attempt to settle what was at that time believed to be an island called Santa Cruz, it began with the captain of the expediition, Diego Becerra, being murdered by his crew in 1533 just before a landfall was made. Shortly after landing, the new leader, Fortún Jimenez, and 22 of his soldiers were slain by the Indians. The sirvivors fled back to the mainland. Two years later, Hernán Cortéz himself led a group of soldiers and colonists to La Paz. This group too had to return when political turmoil on the mainland caused a cessation of supplies.

Just prior to the 1600's another attempt was made, only to end when fire destroyed most of the supplies and buildings. The year 1683 saw another colony fail when rebellion by the Indians followed the murder of several of their number — at a banquet in their honor given by the Spaniards.

In 1734 another attempt ended in disaster when the southern portion of the peninsula erupted in the rebellion of the Indians against their conquerers. The colony was restocked, only to collapse again when epidemics swept the Indian population in 1749.

The first permanent residents were in 1811 following a land grant to Juan José Espinoza, a retired soldier. In 1829 La Paz was named the capitol of the Southern Territory of California following the virtual annihilation of Loreto by a fierce storm. During the war between Mexico and the United States in 1847, La Paz was occupied by American troops and a number of skirmishes resulted. The soldiers withdrew after the treaty of Guadalupe Hidalgo returned Baja California to Mexico.

Violence again visited La Paz when the self-styled American adventurer William Walker, made a brief stand before being driven out.

The prime lure of the colonists were the rich pearl oyster beds in the nearby gulf. In the 18th Century, many of the finest pearls of the royal treasury in Spain came from La Paz. Pearling continued until the early 1940's when a mysterious disease destroyed nearly all oyster beds in the Sea of Cortez.

In the 1950's, sportfishermen from the United States discovered the rich bounty of gamefish in the nearby waters. La Paz quickly acquired the reputation of being one of the billfishing centers of the world. Countless articles in publications throughout America about La Paz, the East Cape and Cabo San Lucas assured a steady stream of visitors.

Improvements in transportation, ferries, jetliners and the Baja highway, have made perishable supplies more available and La Paz residents now number nearly 100,000.

El Triunfo....came into existence with the discovery of silver in 1862. Within a few years the mines, stamping mills and smelter provided livelihood for nearly 10,000, before playing out. Today the 600 residents nearby live in a quiet, ghost town environment. Situated in the mountains and in a cooler, wetter climate than La Paz, it has recently attracted the attention of several Americans who are restoring homes.

San Antonio.. had its beginnings in 1756 when Gaspar Pisón opened a silver mine. Its nearly 1000 residents now engage in agriculture. Here too are some relics of the past.

San Bartolo.. strung out along a narrow canyon, the area has many small farms that raise sugar cane, mangoes and citrus. A number of stands sell produce. Those who passed through here prior to late 1986 will be happy to know that the speed bumps, *topes,* are gone.

Santiago...it began around the now-gone mission and has remained as a prosperous farming community. Its nearly 2500 residents even have a zoo — the only one in Baja! A bear, monkeys, goats, birds and numbers of native critters. The sign out on Mexico 1 showing an elephant crossing is a classic. The town plaza is surrounded by various stores. The Palomar Hotel has eight rooms and a fine restaurant (closed Sundays).

Miraflores...farming and cattle center where fine leatherwork may sometimes be purchased. Several families provide informal backpack and burro trips into the nearby mountains.

San José del   )o...once a supply station for the Manila galleons and a mission site, San José is now a thriving tourism center of 22,000. A beautiful town of many trees, it is tempered somewhat by ocean breezes and enjoys a mild climate. A large international airport six miles north of town brings thousands of visitors to hotels throughout the area. A number of fine restaurants and gift stores are to be found in downtown San José.

Cabo San Lucas...the town (which now officially has the same name as the rocky ridge extending south into the ocean), in the view of many of us, has grown in past the small, intimate little Baja village of yesterday. The streets are crowded most of the time; new buildings are everywhere; the harbor will soon have a fullfledged yacht basin; hotels and restaurants flourish. Condos, luxurious homes and a few timeshares are proliferating in a general atmosphere of organization and planning — a good sign. Actually it is still a fine place to visit, maybe even settle. It is just hard to keep up with, even in 3 or 4 trips per year. The fishing and the weather continue to attract people from all over the world.

El Pescadero...a quiet farming community of about 2000 located a short distance from the Pacific. There is good hunting for dove and duck in the vicinity. The beaches west of here are fine for camping and some fishing.

Todos Santos...it began as a farm and mission visiting station in the early 1700's, finally gaining mission status in 1734. Today, it is a busy producer of a wide variety of fruits and vegetables. Mangoes are one of the top crops. Some good beaches are reached by roads west of town. Most services are available, including a restaurant and two small hotels. Several Americans have built homes here, and others have become involved in farming the very rich soil.

Offshore fishing is excellent, while casting lures from shore can bring a wide variety of smaller species. Punta Lobos beach has a large fleet of pangas, some of which can be hired for fishing.

BLUE PALM

BAJA'S PALM CANYONS

The road south along the west side of the Laguna Salada leads to a series of palm-studded canyons that descend sharply from the eastern side of the Sierra Juarez. A number of these canyons have small streams fed by winter snows and summer thunderstorms. Though the water disappears into the sandy soil long before reaching the *laguna*, its presence in the narrow canyons has created beautiful oases of palms, flowers, ferns and the many forms of animal life that thrive in such an environment. Even the desert bighorn *(borrego)* and deer *(venado)* visit regularly for their share of the lifegiving water in this otherwise hostile country.

Generally, the road is passable for a standard automobile to both Cantú Palms, 19 miles from Mexico Highway 2, and to Cañon de Guadalupe 16 miles further on. Access to the others, such as Santa Isabel, Tajo and Palomar, is much more difficult and should not be attempted except with specialized equipment, and then never alone.

Cantú was once a gathering place for the Cocopah Indians, as evidenced by the petroglyphs and mortars for grinding seeds to be found on a number of rocks. Miners also visited here in times past, along with woodcutters, and evidence of their presence still exist. The beauty of the canyon is something very special, and hopefully it will remain free of man on a permanent basis.

Cañon de Guadalupe already has a small commercial development to take advatage of the hot springs and the cool sparkling stream that tumbles from the 6,000 foot mountains immediately to the west. Here again, palms line the floor of the *arroyo* with hundreds of species of plants and animals crowded into a stretch of only a few miles. Waterfalls and pools are in the upper portions of the canyon, and some evidence of the Indian's visits may be found.

There is is an area for campers, and rates for the use of the facilities, including the swimming pool and hot springs, are very reasonable. The region is best visited in the spring when the flowers are at their peak and the weather is still mild.

BEACHCOMBING

If you are the type that likes to walk along the ocean shore...inspecting what has been washed above the water line, and occasionally collecting several of the more interesting specimens of shells, driftwood and other debris...you can spend a lifetime along the nearly 3,000 miles of coastline encompassing Baja California and Baja California Sur.

Shell collectors will find many varieties from which to choose, sometimes in incredible numbers. Wide windrows occur along several beaches — west of Punta Chivato, north of Scammon's Lagoon, and east of El Golfo de Santa Clara. The urge to load up the car with colorful conch, clam, oyster and abalone shells is almost irresistible, and each succeeding beach visited will seem to have even more to offer.

The beaches along Baja's Pacific side collect flotsam from the entire northern Pacific Ocean. It is possible to find giant redwood logs from the northwest United States, white cedar stumps from Canada and Alaska, hatch covers from the ships of the world, bottles-old and new. Occasionally, a glass net float will survive the journey from the Japanese fishing grounds. Here, too, is evidence of man's carelessness in the growing mountains of our plastic age — cups, bottles, bags, egg cartons, etc.

The beaches on the Cortez side yield numbers of intricately sculptured driftwood — torn from some distant canyon by an infrequent deluge of rain and bleached by the Baja sun. The skeletal remains of seabirds, fish, whales and seals are scattered throughout the coves and rocky headlands that comprise much of the shoreline.

Eventually, all but the most remote shores will be picked clean of their treasures. But, by taking only a few rememberances for the bookshelf back home, the supply may last long enough for many to experience the exhilaration of an exciting "discovery".

MINI-TRIPS: TAKE YOUR PICK

Though driving Mexico 1 may be the most popular way to go to Baja, there are an increasing number of special package tours catering to fishing or other special interests.

The following fly non-scheduled charters into all parts of Mexico from nearly airport:

Gunnell Aviation, write or call: 3000 Airport Ave., Santa Monica, CA 90405. Phone: (213) 391-6354.

Jimsair, 2904 Pacific Highway, San Diego, CA 92102. Phone: (619) 298-7704.

Several companies specialize in a variety of tours to Baja, many of which include fishing. They include:

Baja Adventures, 16000 Ventura Blvd., Suite 200, Encino, CA 91436. Phones: inside CA 1-800-345-2252; outside CA 1-800-543-2252.

Baja Safari, PO Box 1827, Monterey, CA 93942. Phones: 408-375-2252; CA only 1-800-248-9900.

Tony Reyes Fishing Tours, 4010 E. Chapman, Suite D, Orange, CA 92669. Phone 714-538-8010.

Baja Fishing Adventures, 2221 Suite 1T, Palo Verde Ave, Long Beach, CA 90815. Phone 213-594-9441.

"Ole" Baja Fishing Trips, 2430 E. Pacific Coast Hwy., Long Beach, CA 90804. Phone 213-0439-9906.

For those with a deeper interest in more nature-oriented travels in Baja California and its seas will find the following operators of interest — all emphasize marine mammals, and on any trip you might have an opportunity to pet a California gray whale!

Baja Expeditions Inc., Box 3725, San Diego, CA 92103, (714) 297-0506. Boat trips out of La Paz guided by Tim Means and his staff spotlight the Cortez and Bahía Magdalena, a major calving ground for the California gray whale.

H&M Sportfishers, 2803 Emerson St., San Diego 92106. Phone; 619-222-1144.

Fisherman's Landing, 2838 Garrison St., San Diego, CA 92106. Phone 619-222-0391.

A number of colleges and universities offer credit and non-credit classes that include trips to Baja. A check of the schedules of your local schools might turn up a unique destination.

BUSHOPPING IN BAJA

The long-range public transportation in Baja is growing by leaps and bounds. Today there is an almost steady stream of busses departing for La Paz from Tijuana's new bus terminal east of town. Most are modern, many even having restrooms. There are also a variety of local schedules for shorter trips. Though they are rarely "scenicruisers," they go almost anywhere for little cost.

One-way fares as far as La Paz have been ranging around $20. Confirmed reservations are difficult to come by. The easiest way is to go with the system and be at the depot early in the day, and with the number of busses, you will fit in somewhere. The entire trip takes less than 24 hours, with brief food stops. (A tip — take a small ice chest and a few sandwiches, just in case.) Tickets may also be purchased for intermediate destinations such a Mulegé, but you cannot get off and resume your trip later on the same ticket as you can in the U.S.

We know several groups who have bussed themselves to Loreto, spent 3 or 4 days days fishing, then loaded up their ice chests with frozen fillets and returned to Tijuana. They said they had a blast.

Bussing through Baja could be considered a bit rugged for most, but it's a hit with the sleeping bag set, and the price is right.

FLYING, AN OVERVIEW

Though one cannot classify Baja as being overrun with international airports, there are more than there were when **The Baja Book** first hit the stores in 1974. International arrivals and departures include Los Cabos (Cabo San Lucas and San José del Cabo), La Paz, Loreto, Mexicali and Tijuana, with Mulegé not far behind if the work on the runway continues. Stories persist that San Felipe will soon join the number, but we don't see it for some time to come.

The scheduled airlines currently serving Baja from American airports are Aeromexico, Mexicana and PSA. Another, Aero California, a domestic Mexican airline, flys out of Tijuana to a variety of destinations in Baja and Mexico's west coast. At the moment San Francisco, Los Angeles, Tucson and Houston serve as gateway cities.

There are several Baja-oriented charter services and air taxis to take you to many of the hundreds of dirt strips in the peninsula: Gunnell Aviation, 3000 Airport Ave., Santa Monica, CA 90405, (213) 391-6354. Another is Jimsair Aviation, Inc., 2904 Pacific Hwy., San Diego, CA 92101, (714) 298-7704.

BAJA'S NUMERO UNO PILOT

Few people become legends in their own time, but Captain Francicso Muñoz became one nearly a half-century ago. And though Capt. Muñoz has retired and now flies only for his own pleasure, his story is still worth telling:

A large percentage of the small dirt stips in Baja, and some of the paved landing fields, would probably not exist had it not been for this amazing man. His expertise in getting in and out of tight quarters has led to many stories, one of which is that that Captain Muñoz can make a wheelbarrow fly and can land a DC-6 in a sand trap. But his true exploits are in the supplying of remote ranchos and fishing villages, and his roles in countless search and rescue missions.

He last worked for the evaporative salt works, Exportadora de Sal, at Guerrero Negro as their chief pilot. Between flights he took time to make census reports for scientists studying the California gray whale's calving and mating behavior in the Baja lagoons of Guerrero Negro, Scammon, San Ignacio and Magdalena.

He and his wife Lisle have also established themselves as experts on the nearby early Indian settlements. And their interests in everything from glass floats to relics from old sailing ships has turned their home into a fascinating display of what Baja's beaches hold for the inveterate beachcomber.

THE LONG RANGE BOATS

Much of the October-April activity at the San Diego sportfishing docks is centered around the eight to ten large deluxe sportfishing boats that specialize in fishing the waters along Baja's Pacific coast. Ranging as much as one thousand miles south of their home port, they offer some of the world's finest fishing in an atmosphere of luxurious comfort.

Private or semi-private staterooms, air conditioning, stereo music, great food and efficient crews, added to the quality fishing, brings people back time and time again.

Popular too are the January to March trips into such wildlife sanctuaries as Scammon's Lagoon and Laguna San Ignacio where the life cycle of the California gray whale may be studied along with other marine mammals and a wide variety of bird and sealife.

Reservations are a must for any of the above trips. Rates run $120-150 per day, plus possible fuel surcharge.

Contact: Lee Palm's Sportfishing, 2801 Emerson St., San Diego, CA 92106, (619) 224-3857.

Fisherman's Landing, 2838 Garrison St., San Diego, CA 92106, (619) 222-0391.

H&M Sportfishers, 2803 Emerson St., San Diego, CA 92106, (619) 222-1144.

Point Loma Sportfishing Assoc., 1403 Scott St., San Diego, CA 92106, (619) 223-1627.

FIRST TASTE OF THE CORTEZ

My first romance with the Sea of Cortez came as a result of an article by Ray Cannon in the early 1950's. He wrote glowingly of the great size of the *totuava* and described how the fish would migrate north past San Felipe on their journey to deposit millions of eggs in the brackish water of the Colorado River delta. Cannon had worked out their timetable so that one could take advantage of their ravenous nature following the spawn. In 1953, I ventured into that primitive gulf port as he directed. The first fish was the largest I had ever taken, about 75 pounds. The weight turned out to be unimportant a short while later when the second totuava topped a hundred pounds. I was hooked on the Cortez.

— Tom Miller

CAGUAMA

GREEN SEA TURTLES

FISHING BAJA — NO FISH STORY

The first thought most people have about Baja Calfiornia is its reputation for being a giant fishing platform, from which are tapped the great riches of the Sea of Cortez and the Pacific Ocean. And this is true, for Baja's boundless sea bounty consistently provides more than just "fish stories."

The waters surrounding the Baja peninsula vary from cool upwellings just south of Ensenada, offering shallow-depth rock fishing similar to that found off central California, to tropical climes where sea temperatures rarely drop below the 70 degree mark and can top 90 in the late summer.

The great tidal movements of the middle and upper gulf cause a continuous upwelling of cool nutrient-laden water into the warmer surface water, bringing about conditions that nurture incomparable concentrations of sea life. Dozens of major species of fish have their beginnings in these regions.

Although known primarily for its saltwater fishing, Baja, through its eons of isolation, produced an indigenous fresh water trout similar to the rainbow, but more brightly colored. Though their present status is somewhat clouded, they inhabited several streams in the shadow of the Picacho del Diablo mountain east of the Meling Ranch. Other freshwater action is found south and east of Mexicali in the Río Hardy and Laguna Salada areas. But it is the hundreds of species of saltwater fish that really put meat on the table and money in the pockets of those who live and work along the coasts of Baja.

An incredible mixture of sea animals in every stage of development creates a great smorgasbord for billions of living things, each feeding on one or more of his neighbors. For man to reap the benefits of the many life sources around Baja California, he needs little more than a willingness to exercise a bit of patience.

The results can be astounding, especially in the varieties which may be taken both on the Pacific Ocean side of the peninsula and in the Sea of Cortez.

Beginning on the northern Pacific side of the pensinsula, here is what you might expect to find, with more exact locations noted in the map text and on the maps. We have also printed a more exact guide to all of Baja's fishing in the book, **Angler's Guide to Baja California**. (see back of book for ordering information.)

*Tijuana to Abreojos...*The inshore species of rock and surf fish found around Southern California (perch, croaker, corbina, opaleye, etc.) are generally more plentiful in Baja than in the States. Surf rigs with clams or mussels usually do the job. Offshore fishing boats from San Diego and Ensenada, plus scattered skiff operations, offer vayring degrees of comfort while garnering catches of yellowtail, white seabass, rock cod, giant (or black) sea bass and bonito. Unless you depart from San Diego or Ensenada, plan to use your own jigs and feathers — plus whatever dead bait *(carnada)* your guide may have. With the help of local fishermen, the bays *(esteros)* at San Quintín, Manuela, La Bocana and El Coyote produce all manner of sport, either from shore or small boat.

*Abreojos through Bahia Magdalena and Puerto Chale...*The many lagoons and warmer waters of this bring about a mixing of the northern species with those that thrive in a more tropical habitat. Croakers and corbina are joined by the triggerfish, corvinas, snook and others that take clams, cut bait and lures on many of the beaches and in the lagoons.

The Magdalena complex of bays has hardly been touched by the sport angler; over 150 miles of inland waterway and hundreds of baylets and estuaries have yet to be thoroughly tested. Resident and migrating populations of waterfowl make this region one of great interest to the naturalist. A fall or winter trip to this area produces a potpourri of fishing, whale watching, birding, exploring and clamming.

Except for a few private boaters with appropriate equipment, the only organized access to offshore waters at the present comes from the dozen or so long-range San Diego-based sportfishing boats. (See list on Page 145) The area around the mouth of Bahía Magdalena and numerous offshore reefs yield good catches of the same fish taken to the north, plus yellowfin tuna, wahoo, dorado (dolphinfish) and billfish. Inside, small boats are best suited for the numerous mangrove channels and flats of this huge inland waterway. Here look for black snook *(robalo)*, halibut, varieties of corvina, cabrilla, grouper and a number of jacks.

*Below Magdalena to Cabo San Lucas...*The many sandy beaches and pounding waves throughout most of this distance hold many of the species also found in the lower portions of the gulf. Lures cast past the surf line could connect with roosterfish, toro (jack cravalle), pompano or any of dozens of other roving varieties. Baits are also productive for a number of species.

Here too, the San Diego boats provide the main offshore fishing access, due to so few good anchorages or launching areas. Minimal coverage of offshore reefs from pangas, though, can be arranged at Punta Lobos just west of Todos Santos. Fish taken are the same as noted in the Madgalena region.

Many species caught in the shallows will be the immature versions of the larger ones found in deeper water. Occasionally, however, a 50-pound roosterfish or a 20-pound toro will come almost onto the beach to grab your lure.

*Cabo San Lucas to La Paz...*Here the true character of the storied Sea of Cortez begins to unfold — calm seas and sheltered coves afford bases of operation for the many fishing fleets of the Baja resorts. The bays, islands, reefs and channels are within range of the visiting angler. Here visitors have the choice, almost any time of year, of fishing for a marlin, sailfish, wahoo, dolphinfish, tuna, roosterfish, amberjack, pargo or yellowtail. There are also sierra, barilette, pompano, cabrilla, bonito, corvina, shark and hundreds of other species that join their larger cousins in accommodating the angler, whether he walks the surfline or uses a boat. It is rare when some type of fish cannot be taken by any sportfisherman somewhere along this section of Baja.

*La Paz to the Midriff Islands...*The smorgasbord continues — although the migrations of the greater fish bring a more seasonal aspect to fishing. These regions are visited by schools of dorado, tuna and some billfish during the summer months (wahoo are rarely found this far north), then as summer wanes, are replaced by ravaging schools of yellowtail and some sierra mackerel. The cabrilla, pargo and grouper, often neglected during the summer, also move in to fill the void. Many of the inshore species are on a continual rampage, and the trick is to locate where they are at any particular time.

Bays and shallow reefs around the islands and along the coast are places of fascination for anyone with a love of the water and an interest in its inhabitants. Months could be spent exploring Bahía Concepción alone. The narrow entrances to bays such as Puerto Escondido and the lagoon at the south end of Isla San José contain enough varieties of brightly colored fish to stock a major metropolitan aquarium.

The region north of La Paz tosses in a teaser which frustated avid anglers for years. The late Ray Cannon wrote that the brackish waters of the Río Santa Rosalía at Mulegé contained black snook *(robalo)* that would break all existing fishing records for that species. They were most often taken by the local residents by spearing, but they eluded all but the most astute angler by either not biting or taking off for the mangrove roots as soon as they felt the hook. Though small robalos are still caught occasionally, there is no evidence that any record-size black snook remain.

*The Midriff...*Its narrow width, plus the numerous islands between the Mexican mainland on one side and Baja on the other, generates great surges of tidal movement, creating a unique environment. Cool waters from the deep subsurface canyons mix with oxygen-rich, warm surface waters, causing a population explosion of microscopic plankton. This is devoured by the tiny fish, who are in turn eaten by their larger neighbors. At times, great hordes of birds and fish, and small groups of anglers, arrive at the same place at the same time. It is difficult to maintain your perspective when witnessing such an event...you are torn between getting away for fear of being overwhelmed, or wading in and filling the boat with limitless numbers of frenzied fish.

Yellowtail, particularly, consider the Midriff their domain. Summer residents of this region, their migrating schools sometimes extend for several miles. Here too, are found a large portion of the gulf's population of white seabass. Cabrilla, grouper and giant (black) sea bass proliferate in the cooler water and abundant food supplies of the Cortez Midriff. The region also abounds with sea lions and several pods of finback whales call the Midriff home. These plankton-eating baleen whales have forsaken their normal migrations into Arctic seas for the rich bounty of krill and small forage fish found here.

*Above Midriff to Rio Colorado...*Once again the sea warms up, heated by its shallowness and the blistering heat of the desert. The higher temperatures (into the 90's during the summer) acts as a barrier for some species and a playground for others. Sharks and corvina thrive, but many other species retreat into the cooler waters of the Midriff. The upper gulf offers seasonal fishing for white seabass (winter and spring), sierra (fall and spring) and yellowtail (spring and summer south of Puertecitos).

Today, the visitor to San Felipe will rarely see the once abundant totuava. Long the main attraction of the northern Gulf, the loss of suitable spawning areas and overharvesting by commercial netters has reduced this giant (to 250 pounds) cousin of the white seabass to the brink of extinction.

TACKLE

Any size of rod, reel and line you might take will be right for some of the fishing to be had, wrong for the rest. It doesn't make sense to try for the big ones with a 4-pound test outfit, unless you are an expert and willing to lose a lot of fish. But that same trout-type tackle will provide great sport around the rocks, using small lures or tiny pieces of bait.

A good versatile rod/reel combination would be a 6 1/2 to 7-foot rod capable of casting 4 to 6 ounces of weight, and either a conventional or spinning reel with several several extra spools loaded with 15 to 30-pound test line. This will handle any but the roughest of customers. A rig balanced for 8 to 12-pound line will provide even more sport for the experienced angler.

Should you plan to go billfishing, it is not necessary to take heavy marlin tackle with you as it is standard equipment on most resort boats. The boat gear is much better than it was in times past, but if you are a serious billfisherman, you'll want to bring your own outfits, with fresh line and a smooth-working drag.

LURES

With few exceptions, live bait is hard to come by in Baja, thus lures play a big part in fishing Baja waters. Clams, shrimp and chunks of fish do well as attractors for some species, but often the action is found by casting or trolling the artificial lure.

Today the marketplace is filled with lures specifically designed, on paper at least, to take any kind of fish. It is not to say they will not, but we have only so much space and money to dedicate toward lures, so here are some basics.

Trolling jigs such as albacore feathers, in whites, yellows and greens are effective for yellowtail, cabrilla, tuna, etc. when trolled over rocky structures and in the offshore migration routes. Sometimes, it pays to string 2 or 3 feathers together on one leader, providing a longer target for the attacking fish.

A most effective family of jigs are those made out of a variety of metals with a shape similar to that of a candy bar. Flat on one side with curved top and tapered sides, they do a good job of simulating the action of live bait. Although they are sometimes trolled, a fast retrieve near the surface or angled up from a greater depth will often give you the best results. For some species, a heavy jig bounced, or "yo-yo'd", near the bottom will prove irresistible. Names of typical proven jigs of this type include Seastrike, Salas, Tady and Yo-ho-ho, with many similar styles with lesser names also in the stores.

A third class of effective lures are those more closely resembling the shape and color pattern of a natural fish. These types often prove deadly when no others will work. While their light weight makes casting difficult, it does not affect their ability to be trolled. Manufacturers such as Rapala, Rebel and Bagley make fine lures for Baja fishing. Silver and blue, dayglow pink and mackerel patterns are usually the most consistent producers. What size is best? From the jointed 4-inchers to the 9-inch deep-running magnums — they will all take their share. But remember: smaller lures usually have weaker hooks and you may wish to consider putting on new ones.

Spoon-shaped wobbling lures are another class to be included. Such product names as Krocodile, Tady, Castmaster and Hotshot have shown themselves as effective. Slow to moderate retrieval speeds often better suit the mood of the fish..

The light tackle buff who enjoys being on the beach at first light will find many places where he can cast small spinners into all manner of fish as they feed on small baitfish next to shore. Later in the day, sporadic action may be found on the tidal changes around the mouths of the *esteros* and rocky points — wherever the current movement stirs up the morsels of food that triggers the "eat and be eaten" cycle. Small lures such as the Roostertail and Abu Reflexe, and their larger 3/4 to 1 ounce versions, will produce lots of action. Copper, gold and silver spinners too, work well, especially if the trailing streamers are white or yellow.

Although there are a few tackle stores in major fishing centers, they are limited in selection, so it is still advisable to have an extra supply of line, lures, sinkers, hooks, etc.

Other items that are wise to include are hooks with wire leaders and a few short wire leaders for use with jigs. There are lots of "toothy" fish in the Cortez ready to slash even the heaviest monofilament.

You are likely to come up with many types of fish that you have never seen before, plus the more familiar species. Following are some fish that might be taken or seen. Following that are several pages of how to eat them, plus a number of Baja critters. For more complete books on the subjects, see the list in the back of the book.

FOOD FOR THOUGHT

The Sea of Cortez abounds with the fixin's for a wide variety of fine meals. From the highly-prized *dorado, cabrilla* and grouper to the succulent chocolate clam, they await only a bit of effort on our part.

TRIGGERFISH

The finescale trigger fish is easily caught almost anywhere in the Cortez, shallow or deep. If there are rocks there are usually triggers. The take both lures and bait (use wire leaders as their teeth are sharp) and will put up a stiff fight. Their armor-like hide can easily dull a knife (tip: puncture the skin with knifepoint and then cut from inside), once the fillet is removed, it is great when fried or steamed.

Fried Triggerfish: Brush meat with soy sauce and let stand for about 1/2 hour. Pat dry, dredge in seasoned flour and fry quickly.

Steamed Triggerfish: When done this way the meat takes on a crab or lobster-like flavor. Delicious with a seafood cocktail sauce. Simmer fillets in or over water containing boiling spices (allspice, peppercorn, several dry chiles, bayleaf and the rinds of one or two limes). Do not overcook. When cool, break into bite-sized pieces and add to sauce. Get ready for the stampede.

SEAFOOD COCKTAIL SAUCE

1/2 cup chili sauce
4 tbsp lime juice
1 tbsp horseradish
Tabasco sauce to taste
1/2 tsp celery salt
2 tbsp onion, finely chopped

Salt and pepper to taste. Blend all ingredients and chill. Serves 4-6.

BAJA MARINE MARINADE

This marinade works like a charm on bonito, yellowtail, sierra and many other species where the fish can be quarter-filleted and the dark meat removed.

    2 lbs fish fillets
    1 cup Italian dressing
    juice of 6-8 limes (or 2-3 lemons)
    1/2 cup dry white wine
    1/2 to 1 onion, thinly sliced
    parsley or *cilantro* to taste

Marinate fillets in mixture and store in cool place for 1-3 hrs, turrning occasionally. Lay directly on grill over hot coals. Turn once when lightly browned. Cage-like hamburger or hot dog grills work well here. We have done hundreds of pounds of fish in this manner without a complaint.

USE THAT BARBEQUE

In addition to fixing fish, a bed of hot coals will do wonders for clams, lobster and shrimp.

Lobsters, when available, are delicious when basted with lime juice and garlic butter and sprinkled with paprika. Split the tails and start with shell side up, turning once.

Both coasts of Baja offer a number of species of clams or cockles (2-3 inches in diameter) that, after being allowed to cleanse themselves in sea water for several hours, are ready to be put directly on the grill. Just as they open or start to drip juices, remove and serve with a hot sauce or garlic butter and lime.

Shrimp may be skewered, brushed with a small amount of butter or bacon grease and lime juice, then cooked until barely done. Scallops, too, respond well to this treatment.

SAN QUINTÍN STEW

This was invented out of necessity one evening while camped on a clam beach west of San Quintín. Just before sunset a small group set up their last camp before heading home. They had a few miscellaneous canned goods left so Carlton Bishop and I tossed in what we had, as did two Japenese anglers who appeared a few moments later. To all the cans of stuff we added the better part of a bucket of pismo clams. Though the combination might appear odd, the results were dynamite.

    2 cans each potatoes and tomatoes
    1 large can pork and beans
    1 can each creamed corn, regular corn, kidney beans
    2 onions chopped
    1 large can condensed milk
    2 dozen pismo clams, more or less, cleaned and cut into bite-sized
        pieces. (Put round, reddish muscles or "buttons" aside.)
    salt and pepper to taste

Saute onions in a little oil. Open all cans and put everything but clams into a big pot. Cook until mixture thickens. Add clam pieces and bring back to a simmer. Remove from heat and serve. It fed four campers, the four fishermen (Bishop, Miller and the two Japanese), a young couple who were lost and showed up as we started to eat, and a family of three appeared as we finished. San Quintín Stew has been our camp dinner a number of times since.

PISMO CLAM "BUTTONS"

Slice the "buttons" crosswise and cover with lime juice. Add a little finely chopped *cilantro* and a sparing amount of very thinly sliced serrano chile. Marinate 1-2 hours in a cool place. Just before serving, add a teaspoon of soya sauce and stir. Drain and serve on crackers. Great!!

COOKING WITHOUT HEAT

A way to beat the energy shortage is to get the *cebiche* habit. *Cebiche,* or *seviche,* is a dish consisting of a variety of mild flavored fish or shellfish marinated in mixtures of lime juice, tomatoes, onions and chiles. It requires no heat, as the limes "cook" the seafood sufficiently. In fact, it is best refrigerated before serving.

    1 pound of sierra (or similar fish) fillets
    Juice of about a dozen limes
    (or enough to almost cover)
    2 medium tomatoes
    1 or 2 pickled jalapeno chiles
    1 small onion, thinly sliced
    1/4 to 1/2 tsp oregano
    chopped *cilantro* to taste
    (parsley is also good)
    Pepper to taste

Cut the fish into small pieces, add lime juice and refrigerate for several hours, or until fish loses transparent look. Stir occasionally. Peel and chop tomatoes, removing seeds. Finely chop chiles after removing seeds. Add onion, oregano and cilantro. Pour off excess lime juice and combine all ingredients with semi-drained fish. Let stand for a bit longer if you can. It is great on crackers or chips. Add avocado if you have it. You can substitute shellfish, such as shrimp (peeled and deveined), scallops and lobster for the fish if you choose.

EASY SHRIMP

    2 1/4 pounds (1 kilo) medium shrimp
    1/4 lb butter or margarine (or 1/2 cup of cooking oil)
    2+ cloves garlic or 1/4 tsp garlic powder

Wash and drain shrimp well, leaving shells on. Heat oil and garlic in frying pan. Add shrimp and cook quickly until they turn pinkish (1-3 min.). Remove from oil, drain and serve hot. Let guest remove shells and put in "bone dish". Messy, but great eating. Have plenty of paper towels handy.

SCALLOPS IN WINE

    1 lb. scallops (1/2 kilo)
    1/4 cup dry white wine
    1/2 cube butter
    garlic to taste
    1/4 cup grated parmesan cheese

Marinate scallops in wine 1-2 hours. Melt butter in frying pan, add garlic, then scallop-wine mixture. Simmer gently about 4 minutes. Sprinkle with parmesan cheese. Serve hot with bolillo to sop up juice. Great as a main dish or hors d'oeuvres.

COCKTAIL TIME

For many regular visitors to Baja, a cocktail made from *tequila,* the beverage synonymous with Mexico, is the only way to start the evening.

Made from the fermented and distilled juices of the heart of the *maguey* cactus, this fiery liquid is usually served in one of the following ways:

STRAIGHT

This can be rather hazardous, and is best left to the old hands who have measured well their capacity, but if you gotta try, here is the traditional way.

Moisten the skin on the back of your hand between the thumb and forefinger. Sprinkle salt on the area. Holding a wedge of lime with the "salted" thumb and forefinger and the jigger in the other hand, lick the salt, down the tequila and suck the lime. Then take a deep breath — you may need it.

WITH SANGRITA

This method too is popular, and devastating if not careful. Sangrita is a highly-spiced concoction of orange juice blended with lime, a little grenadine and enough Tabasco sauce to make it a bit too hot for comfort. Some also add onion juice, though we usually leave it out. Stick it in the refrigerator, it will keep for several weeks. Use as a chaser for the *tequila* — or is it the *tequila* as a chaser for the *sangrita?* It's not too important with this one.

BAJA MARY

A variation on the Bloody Mary introduced to Baja resorts by Elmar Baxter over 25 years ago, this is a much more benign libation. Lime and salt the rim of a tall glass, add a jigger or two of tequila and fill with tomato juice or your favorite Bloody Mary mix. Squeeze in a section of lime, season with salt, pepper, Worchestershire and Tabasco. Ole!

BAJA LOVE POTION

The liqueur, *damiana,* is flavored with the leaves of a shrub that grows only in Baja deserts. The Indians believed that the leaves of the *damiana* plant contained a powerful aphrodisiac, and many swore by its powers. So too did the bottlers of diamana-flavored liqueurs, until the Mexican government made them change the claims, but some labels still allude to its powers. We can, however, vouch for the fact that it makes an excellent Baja Margarita.

BAJA MARGARITA

Perhaps the classic form of the world-famous Margarita is made by the resorts in the southern portion of the Peninsula. The difference is that Baja-produced Damiana liqueur is substituted for the usual Cointreau or Triple Sec. Like Tequila, Damaina is derived from a plant native to Mexico. For a variation unique to Baja mix together two parts lime, three parts Damiana and six parts tequila. Add lots of ice and blend well. If a little frost forms on the glass, it's perfect.

A1

RESORT ROUNDUP

Hotel rooms between the border cities of Tijuana and Ensenada and the main touristic destinations to the south — Loreto, La Paz, the East Cape and Los Cabo — though not plentiful, are adequate for all but the most crowded holiday times. Accommodations range from modest to comfortable. It is rarely necessary to have reservations as many Baja visitors travel by camper, trailer or motorhome, and a hotel room is often only for that occasional time when a thorough "sprucing-up" is in order.

Telephones now reach almost all populated portions of central Baja except Guerrero Negro. Where phones are lacking, sometimes govenment radio stations can relay emergency messages.

In all of the 400-mile mid-Baja wilderness — between San Quintín and Mulegé — we count little more than 200 rooms. Most are in the so-called "3-star" category, making them adequate for overnighting, but providing little in the way of amenities, other than occasional meals. Trailer accommodations are marginal at best. If you were to drive from sunup to sunset, you could barely cross those 400 miles in daylight, so plan an overnight stop somewhere along the way.

Another great help to the traveler is the fact that the main roads of Baja are patroled during the day by Mexico's famed Green Angels (see page 19). Bilingual, they are equipped to do many minor repairs on the spot, and put you back on the road. Stories of the assistance they have rendered are part of the legends of Baja.

Try to plan your trip so you will be checked into a room or camped well before dark. It is risky to drive at night in Baja as wideroaming livestock, plus busses and trucks on narrow highways all combine to present many hazards.

Once on the Sea of Cortez below Santa Rosalía, at Mulegé, accommodations are easier to find.

HOTELS...

TIJUANA
Hotel Fiesta Americana...430 rooms. Near racetrack. Deluxe, rest, etc. Box BC, Chula Vista, CA 92012. (800) 223-2332.
Hotel Paraiso-Radisson...200 rooms. Formerly the El Presidente. Near racetrack. Air cond., TV, pool, jacuzzi, sauna, etc. Rest, bar. Box 1588, San Ysidro, CA 92073. (800) 228-5050.
Hotel El Conuqistidor...110 rooms. Near racetrack. Air cond., TV, pool, disco, rest, bar. Box 4471, San Ysidro, CA 92073. Ph: 011 526 686-4801
Hotel Lucerna...130 rooms, air, suites, pool, rest, bar. Box 4471, San Ysidro, CA 92073. Ph: 011 526 686-4801.

TECATE
Rancho La Puerta...125 rooms. A famous health spa. Vegetarian food, air cond., pools, spas, ranch-like atmosphere. Weekly rates. At K136+ west of town. Res: 3085 Reynard Way, San Diego, CA 92103. (619) 294-8504.
El Dorado Motel...41 rooms. Air cond. with pool on Avenida Juarez 1100. Box 7, Tecate, B.C., Mexico. Ph: 011 526 654-1102

MEXICALI
Hotel Calafia...170 rooms. Several miles SE of center of town. Air cond., pool, TV, phones, rest. Calzada Justo Serra 1495, Mexicali, B.C., Mexico. Ph. 011 526 568-3311 (dir), (800) 238-8000 in CA, (213) 462-6391 elsewhere.
Hotel Lucerna...200 rooms. Air cond, two pools, rest, bar. Blvd. Benito Juarez 2151. Box 2300, Calexico, CA 92231, Ph. 011 526 564-1000.
Holiday Inn...125 rooms. Air cond., pool, rest, bar. P.O. Box 5497, Calexico, CA 92231. 011 526 568-1300 (dir), or (800) 238-8000.
Campo Rio Hardy...10 rooms. Boat ramp, fishing, hunting. Cafe and store. Box 43, Calexico, CA 92231.

SAN FELIPE
El Capitan Motel...39 rooms. Air cond., pool, hot showers, inexpensive. Box 1916, Calexico, CA 92231. Ph. 011 526 577-1303
Motel Villa del Mar...40 rooms. Air cond., pool, rest. Mar Baltico, San Felipe, B.C., Mexico. Ph. 011 526 577-13-33.
Hotel Castel San Felipe...120 rooms. Modern hotel on water. Air cond., rest, bar, pool, disco. Ph. 011 526 577-12-80 (dir). Res. 664 Broadway, #G, Chula Vista, CA 92010. (800) 336-5454 in CA, (619) 422-6900 elsewhere.
Hotel Riviera...44 rooms. Air cond., pool, rest, bar. Box 102, San Felipe, B.C., Mexico. Ph. 011 526 577-11-86.
El Cortez Motel...40 rooms on beach. Air cond., pool, rest. Box 1227, Calexico, CA 92231. Ph. 011 526 577-10-55.

ROSARITO BEACH
Quinta del Mar Hotel...71 rooms. Pool, rest, bar, tennis. Box 4243, San Ysidro, CA 92073. Ph: 011 526 612-1300.
Rosarito Beach Hotel...73 rooms. Rest, bar, two pools, tennis. Box 145, San Ysidro, CA 92073. Ph. 011 526 612-1106.

ENSENADA
Casa del Sol...40 rooms, A Best Western Hotel. Center of town. TV, pool, rest, phones. Box 557, Ensenada, B.C., Mexico. Ph: 011 526 678-1570 (dir), or (800) 334-7234.
Cortez Motor Hotel...80 rooms. Best Western Hotel. Pool, phones, TV, rest, bar. Box 396, Ensenada, B.C., Mexico. Ph: 011 526 678-2307 (dir), or (800) 334-7234.
Ensenada TraveLodge...41 rooms. Pool, color TV. Rest, Bar. Ave Bancarte 130, Ensenada, B.C. Mexico. Ph: 011 526 678-1601 (dir), (800)255-3050 elsewhere.
San Nicolás Hotel...120 rooms. Pool, rest, bar, disco. Box 19, Ensenada, B.C. Mexico. Ph: 011 526 676-1901 (dir), or (800) 532-3737 in CA, (800) 854-2900 elsewhere.
El Cid Motor Hotel...36 rooms. Pool, air, rest. Box 1431, Ensenada, B.C., Mexico. Ph: 011 526 678-2401.
Hotel La Pinta...52 rooms. Pool, rest. 3838 N. Belt East, #280, Houston, TX 77032. (800) 472-2427
Villa Marina...Older well-kept motel in center of town. Reasonably priced. P.O. Box 28, Ensenada, B.C., Mexico. Ph: 011 526 678-3321.
Estero Beach Resort Hotel...87 rooms. 8 miles south of Ensenada and 2 miles west. Bayfront, boat ramp, rest. Write: Apartado Postal 86, Ensenada, B.C., Mexico. Ph: 011 526 679-1001.

COLONIA GUERRERO
Motel Sanchez...24 rooms. at K173. Small, clean, inexpensive, hot showers.

SAN PEDRO MARTIR MTNS.
Mike's Sky Rancho...American Plan, camping, pool, hiking, hunting. Popular Off-road destination. Box 5376, San Ysidro, CA 92073. Ph: 011 526 685-4995

SAN QUINTÍN
Motel Chavez...12 rooms. Near K191. Limited space. Clean, hot showers.
Molino Viejo...12 rooms. Some w/kitchens, spotless, rustic. Hot showers. Interesting hosts. Box 90, Valle de San Quintín, B.C., Mexico.
Cielito Lindo Motel...24 rooms. Rest, bar, trailer park with limited facilities. Write: Santa María, Valle de San Quintín, B.C. Mexico.
Hotel La Pinta San Quintín...60 rooms. Rest, and bar, on beach. Box 179, San

Quintín, B.C., Mexico. Res: 3838 N. Belt East, #280, Houston, TX 77032. (800) 472-2427

SANTA INES
Hotel La Pinta Catavina...28 rooms. Pool, rest, bar. Res: 3838 N. Belt East, #280, Houston, TX 77032. (800) 472-2427
Rancho Santa Ines...located just off highway 1/2 mi. south of hotel. Bunkhouse style accommodations, good food and friendly atmosphere.

BAHÍA DE LOS ÁNGELES
Casa Diaz...26 rooms. Fishing. Boats and boatramp. Write Antero Diaz, P.O. Box 579, Ensenada, B.C., Mexico.
Villa Vitta Motel...30 + rooms. Modern with air-conditioning, pool, jacuzzi, rest, bar. Fishing. Res. 2904 Pacific Hwy., San Diego, CA 92101. (619) 298-7704.

GUERRERO NEGRO
El Morro Motel...20 rooms. Formerly Baja Sur Motel. Clean, hot showers, inexpensive. Box 6, Guerrero Negro, B.C. Sur, Mexico.
Hotel La Pinta Guerrero Negro.. 28 rooms. Air cond., rest, bar. 3838 N. Belt East, #280, Houston, TX 77032. (800) 472-2427
Dunas Motel...30 rooms. One mile east of town. Adequate. Dom. Con., Guerrero Negro, B.C.S., Mexico.

SAN IGNACIO
Hotel La Pinta San Ignacio...28 rooms. Air cond., pool, rest, bar. 3838 N. Belt East, #280, Houston, TX 77032. (800) 472-2427.
La Posada Motel...6 modest rooms. Clean, cheap. Owner, Sr. Fischer takes groups into painted caves. La Posada, San Ignacio, B.C.Sur, Mexico.

SANTA ROSALÍA
Hotel El Morro...20 rooms. Air cond., cocktails and dining room. Box 76, Santa Rosalía, B.C.Sur, Mexico. Ph: 011 526 852-0414.
Hotel Francés...16 rooms. Air cond., rest., bar. Old, restored hotel — lots of memorabilia. 30 Avenida 11, Santa Rosalía, B.C. Sur, Mexico. Ph: 011 526 852-0829.

PUNTA CHIVATO
Hotel Punta Chivato...Air cond, rest, bar, pool, fishing, on bluff. Airstrip. Box 18, Mulege, B.C.Sur, Mexico. Ph: 011 526 852-0188.

MULEGÉ
Hotel Las Casitas...6 rooms. Small and clean, excellent rest., bar. In center of town. Madero 50, Mulege, B.C.Sur, Mexico. Ph: 011 526 853-0019.
Hotel Vista Hermosa...22 rooms. Air cond., pool rest, bar. On hill overlooking bay, town, etc. Res: 4440

Cattle Dr., Redding, CA 96003. (800) 538-8000 in CA, (916) 221-4430 elsewhere.
Hotel Serenidad...35 rooms. Air cond., rest, bar, fishing, airstrip (4100 ft.), Res: Box 9, Mulege, B.C.Sur, Mexico. Ph: 011 526 853-0111.
Hotel Terrazas...20 rooms. Air cond., Rest, bar' w/sattelite TV. Clean, in town. Dom. Con., Mulege, B.C.Sur, Mexico. Ph: 011 526 853-0019

LORETO
Hotel La Pinta...45 rooms. Air cond., rest, bar, pool, tennis, fishing. 1 mi. N town on beach. Box 28, Loreto, B.C.Sur, Mexico. Ph: 011 526 833-0025 (dir.). 3838 N. Belt East, Houston, TX 77032. (800) 472-2427
Motel Salvatierra...18 rooms. Small rooms, inexpensive, away from beach. Hot showers.
Hotel Oasis...33 rooms. Amer. Plan, air cond., rest, bar, pool, fishing. Box 17, Loreto, B.C.Sur, Mexico. Ph: 011 526 833-0112.
Mision Loreto...32 + rooms. Air cond., good rest, bar, pool, fishing. Box 49, Loreto, B.C.Sur, Mexico. Ph: 011 526 833-0048.
El Presidente Loreto...250 rooms. Air cond., 2 pools, tennis, rests, bar. 8 mi. S of town. Box 28, Loreto, B.C.Sur, Mexico. Ph. 011 526 833-0025 (dir.). 3838 N. Belt East, Houston, TX 77032. (800) 472-2427

CIUDAD CONSTITUCIÓN
Hotel Casino...36 rooms. Air cond., rest, bar. Avenida Guadalupe Victoria, Ciudad Constitucion, B.C.Sur, Mexico. Ph: 011 526 832-0004.
Hotel Maribel...39 rooms. Air cond., rest, bar. Avenida Guadelupe Victoria 156, Ciudad Constitucion, B.C.Sur, Mexico. Ph: 011 526 832-0155.

LA PAZ
Hotel Los Arcos...130 rooms. On Malecon, air cond., pool, phones, rest, bar. Box 112, La Paz, B.C.Sur, Mexico. Ph: 011 526 822-2792. Res: 4332 Katella Ave., Los Alamitos, CA 90720. (800) 352-2579 in CA, (800) 421-3772 elsewhere.
Cabañas Los Arcos...52 rooms. Air cond., pool, phones, TV. Box 112, La Paz, B.C.Sur, Mexico. Ph: 011 526 822-2744. Res: 4332 Katella Ave., Los Alamitos, CA 90720. (800) 352-2579 in CA, (800) 421-3772 elsewhere.
Hotel Palmira...120 rooms. Air cond., pool, rest, bar, tennis, and disco. Box 442, La Paz, B.C.Sur, Mexico. Ph: 011 526 822-4000. Res: 1717 N. Highland Ave., #512, Los Angeles, CA 90028. (800) 421-0767 in CA, (213) 462-6391.
La Posada...25 rooms. Next to Gran Baja. Air cond, pool, good rest, bar. Box 152, La Paz, B.C.Sur, Mexico. Ph: 011 526 822-0663

El Presidente La Paz...109 rooms. 3 mi. NE of town. Air cond, phones, pool, beach, rest, bar. 4 mi. NE of town. Ph: 011 526 822-6544 (dir). Res: 3838 N. Belt East, #280, Houston, TX 77032. (800) 472-2427

Gran Baja Hotel...250 rooms. The highrise 2 mi. west of downtown. Air cond., pool, tennis, phones, beach, rest, bar. Disco. Box 223, La Paz, B.C.Sur, Mexico. Ph: 011 526 822-0663 (dir). (800) 228-2828.

Hotel Gardenias...56 rooms. Air cond., pool, rest. Clean and very nice. Good parking for those towing boats and trailers. Box 197, La Paz, B.C.Sur, Mexico. Ph: 011 526 822-3088.

Hotel Perla...30+ rooms Air cond., phones, open-air rest. on Malecon. Box 640, La Paz, B.C.Sur, Mexico. Ph: 011 526 822-0777.

LOS PLANES

Hotel Las Arenas...40 rooms. Amer. plan. Fans (no air cond.), pool, tennis, beach, rest, bar, fishing, snorkeling. 10% serv. chg. Airstrip. Box 3766, Santa Fe Springs, CA 90670. (800) 352-4334 in CA, (800) 423-4785 elsewhere.

EAST CAPE

Punta Pescadero...25 rooms. 8 mi. N of Mexico 1 at Los Barriles. Fans, pool, tennis, beach, fireplaces, rest, bar, fishing, diving. 15% serv. chg. Airstrip. Box 362, La Paz, B.C.Sur, Mexico. No phone. Res: Box 1044, Los Altos, CA 94023. (415) 948-5505

Playa Hermosa...18 rooms, soon 26. Amer. plan. 0.9 mi. N of Los Barriles. Air cond., beach, rest, bar, fishing. Box 1827, Monterey, CA 93942. (800) 248-9900 in CA, (408) 375-2252

Palmas de Cortez...32 rooms. Amer. plan. 0.4 mi. off highway. Air cond., pool, tennis, beach, fishing, hunting, rest, bar. Box 1284, Canoga Park, CA 91304. (818) 887-7001

Rancho Buena Vista...50 rooms. Amer. plan. Air cond., pool, tennis, beach, fishing, hunting, rest, bar. 10% serv. chg. Airstrip. Box 673, Monrovia, CA 91016. (818) 303-1517.

Spa Buena Vista...40 rooms. Amer. plan. Air cond., pool, mineral baths, tennis, beach, fishing, hunting, rest, bar. Box 2573, Canoga Park, CA 91306. (818) 703-0930.

Punta Colorada...30 rooms. Amer. plan. 12.5 miles east of Hwy from Las Cuevas. Most air cond, large rooms, beach, fishing, snorkeling, rest., bar. Airstrip. Box 1284, Canoga Park, 91304. (818) 703-1002

SAN JOSE DEL CABO

El Presidente Los Cabos...250 rooms. On beach below town. Air cond., pools, tennis, fishing, golf nearby, water sports, rest, bar, disco. Ph: 011 526 842-0211 (dir). Res: 3838 North Belt East, #280,

Houston, TX 77032. (800) 472-2427

Hotel Castel Cabo...150 rooms. On beach. air cond., pool, tennis, golf nearby, fishing, rest, bar. Ph: 011 526 842-0155 local. Res: Box 8193, Chula Vista, CA 92012. (800) 336-5454 in CA, (619) 422-6900 elsewhere.

Hotel Calinda Aquamarina...90 rooms. On beach. Air cond., pool, golf nearby, fishing, rest, bar. Ph: 011 526 842-0155 local. Res: Box 3009, Silver Springs, MD 20901. (800) 228-5151

Hotel Palmilla...70 rooms. On bluff above beach. Some air cond., pool, beach, tennis, fishing, hunting, snorkeling, rest, bar. 15% service charge. Box 52, San Jose del Cabo, B.C.Sur, Mexico. Res: 4577 Viewridge Ave., San Diego, CA 92123. (800) 542-6082 in CA, (800) 854-2608 elsewhere.

CABO SAN LUCAS

Hotel Cabo San Lucas...70 rooms. At K14+ on Chileno Bay. Great view. Most air cond., pool, tennis, beach, diving, fishing, hunting, rest, bar. 26.5% service charge. Box 48088, Los Angeles, CA 90048. (800) 282-4809 in CA, (800) 421-0777 elsewhere.

Hotel Twin Dolphin...50 rooms. At K12+ overlooking ocean. Amer. plan, air cond., pool, tennis, beach, balconies, fishing, horses, rest., bar. 15% serv. chg. 1625 W. Olympic Blvd., #1005, Los Angeles, CA 90015. (213) 386-3940, or (800) 421-8925 outside CA.

Hotel Cabo Baja...125 rooms. At K6 on bluff. Air cond., pools, balconies, beach, fishing, rest, bar. 10% serv. chg. Ph: 011 526 843-0044 (dir). Res: Box 3009, Silver Springs, MD 20901. (800) 228-5151.

Hacienda Beach Resort...114 rooms. Swimming beach. Some with air cond. Pool, swimming beach, tennis, scuba, fishing, hunting, horseback, water-sports, rest, bar. 26.5% serv. chg. Ph: 011 526 843-0122 (dir). Box 48872, Los Angeles, CA 90048. (800) 282-4809 in CA, (800) 421-0645 elsewhere.

Hotel Solmar...65 rooms, plus condo-type suites. On beach, Pacific side. Air cond., balconies, pool, fishing, beach, diving, rest, bar. 10% serv. chg. Ph: 011 526 843-0022 (dir). Box 383, Pacific Palisades, CA 90272. (213) 459-3336.

Hotel Finisterra...76 rooms. Perched on cliff overlooking Pacific. Beach 140 steps below. Pool, balconies, tennis, fishing, diving, rest, bar. 15% serv. chg. Box 1, Cabo San Lucas, B.C.Sur, Mexico. Ph: 011 526 843-0100 (dir). Res: 4332 Katella Ave., Los Alamitos, CA 90720. (800) 352-2579 in CA, (800) 421-3772 elsewhere.

Hotel Mar de Cortez...72 rooms. In town away from water. Air cond., pool, fishing, rest, bar. Ph: 011 526 843-0032 local. Res: Box 1827, Monterey, CA 93942. (800) 248-9900 in CA, (408) 375-4755.

TODOS SANTOS

Mision de Todos Santos...13 rooms. Rooms are an interesting jumble of shapes, sizes. Hot showers, inexpensive. Domicillo Conocedo, Todos Santos, B.C.Sur, Mexico.

Todos Santos Inn...5 rooms. Bed and breakfast. Very old building has been restored by American owner. Trips into sierras from here. 17 Calle Obregon, Todos Santos, B.C.Sur, Mexico.

TRAILER PARKS...

TIJUANA/ROSARITO

KOA Trailer Park...on hill overlooking ocean. Turn off at San Antonio del Mar toll road exit, K22. Clean, hookups. Box 2082, Tijuana, B.C., Mexico.
La Siesta Trailer Park...K35+ at S end of Rosarito, near ocean. Many permanent spaces, showers, toilets.
Popotla...at K33 Mexico 1. Mostly permanents, restaurant, beach. Full facilities.
La Salina...K72+Open camping. Lots of beach. Popular during summer. Showers, water.

ENSENADA AREA

Playa Saldamando...K94 above Ensenada. Perched on narrow piece of land above ocean. Cozy, beautiful view, showers, toilets. Good surf fishing.
San Miguel Village...K100 N of town. All facilities, restaurant. Box 55, El Sauzal, B.C. Mexico.
Granada Cove...K109 just before "Y" in road. Toilets, showers.
Campo Playa Ensenada RV Park...1 mi. S of downtown across street from beach. All hookups and facilities. Box 21, Ensenada, B.C. Mexico.
Rancho Todos Santos Trailer Park...just S of town. Toilets, showers, nice beach.
Estero Beach Trailer Park...at K15, 5 mi. S of town, follow paved road to bay. A nice resort, full facilities, good restaurant. Gift stores. Box 86, Ensenada, B.C. Mexico. (706) 676-6225
La Jolla Beach Camp...8 mi. W of Mexico 1 on road to Punta Banda. Some sites with full hookups. Toilets, showers, some hookups. Lots of residential homes here. Box 953, Ensenada, B.C. Mexico.
Campo Villarino...next to La Jolla Camp. About 100 sites, tents and trailers. Toilets, showers.

SAN FELIPE

Playa Bonita...1 mi. N of town. 40+ sites with hookups. Toilets, showers and restaurant.
Ruben's Trailer Park...N of downtown San Felipe on main street. 50 sites with hookups, showers, boat launch (of sorts), restaurant.
Playa de Laura Trailer Park...on beach in town. 61 sites with hookups.
Victor's El Cortez...next to El Cortez Motel. Hookups, toilets, showers, beach.

Club de Pesca...1 mi. S of town on beach. Many sites with hookups. Full facilities including laundry and store. Box 90, San Felipe, B.C., Mexico.
Mar del Sol RV Park...next to Castel San Felipe Hotel. Use of swimming pool at hotel included with camping. Full hookups, on beach. Hotel facilities available to guests. Res: 664 Broadway, #B, Chula Vista, CA 92010.
El Faro Beach Trailer Park.. out of town on road S. of airport. Lovely view but sometimes windy. Pool, bar, tennis. Full hookups. Box 107, San Felipe, B.C., Mexico.

SANTO TOMÁS

El Palomar Trailer Park...tree-shaded park with hookups, store, pool, toilets and showers. Box 595, Ensenada, B.C., Mexico

COLONIA GUERRERO

Posada don Diego...K172+ Baja Highway, just past bridge. Clean, with hookups on 50+ sites, water and electric only on 50. Toilets, showers, restaurant. Box 126, Colonia Guerrero, B.C. Mexico.
Don Pepe Trailer Park...K172+ Baja Highway. Smaller park with about 20 hookups. Toilets, showers, restaurant. Box 7, Colonia Guerrero, B.C., Mexico.

SAN QUINTÍN AREA

Cielito Lindo Trailer Park...at K10 take paved road west and follow signs. Showers (cold?), toilets, fronting wide beach.
Honey's RV Park...right at K16 toward El Pabellon Beach. Toilets, showers, water. Great for fishing, clamming.
El Socorro...toward ocean at K25. Toilets, showers. Quiet, off beaten track.

CATAVIÑA

Parque Nacionál Desierto...Next to La Pinta Hotel. Fenced, landscaped with desert plants.

BAHÍA DE LOS ÁNGELES

Guillermo's Trailer Park...on beach near launch ramps. toilets, showers, some hookups.
La Playa Trailer Park...adjacent to Villa Vitta Motel. Clean and well kept, hookups. Res: Jimsair, 2904 Pacific Highway, San Diego, CA 92101.
La Gringa Camp...6 mi. N of town. Most spots have been leased, but if owners not there the guard may allow you to camp for a small fee. No facilities, dry camping. Good for boaters, but watch the high tides.

VILLA JESUS MARÍA
Beach camping at Laguna Manuela, 6 mi. W of town is highly recommended. Good fishing, lots of beach. Sometimes windy.

GUERRERO NEGRO
Paralelo 28 Trailer Park...next to La Pinta Hotel, it probably won't be open.
Malarrimo Restaurant...overnight area behind restaurant. Toilets, showers, some hookups.

SAN IGNACIO
San Ignacio Trailer Park...On highway at junction with paved road to San Ignacio. 20 sites with hookups. Next to gas station. Several other informal parks are found on road into town. Outhouses, small palapas in some.

SAN LUCAS COVE
San Lucas Trailer Park...10 miles south of Santa Rosalia on San Lucas Cove. Facing on beautiful cove, fishing, shelling, some clamming, snorkeling. Box 131, Santa Rosalia, B.C.Sur, Mexico.

PUNTA CHIVATO
Camp Punta Chivato...at K156 take road east and north 14 mi. to area. One of the most beautiful spots in Baja. Clean outhouses, trash pick up, shower. Adjacent to hotel.

MULEGÉ AREA
All of the following are on Río Santa Rosalía, Mulegé. All cater to permanents, but most still have some day camping.
Jorge's Lado del Río; La Fortuna; Huerta Saucedo, Oasis Río Baja; Ponchos; and Villa María Isabel...last one has pool and excellent bakery.
Hotel Serenidád...small park next to hotel. Toilets, showers, restaurant/bar.
Playa Santispac...a playa publica on Bahía Concepción at K114+. Very popular with self-contained campers. Pit toilets, trash pick up, some palapas and two restaurants.
Posada Concepción...at K112 below Mulegé. Caters mostly to permanents.
Bahia El Coyote...K108. A playa publica. Limited facilities, but people love the place. Fine beach for swimming.
El Requesón...a playa publica at K92+. A personal favorite. Dry camping, few palapas, pit toilets.

LORETO AREA
Nopolo...playa publica 9 mi. S of town. Beach with few palapas.
Notri.. playa publica at 10 mi. No facilities.
Juncalito...at 14 mi. Grove of palms with palapas and trash cans.
Tripui RV Park...at Puerto Escondido near marina. Well landscaped, pool, restaurant, laundry, sports complex, etc. One of the best in Baja. Soon to be...an adjoining motel. Reservations advisable. Tripui RV Park, Loreto, B.C. Sur, Mexico. 011 526 833-0413.

CIUDAD CONSTITUCION
Campestre La Pila...2 mi. south of town and .5 mi. west. Toilets, showers and fine pool. No hot water, good summertime stop. Clean.

LA PAZ
Oasis Los Aripez RV Park...K15 in area known as El Centenario. On bay, long way from entrance. Hookups. Clean, friendly operators.
El Cardon Trailer Park...2.5 mi. W of town center. Long a popular spot. Pool, laundry facilities, well shaded. All hookups.
La Paz Trailer Park...before town adjacent to water. 30 sites with full hookups. Pool, clubhouse. Very well run. Box 482, La Paz, B.C.Sur, Mexico. 011 526 822-8787
Gran Baja Trailer Park...adjacent to Gran Baja Hotel and use of facilities. Some hookups, toilets, etc.

VENTANA AREA
There are a number of playas publicas in this area E of La Paz. Los Muertos along beach and on muelle; Punta Arena, just N of Hotel Las Arenas and near lighthouse; also around El Sargento.

EAST CAPE AREA
Verdugo's Trailer Park. Turnoff at K110 and go N. On bay, 23 sites with hookups. Toilets, restaurant and bar. poor launch ramp. Box 477, La Paz, B.C.Sur, Mexico.
Playa de Oro RV Park...just N of Hotel Palmas de Cortez. Toilets, showers, on beach. Iffy launch ramp. 3106 Capa Dr., Hacienda Hts., CA 91745.
Vista del Mar...About K108+ N of Rancho Buena Vista. Nice park, but most sites are permanent. Self-contained vehicles only when there is room. Another iffy ramp, toilets, showers and laundry.
La Capilla Trailer Park...K102+ signed dirt road W., then about 1 mi. Electric and water. Boat launching over reinforced sand! Beautiful location.

LOS CABOS AREA
Brisa del Mar Trailer Park...K30 just E of hotels on Highway 1. Good park with full facilities, pool, laundry, groceries, rest, bar, fishing. Box 45, Cabo San Lucas, B.C. Sur, Mexico.
Los Arcos Trailer Park...K6 behind restaurant. Good view. Limited spaces. Full hookups.
San Vicente Trailer Park...At K5. Over half is permanents, nice pool, laundry, showers, etc. Nice management. Box 20, Cabo San Lucas, B.C.Sur, Mexico. 011 526 843-0712.
Faro Viejo Trailer Park...Not on water. Up a dusty road from center of town of Cabo San Lucas. Clean with showers, laundry and excellent restaurant. Box 64, Cabo San Lucas, B.C.Sur, Mexico.

The fact that the Baja California peninsula extends nearly a thousand miles with only the one arterial highway has a tendancy to turn some people off because of having to return on the same road past what they see as the same scenery. They want something new. And there is a way to do just that — take one of the ferries connecting Baja with Mexico proper.

Once on the mainland you may head for the border, or turn south to experience a new and different part of Mexico. Though the ferries need improvements in such areas as cleanliness, food and accommodations, they do run on a regular basis, are safe, and can get you and your rig across the Cortez for a very reasonable cost (see page 26).

Once on the mainland there is the main coastal highway, Mexico 15, to take you to the border. In places it shows wear and tear from too many heavy truck and busses, but it will get you to Nogales, etc., past lots of farms, more desert and a variety of touristic centers — Puerto Vallarta, Mazatlan, Los Mochis/Topolobampo, Guaymas and Kino. Among them there is enough resort living, fishing, sunning, etc., to keep one around for several extra days, weeks or months.

And there is more for those willing to take a few short sidetrips off Mexico 15. Just south of Mazatlan, on the Mazatlan-Durango highway, are several historic villages, Concordia, a furniture and pottery center, and the 450 year-old silver mining area of Copala. Both within an hour's drive of Mazatlan, they are well worth a visit. You may even stay in Copala at a funky little hotel overlooking the plaza for about $12. If you wanted to stay a month (October '86), a double room was under $200!

Another mining center, Alamos, is located 35 miles east of Navajoa. The early colonial Spanish architechure here is beautifully preserved. Several hotels and a trailer park give you an opportunity to take in the sights and sounds of this quiet and historic little village. At Los Mochis you have a number of alternatives. If you wish to hunt (see page 15), the area has the finest whitewing dove shooting in the world. Considered a pest by the farmers, you do them a favor by filling out the very generous limits. Ducks too are plentiful.

At Mochis you can put your rig aboard a flat car and take one of the world's most spectacular railroad journeys, up the famous Copper Canyon to the mountain plateaus in the state of Durango.

Increased farming in the coastal plains of Sonora, Sinaloa and Nyarit has resulted in the building of numbers of large storage reservoirs, which in turn have become top largemouth bass fisheries. Today, bass fishermen travel thousands of miles to fish in lakes such as Fuerte, Dominguez, Mocuzuri and Baccarác. And the word is just getting out.

We think it appropriate here to pass on a word of warning...many of the smaller, newly-paved, or graded roads leading east from the region's main tourist corridor into the mountains, have little in the way of services, and some come rather close to known drug areas. We suggest you check with tourism officials or resort operators before going much beyond what is outlined above.

LAUNCHING YOUR BOAT IN BAJA

To begin with, there are curently only nine maintained concrete boat launching ramps in the Baja peninsula — Ensenada, Bahia de Los Angeles (2), Mulege (2), Puerto Escondido, La Paz, Cabo San Lucas and San Carlos on Magdalena Bay. The rest depend on what nature might provide for surface, protection and maintenance. Obviously the size and weight of your boat, and the traction capability of the towing vehicle will make a lot of difference. Let's take a few typical boat combinations and outline localities where you might launch and retrieve a boat.

CARTOPPERS AND INFLATABLES

If you own one of these the Sea of Cortez, the esteros, bays and sheltered coves of the Pacific side provide innumerable opportunities. Other than cliffs, sandhills, heavy swells and heart conditions, little should stand in your way of getting on the water wherever you wish. Just keep in mind tide conditions and prevailing winds, plus the fact that the boat has to return up the same slope it came down. For most, the small craft are the best way to go.

TRAILERED BOATS TO 1,000 POUNDS

There are still many beaches where the surface conditions allow you to either hand launch or drive right in. Check out the surface conditions carefully. 4-Wheel Drive and wide flotation tires may extend your capabilities, as will many friends, winches, ropes, a wheel for the tongue, etc. The final judgement must be yours.

Some of the areas where we've launched, helped launch, or seen launchings...

San Felipe's ramps are nearly useless over the long haul due to sanding in, or sand being washed out, plus the tidal extremes. Best bet here is to be patient and wait for the right tide, wind, etc.

Below Ensenada at La Jolla Camp and Villarinos...a northwest facing beach, there is little surf except during a stiff onshore breeze.

San Quintín's Molino Viejo Motel has a sand/gravel/clay spot that can launch boats to 24 feet. Located 4-5 miles west of the highway it is the gateway to the San Martin area and fine late summer and fall fishing.

Bahía de Los Ángeles has two ramps to accommodate most any boat. One is at Casa Diaz's, the other adjacent to Villa Vitta and Guillermo's.

Laguna Manuela, 5 miles SW of Villa Jesus María is marginal, while Estero Coyote, on the road to Abreojos, offers a good sand base.

Punta Chivato, above Mulegé has a cement ramp next to the hotel. Mulegé's ramp is just above the Hotel Serenidád. Several other small private ones are in the river. Beach launches are at Santispac (shallow), and Posada Concepción (also shallow).

At Puerto Escondido near Loreto the new double wide ramp is a beauty and conveniently located near the Tripui RV Park.

The La Paz ramp is at Mac and Mary Shroyer's new marina. They also have some limited storage space. Write them at Box 290, La Paz, B.C.Sur, Mexico.

The East Cape ramps, including La Capilla Trailer Park, are continually under stress from wave action and we see none as being reliable.

Lastly, the Cabo San Lucas Harbor launching ramp is a fine one, and the San Carlos ramp at Magdelena Bay is adequate. And that's about it.

Mexican Consulates (a partial list)

El Paso, TX 79901 (915/533-3644)
910 E. San Antonio Ave.

Los Angeles, CA 90012 (213/624-3261)
125 Paseo de La Plaza

San Francisco, CA 94102 (415/392-2897)
870 Market St., Suite 528

Seattle, WA 98101 (206/682-3634)
1425 Fourth Ave. #612

Washington, D.C. 20009 (202/234-6000)
2829 16th Street, NW.

Montreal, Que Can. (514/288-2502)
3450 Drummond Ave.

Vancouver, B. C., Can. (604/684-3747)
310-625 Howe St. Suite 502

Mexican National Tourist Council Offices

Los Angeles, CA 90067 (213/203-8151)
10100 Santa Monica Blvd. Suite 224

Chicago, IL 60601 (312/565-2785)
233 N. Michigan Ave., Suite 1413

Houston, TX 77008 (713/880-5153)
2707 N. Loop West, Suite #450

New York, NY 10022 (212/755-7212)
405 Park Ave. #1002

Montreal, Que. H3B 3M9, Can.
(514/871-1052)
One Place Ville Mar, #2409

Toronto, Ont M5H 3M7, Can.
(416/364-2455)
181 University Ave., Suite 1112

FIRST AID, BAJA STYLE
BE PREPARED, JUST IN CASE

SUN STROKE AND HEAT PROSTRATION...are things to guard against in the sunny climes of Baja California. High temperatures or long exposure to the sun along with too little fluids bring these problems on. Symptoms are flushes and clammy skin, and a rapid, weak pulse. Nausea, headache, cramps and blurred vision often accompany the condition.

Have the victim lie down in a cool shaded place with the head slightly lower than the rest of the body. Give small quantities of fluids often. Any tight clothing should be loosened and the body sponged with cool water until the body temperature drops. Get to a doctor as soon as possible.

SNAKE AND SCORPION BITES...though not as dangerous as a rattlesnake, a scorpion bite can be very painful, and should be treated immediately.

A venomous snake bite or scorpion sting should be treated with a snake-bite kit. You may also apply a constricting bandage above the bite on the victims arm or leg and an ice pack placed on the bite is of great help. Have the victim move as little as possible until the swelling has stabilized. Keep the injured area below the level of the heart. Get to a doctor as soon as possible.

Scorpions may be found under rocks, wood and layers of leaves, etc. Tents, shoes, clothing and boxes can also be invaded overnight. Before you get going in the AM, make sure the little critters have not joined the group.

NOSEEUMS...also known as *jejenes* and *bobos,* these tiny guys (they can fly through a window screen) love to lay their eggs in your epidermis. A few hours later they begin to itch...and itch...and itch. They are common around mangroves and marshes — the Midriff Islands, Bahia Concepcion, Bahia Magdalena, etc. Best repellant we've found is Muskol, a 100% DEET product, but others swear by Avon's Skin So Soft!

JELLYFISH...have tiny syringelike devices on their long tentacles. If you get hit you will know it...a hot burning sensation. Rub the area well with beach sand, then apply meat tenderizer to the area. Lime juice, ammonia and even urine will also help relieve the pain.

MISSIONS...INTRODUCTION

SANTA MARIA 1823

The 1500's, known as "the century of discovery," was the period when Catholic missionaries fanned out into the New World, putting forth zealous efforts to convert its inhabitants to their "civilized" ways. At this time, the Spaniards had not only acquired most of the land, but they also represented the majority of church delegates sent to establish profitable missions throughout the New World.

Church activities on mainland Mexico kept the Padres busy well into the 17th Century, with only a few cursory attempts to establish a beachhead in Baja. Finally in 1696, the Jesuits, led by Padre Juan María Salvatierra made landfall at the mouth of a palm-lined arroyo. Thus began the arduous task of the building of Misión Nuestra Señora de Loreto, mother of the missions in Baja California.

The Jesuits had an exclusive mandate to convert the natives and to exploit the riches of the western lands for the benefit of the Spanish crown and, of course, the church. In Baja their efforts, and later the work of the Franciscans and the Dominicans, proved particularly unrewarding to their sponsors and disasterous to the inhabitants.

The five major groups of Indians — Diegueño and Cocopah in the north, Cochimi in the central portion, and the Guaycura and Perucué to the south — totaled an estimated 50,000 when the Jesuits established their first mission in Baja. By 1845, there were believed to be less than 6,000 left with the original blood lines.

Despite the difficulties, the mission system was the key to the opening of the Baja peninsula. Restoration of some of the missions — San Borja and south is being undertaken by the Mexican government (pgs. 163-170). In the north, a group of private citizens headed by the late Tom Robertson of San Miguel Village, tried unsuccessfully to raise private funds to restore several of the adobe missions north of Mision San Borja. Another mission, Santa María de Los Angeles, was also under consideration by the owner of the land upon which it stood, but the remoteness of the site has generated many obstacles. Nestled in a canyon east of the Santa Inés Ranch, Santa María would be one of the most interesting of the mission restorations, as the area around it has not changed since Father Victoriano Arnés first visited the site in 1767.

*Misión Santa Clara...*as the story goes, was erected about 1767 by a group of Jesuits who used the mission as a repository for the treasures they acquired in Baja. The mission was supposedly located near placer gold deposits in the Sierra Pintadas of the Vizcaino Desert. While there is considerable doubt that any such treasures actually existed we will continue the story — when the Jesuits were warned they were about to be dispossessed by the Franciscans, they secreted a vast hoard of gold, silver, pearls and other valuables for retrieval later. No records, however indicate that it is true, yet the story persists.

*Misión Santa Isabel...*is another of the "maybe" missions, but of the Dominican era, 1773-1885. Again, valuable vestments and other treasures were reportedly cached on its grounds. The story goes on to say that Santa Isabel was built along the upper Gulf coast region, but numerous observations of the area by foot, dune buggy, airplane and helicopter have failed to locate even one encouraging sign of its existence.

*Misión Descanso...*was established by the Dominicans in 1778. Nothing remains to indicate the exact site, but it is reported to have been located at the entrance into the narrow El Descanso valley just to the east of the highway near the Halfway House Resort on the free road from Tijuana to Ensenada. It is the nearest to the Border of the nine northern missions.

*Misión San Miguel Archangel...*under a deteriorating shelter located on the north side of the old Tijuana-Ensenada road 3.5 miles after turning under the toll road at La Mision, lie the remains of the mission's adobe walls. Founded by Father Luis Sales in 1787, this was the third site for this mission, the previous having been abandoned for lack of enough water and the desire to relocate close to a proposed road linking the Baja California missions with those in Alta California.

*Misión Guadalupe del Norte...*was the last mission to be founded in Baja California. In 1834, Father Felix Caballero established the mission to serve the Indians working in the fertile Guadalupe valley between Ensenada and Tecate. A revolt led by an Indian named Jatnil in 1840 caused the missionaries to flee. Later the site became part of a large rancho. The town of Guadalupe is 25 miles north of Ensenada, one mile west of the highway. An ancient stone foundation near the southeast edge of town is believed by some to be the original site.

SAN JAVIER

Misión Santa Catarina de los Paipais ...was founded in 1797 by Father José Loriente to serve as the supply point for proposed settlements near the mouth of the Colorado River. This mission is located in the mountains five miles east of Heroes de La Independencia, which in turn is 57 miles from Ensenada via the Ensenada-San Felipe highway. Once again, harsh treatment of the Indians led to several uprisings. Deaths from diseases and desertions led to its collapse in 1840. There are stories of the Dominicans taking considerable gold from the surrounding canyons and some evidence of earlier workings were found during the gold rush of 1871. Today the area is the only remaining Paipai Indian tribal center.

Misión Santo Tomás de Aquino...1791 marked the date that Father José Loriente established the Mision Santo Tomás, starting with a small structure just up the arroyo from Puerto Santo Tomas. Several years later, he moved the mission inland to a spot that may still be seen off to the right 3.5 miles from the main highway on the dirt road to Puerto Santo Tomas. Only low mounds of adobe attest to the once-proud mission site. Seven years later in 1801, the final move was completed and the adobe ruins by the side of the road near the north end of town have been identified as the site. Here too are a few palm trees and a large grape vine, presumably planted by the padres. The Santo Tomás mission was one of the more prosperous of the Baja California missions, supporting about 1000 Indians, 1200 cattle and 2600 sheep during its heyday, plus lush vinyards which supplied altar wines for many missions throughout Mexico. Epidemics finally depleted the Indians and the mission slipped from sight in 1849.

Misión San Vicente Ferrér...begun in 1780 a short distance from the present-day town of San Vicente, it floundered almost immediately when attacked by roaming Yuma Indians, then was hit by a smallpox epidemic. The mission was reorganized a year later by Father Luís Sales. San Vicente served as the capital of *La Frontera* and housed the main garrison of troops in northern Baja for 16 years after the mission closed in 1833. Extensive adobe ruins may be found a few miles down the arroyo that crosses the highway just above town. The graveyard overlooking the north side of the stream is believed to contain graves from mission times.

LORETO

*Misión San Pedro Martír de Verona...*one of the least successful of the missions, it was built primarily as a base from which to graze cattle. It was established in a remote mile-high mountain valley deep in the Sierra. Extensive ruins of this mission, which lasted only 11 years, until 1806, can be found after a long horseback ride southeast of the Meling Ranch.

*Misión Santo Domingo...*a year after Misión El Rosario had been dedicated, it was decided that the distance between the new mission and San Vicente was too great to effectively convert the "heathens" living in the hills and along the beaches. Thus, in 1775, a site in an arroyo near what is now Colonia Guerrero was chosen for Santo Domingo. Finding water a problem, they picked up their belongings in 1782 and relocated several miles up the canyon, where an ample supply of water produced abundant crops over about 120 acres of fertile land. Due in part to a reported epidemic of syphillis, the population didn't keep pace with the crops, and as the supply of labor decreased the mission slowly died, with the last entry recorded in 1828. Stone foundations and crumbled adobe walls of the mission and a number of grave markers may still be seen by taking the side road to the east to the small farming community of Santo Domingo.

*Misión Nuestra Señora del Rosario...*like a number of the other missions established in Baja California, Rosario had several locations before settling two miles southwest of the center of today's El Rosario. Many Indians were converted, worked and died here from the time of its inception in 1774 until it was abandoned in 1832.

SAN FERNANDO

*Misión San Fernando de Velicata...*is the only monument, albeit a crumbling one, to the work of the Franciscans during their short tenure in Baja California. Established in 1769 by Father Junipero Serra before he moved on to San Diego in Alta California, it became an important mission, caring for about 1500 Indians. A tragic epidemic during the years of 1777-80 caused such a loss of workers that it finally wasted away by 1818. The mission is in an *arroyo* about three miles west of El Progresso.

Misión Santa María de Los Ángeles ...was founded in 1767 by the Jesuit Priest, Father Victoriano Arnés, only a year before the expulsion of the Jesuits from Baja Callifornia. The general terrain proved inhospitable for farming, in spite of adequate water, and the mission was abandoned by the Franciscans in favor of Misión San Fernando. The adobe walls of Misión Santa Mariá are still in relatively good condition, thanks in large part to its isolation and arid climate. It is located about 12 miles up the *arroyo* from Santa Inés.

*Misión Calamajué...*founded in 1766 by the Jesuit Fathers Victoriano Arnés and Juan José Diaz, who discovered — after completion of the mission buildings — that the water was so mineralized their crops would not grow. They left after only a few months. The faint remains of the foundations are still evident. The ruins can be found near the old Bahía Gonzaga/El Crucero road through the beautiful Arroyo Calamajué. Near the bottom portion of the arroyo a sign points out its remnants.

*Misión San Francisco de Borja Adac...*If the name "Borja" or "Borgia" sounds familiar and conjures up impressions of poisonings and intrigue, you may be surprised to know that the Borja (Spanish spelling) family supplied the money to build this mission, and also those at Calamajué and Santa María. Specifically, it was María, Grand Duchess of Borja, who heard of the mission projects from a servant who had lived in a Baja mission. The Grand Duchess ultimately left a sizeable amount of her estate to the Jesuit Pious Fund. Within a few years after completion in 1762, it served nearly 3000 converted Indians living around the mission, but marginal growing conditions at San Borja forced them to bring in food from other missions. The success enjoyed by the Padres was also dimmed by rampant "white man's" diseases. Less than 100 Indians remained when the Dominicans left in 1818. Poor 21-mile dirt roads come to San Borja from both Rosarito and the highway leading to Bahía de Los Ángeles. The present stone church was built in 1801 to replace several previous adobe structures and is one of the best preserved of the Baja missions.

SAN BORJA

Misión Santa María Magdalena ...it was not until 1966 that the location of this mission became known. During one of the famous Erle Stanley Garner explorations of Baja, his party came across what appeared to be the remnants of a dam in an arroyo. Furter exploration turned up evidence of a building site. According to records, Santa Maria Magdalena was never completed, but the area was described so well that scholars now believe that Gardner did, indeed, find this the old mission site. It is located in almost inaccessible terrain 40 miles south of Bahía de Los Ángeles.

Misión Santa Gertrudis La Magna...a view of this mission site today makes one wonder how it was possible for this location to be the spiritual center for over 3000 novitiates into Christianity. Flash floods have removed most of the tillable land and a small white stone chapel is all that remains of this once extensive mission. There are a few families who still use a portion of the two-century-old irrigation ditches and tend the few old grape vines, olive trees and date palms, along with their own crops. Located some 23 miles east of El Arco, it once served as the main mission for exploration to the north and is in a good state of preservation.

Misión Dolores del Norte...a few years ago it was questionable as to whether Misión Dolores had actually existed. Records were in doubt because they listed its location in an inhospitable portion of the mountainous central section of Baja, and the names of the landmarks were lost in the memories of old-time residents. Then, by accident it was located by a party searching for cave paintings made by an unknown tribe of Indians long before Columbus. Started by Father Fernando Consag sometime before 1745, it closed after about 20 years for lack of water. It is unlikely that many tourists will visit Dolores, due to its inaccessibility.

Misión San Ignacio de Kadakaman (Cadacaaman)...1728 was the year that this mission was dedicated by Padre Juan Bautista Luyando. A few years later, Luyando introduced the Arabian date palms to the region, and these dates are still the primary crop of San Ignacio. Blessed with a good water supply from an underground river, it proved to be one of the most successful of the Jesuit missions. Serving about 5000 Indians in its heyday, disease reduced the number to 120 by the end of the 18th century. Misión San Ignacio is one of the best preserved of the mission buildings, due to its being built from quarried lava rock four feet thick, and its continued use. The mission is located in the center of the town of San Ignacio and is well worth a visit.

SAN IGNACIO

Misión Guadalupe de San Bruno ...in 1683, Jesuit Padres Copart, Kino and Gomi made the first of several unsuccesful attempts to establish this mission. Evidence of one of their efforts is said to be located on the shores of Bahía San Bruno, 13 miles north of Loreto.

Misión San Juan Bautista Londo....was another abortive attempt to bring Christianity to the primitive residents of Baja California. Several miles inland from where the attempts to establish Guadalupe de San Bruno were made, San Juan Bautista Londo started in 1700 and collapsed a few years later.

Misión Nuestra Señora de Guadalupe ...Located in the mountains about 25 air miles due west of Mulegé, Guadalupe was far from a roaring success. Founded in 1720 by Father Juan de Ugarte, its records told of nothing but a downhill struggle for existence. A rugged jeep ride and a number of hours atop a mule are necessary to view the unimpressive stone foundations of the church. Nearly a lost mission, and surely, a lost cause.

Misión Santa Rosalía de Mulegé...The Jesuits founded the mission of Mulegé in 1705 and it attended up to 2000 natives until a flood in 1770 leveled most buildings. Epidemics also did their part to reduce the Indian population to less than 100 by 1782. Rebuilt on a low bluff it now overlooks town half a mile up the arroyo. The tropical atmosphere of Mulegé gives it one of the most beautiful mission settings in Baja California and has proven to be a favorite with visitors to Mulegé since it was restored in the late 1970's.

Misión La Purísima Concepción ...by 1730, eleven years after its beginning, La Purísima was reported to be the most successful of the missions thus far. Records showed that Padre Tamarál had baptized 2000 Indians and produced surpluses of grains, cattle and fruits. The mission workers' skills at road building were also widely admired throughout the adjoining missions. Finally, the harsh treatment at the hands of the Jesuits drove off most of the newly converted natives. In spite of the fertile land and good water, it slowly dwindled to nothing in 1822. Little remains of the mission today in the picturesque little town of La Purísima.

MULEGE

Misión San José de Comondú...was founded by Padre Mayorga in 1708, some 24 miles north of its final location. The town that grew up around the mission after the decimation of the Indians still observes services in the recently restored missionary house-portion of the mission site in present-day San José de Comondú.

Misión San Miguel de Comondú...there is a question as to whether San Miguel de Comondú was any more than a small church building in which visiting padres conducted services. The first records of its existence credit its founding to Fr. Juan de Ugarte in 1718 and is located 1.8 miles up the arroyo from Misión San José de Comondú. It, too, did well for a short period, but as the population dwindled, it was absorbed by San José. Principal crops were sugarcane, grapes and fruit.

Misión Nuestra Señora de Loreto...the site for the mission was chosen by Padre Juan Salvatierra in 1697 with the intent that it would be the capital of the entire mission system to be built in the Californias. It was the first of the 20 permanent missions started by the Jesuits during their 70 years of control. In 1829, a hurricane almost destroyed the town, which had already been rebuilt several times following floods and a huge earthquake. The mission at Loreto has been restored and a small museum opened under the Mexican Government's mission rehabilitation project.

The success of Salvatierra's Loreto effort comes not so much from their ability to survive on what they could raise on the local lands, but from bountiful harvests of valuable pearls, plus Salvatierra's strong friendships with missions in the areas of mainland Mexico now in the states of Sonora and Sinaloa.

Misión San Francisco Javier de Vigge ...in 1699 Padre Francisco María Piccolo of the Loreto mission decided to follow up on stories of numbers of Indians living in a lush valley in the mountains to the west of Loreto. The journey was rugged, and when Piccolo arrived, realizing its potential he asked permission of Padre Salvatierra to build a mission there. Shortly after the ground was dedicated and construction began. Several years later Padre Juan de Ugarte came to the site at a time when revolt appeared imminent. It did not take long for this huge, vigorous man to demonstrate that he was there to stay, and the Indians once again returned to learning how to become Christians. In 1720, five miles south of the original mission, the present building was started, and completed in 1758. This stone church remains as the best preserved and most impressive of all those erected in Baja California during the mission era. San Javier is probably the most rewarding of all the missions to visit, as it is very much as it was over 200 years ago. Check in Loreto as to road conditions, and if it is passable, a trip to San Javier is a fine investment.

*Misión San Luís Gonzaga...*about 25 miles east of Ciudad Constitutión this mission was open only about thirty years (1737-1768) before epidemics eliminated all but about three hundred of the Indians. The present stone church was built by Padre Juan Jacob Baegert in the 1750's. It has been restored under the Mexican Government's mission restoration program. Only a few families live near the church and raise dates, figs, oranges and mangoes.

*Misión Nuestra Señora Los Dolores del Sur...*a bit inland from the shore opposite the north end of Isla San Jose. It closed when the Indians had nearly disappeared. Today it is part of a private ranch and the area, Rancho Dolores is a favorite stopping place for yachts.

Misión Señora del Pilár de la Paz ...even though the La Paz area was the first (1535) to be visited by the Spanish, it was not until 185 years later that they returned to establish permanent quarters. In 1720, Padres Jaime Bravo and Juan de Ugarte began the building of a fort and church, preparatory to baptizing the residents. Diseases took a tremendous toll on the local Indians by 1749. No evidence remains as to the exact location of the fort, but it is believed to have been very near the site of the old post office in downtown La Paz.

*Misión Todos Santos de Santa Rosa...*lasted a considerable time, as its inhabitants were continually augmented by Indians from the other missions as they were phased out. Epidemics and a major rebellion assured a rapid turnover of the natives, in spite of plenty of fertile land and excellent water. Its 120 year existence ended in 1854 with the final expulsion of the Dominican order. The town of Todos Santos has continued to exist and is one of the most charming communities on the peninsula. Little remains of the original dwellings, but the present church — built in 1840 — is near the original site.

*Misión Santiago de las Coras...*was established near present-day Santiago in 1724 after beginning on Bahía de Palmas. It was here that the Pericu Indian revolt began in 1734 with the murder of Padre Cerranco. The fighting spread throughout the southern missions and by the time the missionaries regained control several years later, many on both sides were killed. Soon after, an epidemic practically eliminated the Santiago tribes, reducing their numbers from 1100 to only 40. The mission closed in 1795.

*Misión San José del Cabo...*founded in 1730 by Padre Nicolás Tamarál, this most southerly of the missions served as a supply and refitting stop for the Manila galleons. Within 20 years disease took all but 100 of the original population but the mission continued to operate into the 19th century by importing mestizos from the mainland. Nothing remains of the original church, but the present church is supposed to stand on the same site.

BELLS FROM
EL ROSARIO MISSION

LIVING AND RETIRING IN BAJA

If you were to poll those who regularly travel Baja you would find that many are planning to retire there. For some retirement is a reality, or nearly so. For others it is a dream helping shape their future. We too have those dreams. But maybe, as authors of books about Baja, we already have it. At any rate, the dreams, the thoughts and the plans continue. Someday...

There are a number of ways that you can become a resident of Baja without surrendering your American citizenship. The easiest way is to merely go to Baja and live there on a tourist permit, returning every six months or less and renewing your tourist permit. This method is relatively easy to accomplish because the peninsula's is a "duty free" and "specical status" zone under Mexican law. We know many who have established "vacation" homes in places such as Ensenada, Loreto or Cabo and live there 10 or 11 months of the year, returning periodically to the States to visit relatives, shop, vacation (how about that one!), pay their taxes etc., then returning on a new tourist permit. Under this method you are not allowed to work in Mexico, and, if asked, you must be able to show enough income to meet government requirements. At last check it was around $800 per month for a couple, but as the peso changes it varys, so check with a Mexican consular office. If you wish to become more formal about it there are several avenues open, which may include work permits. These statuses are called, *inmigrado, inmigrado rentista, and visitante rentista.* Here again you should contact the Mexican consul.

FIDEICOMISOS AND THE BAJA LAND BOOM

The issues of land ownership in Mexico have been points of contention and confusion since the 1876-1910 reign of Porferio Diaz. During this time nearly 15% of Mexico's land area came to be owned by foreigners. This changed with the new constitution adopted after the revolution of 1910-14 which specifically banned foreign ownership within 100 kilometers of its borders and 50 kilometers of the coasts.

Finally, in 1971 the government made it possible for foreigners to control, and actually own for a limited time property within the prohibited zones. The specific regulations became law in 1973 and have opened many areas for development. This is done through an instrument called "Fideicomiso," or beneficial trust, which provides for ownership of certain properties by the investor, but it is held in "beneficial trust" by a bank. The ploy meets constitutional requirements, while the purchaser has essentially the rights of ownership. The bank administers the property, paying taxes, title search, transfer fees, etc. in return for a reasonable maintenance fee. Once the fidecomiso is established you have control of the property for up to 30 years, and can build a house, live or retire on it. You may not buy a large amount of property and build, for example, a hotel, condominiums, or other business buildings except under special conditions. As the law now reads, at the end of the fideicomiso the property must be sold to a Mexican national, but you receive the full proceeds of the sale, and there is talk of liberalizing this part of the law.

Today there are many examples of 30-year trust purchases of Baja property. Beginning just below the border at Playas de Tijuana, El Rosario and San Felipe for example. They are also becoming common around Mulege, Loreto, La Paz, the East Cape and Los Cabos.

The Los Cabos area is currently a hotbed of fideicomisos and thousands of lots, parcels, homes and condos are offered for sale — and being sold. We see the Baja land boom as being a reality, and for many, a good investment.

BOOKS ON BAJA

The subject of Baja California continues to be a popular one. Each year a number of new books are published on its people, history, climate, flora, fauna, sealife. And the market for books on Baja continues to expand.

Here we will list some of the books found in bookstores or from the publisher, plus some who are now classics — books that are hard to find, even in large public libraries, but well worth the effort.

GERHARD, Peter and GULICK, Howard, **Lower California Guidebook.** Arthur H. Clark Co., Glendale, CA. 1956. Its first printing came just in time to immerse Tom Miller irrevocably in the Baja California peninsula. He took that first edition and set out to trace every trail listed in this great book. With the opening of the Baja Highway it went out of print, and was replaced by the fine update, **Baja California Guidebook** by *Howard GULICK* and *Walt WHEELOCK*. It too carried on the thorough well-researched tradition of its predecessor.

CANNON, Ray, **The Sea of Cortez.** Lane Publishing Co., Menlo Park, CA. 1966. So well did this beautiful 4-color book present the romance, the people and the fishing, that it became the subject of several TV features. Yes, this is the book that brought the angler, the yachtsman, and ultimately the investors to Baja. It supplied the excitement and the pizzaz to the Baja story, and still does if you can find a copy. Prices for a first edition are now topping $100.

MILLER, Tom, **Angler's Guide To Baja California.** Baja Trail Publications, Huntington Beach, CA 92615. 1978, 5th revised printing 1987. According to the experts, this book has put the finger on Baja fishing making it easy for even the first-time visitor to plan his fishing trip like a veteran. The book tells the when, where, how and what-kind in a manner that leaves little to the imagination. "Miller's 35-years of Baja fishing comes through in a very readable manner." — Bill Beebe, columnist, Western Outdoor News.

MILLER, Tom, **Eating Your Way Through Baja.** Baja Trail Publications. 1986. A lighthearted invitation to step beyond the conventional tourist hotel dining room and join the local Baja people at that special restaurant or taco stand where they eat. Laze in the shade of a palapa and feel the warmth of the people who live there. Eat your way through Baja with Tom Miller and enjoy every bite.

MILLER, Shirley, **Mexico West Cookbook.** Baja Trail Publications. 1983. A unique book which adapts both American recipes to what is available in Mexican markets, and Mexican recipes to American supermarket supplies. Brightly edited, whimsically illustrated.

PATCHEN, Marvin and Aletha, **Baja Adventures by Land, Air and Sea.** Baja Trail Publications. 1981. Adventure comes in many forms in Baja California and the Patchens proved that one's imagination was the only limitation. Included in the ways the Patchens covered Baja are jeep, dunebuggy, canoe, helicopter and airplane, with hiking and diving thrown in. Fun reading with lots of valuable tips.

GOTSHALL, Daniel, **Marine Animals of Baja California,** A Guide to the Common Fish and Invertebrates. Sea Challengers, Monterey, CA. 1982. A fine 4-color reference to the sealife of the Sea of Cortez. Scheduled to be reissued late 1987.

McMAHON, Mike, **Adventures in Baja,** McMahon Press, Los Angeles, CA. 1983. An enteratining and somewhat irreverent look at Baja by a man who obviously has loved every minute of the more than 40 years he has spent in Baja.

BOOKS ON BAJA

HUNTER, Ben, **The Baja Feeling,** Baja Trail Publications. 1976. A classic narrative of love for the land, the people and the feeling. Well written and one you will have trouble putting down.

WHEELOCK, Walt, **La Siesta Press,** Box 230, Glendale, CA 92109. This man, and his publishing company have written so many fine booklets on Baja that you should write for a list.

LEWIS, Leland and *EBELING, Peter,* Baja Sea Guide. An out-of-print classic which is a goldmine of information for the true Baja buff. If you find one, don't let it get away.

COYLE, Jeanette, and *ROBERTS, Norman,* **Field Guide to the Common and Interesting Plants of Baja California.** Natural History Publishing, La Jolla, CA. 1976. Also out-of-print, but scheduled to be expanded and reissued.

SAYING IT IN SPANISH

Spanish is the language of Mexico, though English is widely spoken, particularly by those with whom the traveler ordinarily may come in contact. You can enjoy the country more, however, if you learn even a few phrases of Spanish and use them.

Mexicans, unlike some other nationalities, are not scornful of mispronunciations and errors in grammar; rather, they welcome even the most halting attempts to use their language.

For an English-speaking person, it's easier to learn a smattering of Spanish than of any other language. Many words have the same source: family is **familia,** restaurant is **restaurante,** cathedral is **catedral.**

Spanish is an almost phoentic language. With a few exceptions, the consonants are pronounced as in English. The pronunciation of the exceptions, as well as the pronunciation of the vowels is given below:

A —as the a in father

E —as the e in they

I —as the i in machine

O —as the o in over

U —as the u in rude

Y —as the y in yes

G —with i or e as the h in home

G —with a, o, or u as the g in go

H —always silent

J —as the h in home

LL —as the y in yes, with a silght j to it (jyes)

N —as the ny in canyon

Q —as the c in come

R —has a single trill

RR —has a double-triple-quadruple trill

V —often pronouced b or a combination of b and V

An accent mark over a letter signifies the accent on that syllable. Esta is pronounced ES-tah. Está is pronounced es-TAH.

Almost all words have the accent on the next to the last syllable.

(continued on page 176)

Please—Por favor
Thank you—Gracias
Good morning—Buenos dias
Good afternoon—Buenas tardes
Good evening, good night—Buenas noches
Good-bye—Adiós
How are you?—Cómo está usted?
Excuse me—Perdóneme
Yes, No—Si, No
I don't speak Spanish—No hablo español
I don't understand—No Comprendo
I need—Necesito
You're welcome—De nada
I am sick—Estoy enfermo

We want to eat now—Ya queremos comer
I am thirsty—Tengo sed
Give me a beer—Déme una cerveza por favor
Give me a soft drink—Déme un refresco por favor
What is your name?—Cual es su nombre?
My name is—Mi nombre es
Let's go—Vamonos
What time is it?—Qué hora es?
Where is the road to . . . ?—Dónde está el camino a . . .
Is that road in good condition?—Está en buen estado aquel camino?

Numbers:

			Days:
1. uno	11. once	21. veintiuno	Sunday—domingo
2. dos	12. doce	30. treinta	Monday—lunes
3. tres	13. trece	40. cuarenta	Tuesday—martes
4. cuatro	14. catorce	50. cincuenta	Wednesday—miércoles
5. cinco	15. quince	60. sesenta	Thursday—jueves
6. seis	16. diez y seis	70. setenta	Friday—viernes
7. siete	17. diez siete	80. ochenta	Saturday—sábado
8. ocho	18. diez y ocho	90. noventa	
9. nueve	19. diez y nueve	100. cien	
10. diez	20. veinte	200. doscientos	

Directions:
right—la derecha
left—la izquierda
straight ahead—el derecho
road—el camino
north—el norte
south—el sur
east—el este
west—el oeste or oriente
street—la calle
highway—la carretera
avenue—la avenida
corner—la esquina
block—la cuadra
point—punta
river—rio
mountain range—sierra
valley—valle
ranch—rancho
canyon, wash—arroyo
bay—bahia
cape—cabo
canyon—cañon
hill—cerro
bay—ensenada
lake—laguna
beach—playa
port—puerto
island—isla

Shop Talk:
groceries—abarrotes
beer—cerveza
tires—llantas
market—mercado
cold—frio
hot—caliente
hot (spicy)—picante
clean—limpio
dirty—sucio
for sale—se vende
large—grande
small—pequeño
bad—malo
good—bueno
expensive—caro
more—más
less—menos
high—alto
low—bajo

red—rojo
blue—azul
green—verde
yellow—amarillo
brown—café or moreno
white—blanco
black—negro

In Hotels—Cafes:
bedroom—la recámara
bathroom—el cuarto de baño
single room—un cuarto sencillo
double room—un cuarto doble
dining room—el comedor
hot water—agua caliente
ice water—agua con hielo
key—la llave
towel—la toalla
soap—el jabón
Where is the ladies' room?—Dónde está el lavabo de damas?
men's room?—de señores?
breakfast—el desayuno
lunch—el almuerzo
dinner—la comida
the bill—la cuenta
daily specials—especiales del dia
waiter—el mesero
waitress—la mesera or señorita

"Muchas gracias" **works wonders in Mexico, just like "thank you" brings a smile in the U.S.** Use it often.

INDEX

T
H
E

B
A
J
A

B
O
O
K

III

¡MEXICO WEST!

TRAVEL CLUB Inc.

Now that **The Baja Book III** has given you the **where's** and **when's** of travel in Baja California, you'll need one more thing, a membership in the **MEXICO WEST TRAVEL CLUB, INC.** MWTC offers you tremendous benefits and savings such as:

1. A **Liability Only Auto Insurance** policy for only **$100 a year.** Full Coverage for your vehicle is also available for only a small additional premimum. **Or,** if you plan a short trip you can still **save 20%** over what you'll find at the border.Boat and Hull insurance for your boat, Homeowner's, Personal Effects, Airplane insurance are also available to our members.
2. Each **month** we publish an 8-page newsletter, **¡MEXICO WEST!**, with information about Baja California and west coast of Mexico travel. Exclusive and Enjoyable!
3. Our **Information Service** will help you with your trip planning.
4. Our members receive **10-20% discounts** at over **200 hotels, resorts, RV Parks** and **Sportfishing** spots and **travel packages** in Mexico.
5. In our office we have a supply of **Mexican Fishing Licenses** and **Boat Permits** for sale, and our members can get their **Tourist Visas** from us too.
6. Our **Membership Card** is a highly visible document **recognized** throughout the Baja California peninsula. Both Tijuana and Baja California Sur recognize our members through issuance of a **Visitante Distinguido** (Distinguished Visitor) card.
7. We have occasional **Fun Gatherings** where members can meet and share their trip experiences or plan for new ones.
8. **Group Travel** trips are planned for those who like to see and do new things. Inthe past few years we have traveled to Guadalajara, Morelia, San Miguel de Allende, Guanajuato, Loreto, Mazatlan and Cabo San Lucas.

Each day our members **call** or **write to praise** the Mexico West Travel Club and our **specialized services**, and you will too when you join. Last, but not least, we offer you the opportunity to become a member of a family of travelers who love to explore and enjoy Mexico, especially the Baja California peninsula.

The cost? Only **$35 a year**, and this includes all the benefits. We'll even throw in a **Special Bonus** when you say "**yes!**" Why don't you find out for yourself: Your **Satisfaction is Guaranteed. Send your check today,** or write for a brochure to:

MEXICO WEST TRAVEL CLUB, INC.

P.O. Box 1646, Bonita, CA 92002
or stop by our office at:
3450 Bonita Road, Suite 107, Chula Vista, CA 92010
(619) 585-3033